THE LINCOLN
HYPOTHESIS

THE LINCOLN
HYPOTHESIS

A MODERN-DAY ABOLITIONIST INVESTIGATES THE POSSIBLE CONNECTION BETWEEN JOSEPH SMITH, THE BOOK OF MORMON, AND ABRAHAM LINCOLN

TIMOTHY BALLARD

DESERET
BOOK

Salt Lake City, Utah

For Katherine

© 2014 Rockwell Group Inc.

All rights reserved. No part of this book may be reproduced in any form or by any means without permission in writing from the publisher, Deseret Book Company, at permissions@ deseretbook.com or P. O. Box 30178, Salt Lake City, Utah 84130. This work is not an official publication of The Church of Jesus Christ of Latter-day Saints. The views expressed herein are the responsibility of the author and do not necessarily represent the position of the Church or of Deseret Book Company.

DESERET BOOK is a registered trademark of Deseret Book Company.

Visit us at DeseretBook.com

Library of Congress Cataloging-in-Publication Data

Ballard, Timothy, author.
    The Lincoln hypothesis : a modern-day abolitionist investigates the possible connection between Joseph Smith, the Book of Mormon, and Abraham Lincoln / Timothy Ballard.
       pages cm
    Includes bibliographical references and index.
    ISBN 978-1-60907-863-8 (hardbound : alk. paper) 1. Lincoln, Abraham, 1809–1865. 2. Smith, Joseph, Jr., 1805–1844. I. Title.
    E457.B23 2014
    973.7092'2—dc23   2014005301

Printed in the United States of America
R. R. Donnelley, Crawfordsville, IN

10   9   8   7   6   5   4   3   2   1

Contents

Preface

This is *not* a history book, at least not in the purest sense. (I know this because I have published a few history books.) Rather, this work is an investigative journey—an exploration. Unlike a pure historical work, this book goes beyond the safe recitation of facts and events and opens doors that encourage you, the reader, to wonder, opine, speculate, and hope. This book will contain many valuable facts and sound historical conclusions, but it will also include unsubstantiated, yet compelling, ideas that I believe are also worthy of serious consideration.

Allow me to add some context to what I'm trying to explain. I have spent almost my entire professional life as a Special Agent/Criminal Investigator. In pursuing criminal cases, I have been trained to work around a legal concept called Totality of the Circumstances. This concept promotes the idea that a good investigation gathers *all* evidence: direct, indirect, circumstantial, opinion, conjecture—everything! The prosecutor in any case wants to know it all because the prosecutor knows that although any one piece of evidence by itself may have little meaning, all of it together—the Totality of the Circumstances—could have powerful implications. It is the judge's and jury's job to analyze it all and draw final conclusions.

The pure history books I have written in the past revolve around the scriptural idea that America is a promised land,

foreordained by God Almighty to bless the world with liberty
and truth. While researching and writing on this subject for over
a decade, I would from time to time uncover a fascinating, if not
bizarre, connection between Joseph Smith, the Book of Mormon,
and Abraham Lincoln. Some of the ideas were easily substantiated; others, though highly interesting, were not. And so I set
them all aside.

Through the years, however, the pieces of evidence (whether
fully substantiated or not) began piling up so high that I could
no longer dismiss them all as multiple random links in one long
chain of coincidences. The investigator in me took over, and I
felt compelled to deliver the Totality of the Circumstances to the
court of public opinion—to you! Hence, this book.

As you read, you will, like a prosecutor reviewing a case or a
jury determining a verdict, identify valuable pieces of evidence
that can be fully substantiated. You will also identify pieces of
evidence that cannot. I ask you to consider *all* the evidence and
weigh it all carefully. Through this study, many questions regarding the interplay between the restored gospel and the Civil War
will be answered. New questions may emerge that will not be so
easily answered. To be sure, this is only a hypothesis. Either way,
I invite you to join me on this exhilarating investigative journey
through a most fascinating era, a time when the Restoration of
the gospel intersected with American sociopolitical events like
perhaps no other time in history.

TIMOTHY BALLARD
January 2014

Introduction

For over a decade, I have had a most bizarre job—some might even say it is a calling. I'm not sure how I got here. I certainly never intended to be doing (nor did I ever imagine in my wildest dreams that I would be doing) the things I do. I have never felt qualified enough, prepared enough, or even brave enough. I bring this up only because unless you understand the things I have been forced to deal with over the past dozen years, you will never fully understand how I am able to tell you the story you are about to read in this book.

Perhaps the best way to explain this is to tell you about a real-life event I was part of. The hour was 0545. After several depressing days of working the streets in one of the most ungodly neighborhoods the world has to offer, my team at last had our target directly in our sights. The target looked like a normal middle-aged adult male on the outside, but I knew he was nothing more than a monster on the inside. He was a modern-day slaveholder, even worse than the slaveholders you have read about in history books. For he enslaved children and forced them into the sex industry.

As the team leader, I gave the signal to breach the dirty, off-white door. It was still dark outside, with the exception of the half-lit porch light dangling by its electric cords over the threshold we were about to enter. But the darkness on the outside of the monster's lair was nothing compared to the darkness I was about to feel upon entering.

Boom! One of the agents in front of me slammed his breaching tool (a miniature but powerful battering-ram device we call "the key to the city") into the door, blowing it wide open. The jolting noise alerted all of our senses and almost overdosed my system with adrenaline. Then it was on.

The two agents in front of me entered and swung right but found no targets before them. I took the lead on the left, keeping my Glock 19 (fully equipped with attached pistol light) in the high-ready position. Within seconds, the monster's face emerged from the pitch-black and appeared before my eyes. Seeing that he was caught off guard, and knowing his eyes had not yet adjusted to the pistol light shining in his face, I took advantage of the situation. Before he knew what had hit him, another agent and I had thrown him facedown on the ground. In that moment, I knew he would never be able to touch a child again.

I did not stay long with the monster but let others downline secure and extract him. I was going after a more important target: the only light, the only treasure in the house. I headed down the dark hallway. And there they were: two small boys, ages five and seven. I holstered my weapon and scooped them up in my arms. I just wanted them out of the darkness that had haunted and oppressed them for far too long. I made my way back down the hallway and headed for the front door. As I passed back across the threshold and into the dawning day, the morning breeze calmed me. The younger boy tightened his grip ever so gently around my neck—not out of fear, but almost as if he knew me and loved me, or at least loved what I represented. He instinctively knew we were the good guys.

At that moment, the feeling I had become so accustomed to

in other such situations overcame me. Yes, I had felt it before and would feel it after this particular case. I had felt it multiple times while posing as a child trafficker in Central America. I felt it on the occasions when, after the sting deal went down (and my own mock arrest by foreign authorities saw me facedown on pavement), I could look up and see those poor children I was pretending to buy. Though handcuffed as part of the show to keep my cover, I would always strain to catch a glimpse of those precious souls being scooped up by other loving hands and taken to a safe haven far from danger. That was when the feeling would come.

I suppose this is all just part of the job of serving as an undercover operative for a United States Child Sex Tourism Jump Team. Mine has been the bitter assignment of going undercover as an international broker in the child sex industry in order to infiltrate these abhorrent child-trafficking rings. (With millions of enslaved women and children today, this severe abuse represents one of the fastest growing criminal enterprises in the world.[1]) But, notwithstanding the inherent bitterness of it, at least that feeling always came to enthrall my soul. And I was feeling it again as I held these two boys in my arms and walked them to the recovery vehicle awaiting them. The feeling was something like a burden being instantly lifted—not so much my burden, but that of the innocent. I don't know how to describe it, but one word comes to mind: *emancipation.*

What does any of this have to do with the book you are about to read? You see, my job is not easy. I am in constant need of healing and encouragement to carry on the mission. The Lord and my loving family graciously provide this for me. But I have also been given another tool: heroes from American history. I often remind myself that there were others asked to do far more difficult things. One such person whom I try to emulate—though I always fall far short—is Abraham Lincoln, the Great Emancipator. For over ten years, whether at home, abroad, on an airplane, or in a dumpy hotel room in Latin America, I have carried Lincoln with me. In the unrelenting mission to eradicate modern-day slavery, who better to study than Honest Abe, right? I have found great comfort in reading every book I could get my hands on about Lincoln and the Civil War. And so I read. And when I'm done, I read some more. It's been like some insatiable need I have had to learn what Lincoln knew.

And then something extraordinary happened. I discovered something that shocked my soul. It was something completely unexpected—something that possibly connects me (and every other Latter-day Saint) to Abraham Lincoln in ways that are far more profound than our shared goal of emancipating slaves, though I believe it was that goal that helped direct me to these powerful findings. I learned what I believe to be the sacred secret to Abraham Lincoln's ultimate success. And I learned what that success might have meant for that thing we hold so dear, even the Restoration of the gospel of Jesus Christ. I have written this book with the intent to share with you this secret.

But I must warn you about something. When I first tell you what this secret is, you will think I have been cooking too long in the Central American sun. You will say to yourself, *This is impossible! If this were really true,* you will say, *then certainly I would have heard of it already.*

I don't blame you for being skeptical. I would not have given much credence to the general premise myself. But after more than ten years of investigating the matter, I am left believing. And so, I invite you to explore with me the evidence at hand. If you judge that my arguments have value, then you might agree with me that the lessons in these events carry with them enormous conse-quences for our America today.

And this is perhaps the most important reason I have written this book. You see, I am deeply concerned about America today. We are falling fast. Our liberty, protection, and prosperity are being threatened. These things were also threatened in Lincoln's day—but he pulled the nation out of the mire. He learned this secret I speak of and masterfully employed it. It was the secret to national salvation then and now. It was a secret that arguably ensured that the restored gospel of Jesus Christ had a strong foun-dation upon which to flourish (because, as you shall see, before Lincoln came to town, the Church was suffering immensely).

The problem is that, notwithstanding the hundreds of Civil War books written, this secret and the herculean measures taken to make sure it was invoked and applied have been all but lost to later generations of Americans. I want to bring this secret back. If we don't know what Lincoln *really* did to save the nation, how will we know what to do now? How will we know how to redeem the land in our day? I want America to be redeemed . . . again.

This secret represents the cornerstone of the argument I will make in this book. I uncovered it through a decade-long investi-gation into Lincoln, and it is couched in multiple pieces of infor-mation, evidence, and even some conjecture. Because of its com-plexity, an explanation of the secret cannot be properly summed up in a few words. It will take the length of this book to fully flesh it out. However, in an effort to give you a clue as to where we are headed, I ask you to consider the following questions: What if Abraham Lincoln's mission directly revolved around the prophecies of Joseph Smith? What if Joseph's works and prophe-cies, operating together with Lincoln's revelations and reactions, created the perfect formula for the building up of Zion and for the establishment of temples on the earth? And what if the key that unlocked this knowledge for Abraham Lincoln was a copy of the Book of Mormon that ended up in his possession precisely during the darkest days of the Civil War, right when he needed it the most?

If this were true, would it affect you? Would it change the way you viewed your religion and your country? Would it provide a key today to help preserve both of those sacred institutions in their joint missions to fulfill God's plan of happiness? By the end of this book, I think you may just believe my bold hypothesis, and I believe you just might answer *yes* to all of the above.

CHAPTER 1

Easter Sunday, 1865

The American tears that were shed on Easter Sunday in 1865 were immeasurable! During the week leading up to the hallowed day, Abraham Lincoln's secretary of state, William H. Seward, had been bedridden due to a tragic carriage accident that had almost claimed his life. But that tragedy was severely compounded by the darkness and evil that attacked his own home two days before Easter Sunday. The attack was on Good Friday. The world would never forget that day. Not ever.

As Seward awoke from a state of semiconsciousness that Sunday morning, he could smell blood. He could taste blood. He glanced into a small mirror by his bed, only to jerk away from the awful sight of a man he did not even recognize. He wondered who had done this to his face and neck. He knew he would never fully recover.

As use of his faculties slowly began to return, memories of the dreadful scene that had played out less than forty hours earlier flashed before his eyes. He could still hear the echoed scream of his daughter Fanny as she was knocked to the ground by the vicious assailant. She had tried to defend her father against the demon. And his son Fred! His poor Fred! When he had tried to protect his father, that murderous hand had crushed his skull with the butt of a gun. He was left near death on the stairway outside his father's bedchamber. By some providential occurrence, the gun had malfunctioned when the assailant had first tried to put a bullet through Fred's head. Only that had saved his life. But his pain was not spared. Seward could still hear his anguish. He could still hear his wife scream in agony as she hovered over Fred's broken body.

And the knife. The secretary of state could still see it coming down over his face and neck, cutting through his flesh.[1] Somehow he had survived this horror on Good Friday. Two days later, he would lie there trying not to remember.

Complete darkness and misery. On that Easter Sunday, Seward's own pain was nothing compared to what he felt for Fred, who was still near death, or for his dear wife, Frances, whose frail constitution could not endure the tragedy. She would die shortly thereafter as a result of it all. But there was something else consuming his soul. Some foreboding feeling . . .

Suddenly, instantly, he knew. He turned his aching head to his attendant and opened his mouth. All he could muster was a whisper—though in his mind it was a powerful and frightening proclamation: "The president is dead!" Seward's startled attendant immediately "stammered and changed color as he tried to say nay." The poor fellow did not want to be the bearer of news that might do his patient in. But Seward needed no confirmation. He knew at once that it had all been a conspiracy. The fiend who entered his quarters had had an accomplice—the president had been attacked simultaneously. They wanted them both dead. But the president had not been as lucky. Abraham Lincoln had been struck down on the very night that commemorates the murder of our Lord.

Seward gathered his emotions, then softly spoke his conclusion to his attendant: "If he had been alive he would have been the first to call on me, but he has not been here, nor has he sent to know how I am." His feelings at that very moment were later reported by his journalist friend Noah Brooks: William Seward then lay in silence, "the great tears coursing down his gashed cheeks, and the dreadful truth sinking into his mind."[2]

Of course Seward knew Lincoln would have called on him had he been alive. That was Lincoln. That was the magnanimous spirit who over the course of a few short years had become his best friend.

There was something almost appropriate about the day of this sad revelation—Easter Sunday. Twenty-eight years earlier, Seward's sweet infant daughter, Cornelia, had been taken from him. Smallpox. After her funeral, Seward resumed his work, which at the time placed him far from home. It was a difficult time to be alone. He turned to God. Then he made the decision. On Easter Sunday, 1837, he was baptized a Christian. He wrote his wife of that day, explaining to her that during his baptismal service he thought continually of "our child-angel, 'that left her errand with my heart and straight returned to heaven.'" He resolved on that Easter "to live more in the fear of and under the influence of love and gratitude to God" and to "gradually elevate and refine my motives of action."[3]

That earlier Easter day connects to this one because they both conjure up the memory of a man—Abraham Lincoln. Easter 1865 connects to Lincoln because it forever memorializes his sacrificial death. And Seward's previous Easter experience with tragedy and humility, followed by conversion, God, and salvation, connects to Lincoln because it was a foreshadowing of Lincoln's own experience. In watching Lincoln pass through a similar experience over the last four years of his life (and passing through part of it with him), Seward bonded with Lincoln in ways he never could have imagined. It was part of what made them friends. But

Lincoln's experience was much more profound than anything Seward had endured. For Lincoln's experience, I believe, led to the salvation of an entire nation—perhaps even the salvation of the whole world! Yes, though his story leads us through dark and dreary places (like those just recalled), it is in fact a happy one. In some ways, as you shall see, it *is* the story of Easter, which is why perhaps the timing of Abraham's death—like the timing of Seward's baptism—was somehow foreordained. The Master is indeed at the center of this story. And it ends in glory!

This glory especially applies to Latter-day Saints, who have a particularly deep connection to Abraham—perhaps deeper than they ever imagined. For his sacrifice *directly* led to that thing which is of greatest import. Indeed, his life and death represent a crowning achievement in the building of the kingdom of God and in the development of the Restoration of the gospel.

CHAPTER 2

The Witness

You may wonder why I chose to begin our examination of the evidence tying Abraham Lincoln to the work of the Restoration with a chapter written from the perspective of a historical character you likely know little about. The reason is that he is a principal witness in our investigation.

His name was William Henry Seward (his friends just called him Henry), and he was Abraham Lincoln's secretary of state. When he took up his post in the Lincoln administration, he was not the greatest fan of old Abe. He was a bit uneasy about him. In fact, he hardly even knew the strange-looking, tall, gangly newcomer from the frontier. And he could not fully comprehend how or why the populace had chosen that man as their leader. Much of his early reticence toward Lincoln no doubt stemmed from the fact that Seward was supposed to be the Republican nominee for the 1860 election. Indeed, *he* was supposed to be president—not Lincoln. Seward had, after all, served as a very well-known and well-liked governor of New York, and just prior to the election was serving as perhaps the most popular United States senator of his day. Lincoln, by contrast, had done very little politically, especially on the national scene.

At first Seward refused to consider the opportunity of being secretary of state (arguably the most important position in Lincoln's cabinet). But Lincoln was relentless on the point, and

Seward eventually surrendered, accepted his offer, and subsequently became his most loyal friend and most ardent supporter.[1] Exactly how and why that all played out will be discussed throughout this book.

Because of the important, though underrated, role Seward plays in this historical narrative, I want you to know more about him. Though the only known photos of him depict him in his later years, wrinkled and gray, in his youth he actually had vibrant red hair. And his personality seemed to match. He was described

by his son as a man of "clear blue eyes, red hair, quick, active movements, and merry laugh. . . . The house was always cheerful when he was in it."[2]

Seward was famous for hosting parties, especially when serving as governor of New York, U.S. senator from New York, and secretary of state. He tried to be a friend to everyone—politicians, actors, soldiers, diplomats, and their wives—and many attended his parties and dinners. He liked them all, and they liked him, even though

William Henry Seward, friend and confidant of Abraham Lincoln.

he was a bit quirky. Charles Frances Adams aptly described him as "small, rusty in aspect, dressed in a coat and trousers made apparently twenty years ago, and by a bad tailor at that, lolling against the partition as he talked . . . with a face and head in no way striking."[3] Another friend described him as having "a head like a wise macaw; a beaked nose; shaggy eyebrows; unorderly hair and clothes; hoarse voice; off-hand manner; free talk, and perpetual cigar."[4]

Seward becomes important because Abraham Lincoln did very little to ensure his own personal legacy. He did not begin

A MAN WITH PERSONALITY

Seward could be very serious minded and delivered some of the most profound political speeches in American history. However, he could also be very humorous. At times, after taking the stage and being greeted with thunderous applause, he would receive such adulation, as described by witnesses, in "the least elegant of postures, spreading wide his parenthetical legs and thrusting his hands deep into the pockets of his pantaloons." Many thought his quirkiness hilarious; others did not know what to think. On one occasion, soon after the Whig Party and the American Party were dissolved in the wake of his new Republican Party, he gave an impromptu speech at a train stop in Lockport, New York. Upon taking the stage, he cheerfully asked the crowd, "Is it an auction? I have no party to sell. What do I hear! The Whig Party? Going, going, gone. The American Party? Going, going, gone." He then jumped on the caboose of the train as it carried him away and shouted his final line before his laughing audience, "This train too. Going, going, gone!"[5]

William H. Seward.

a memoir, nor did he keep a regular detailed journal. He simply was not consumed by the power of his position. Though this proves to be a sign of his humility, it also forces us to rely on witnesses to help us understand the enigmatic sixteenth president. One man stood closer to Lincoln than any other during his presidency and war. It was Seward. Many of our discoveries about Lincoln, therefore, are derived from Seward and others of Lincoln's inner circle—even those witnesses who saw the miracles and witnessed the truth of what was happening.

Lincoln knew, and thus stated, that Seward "was the one man in the cabinet [he] trusted completely, the only one who fully appreciated his unusual strengths as a leader, and the only one he could call an intimate friend."[6] And though his wife would scold him for spending too much time chatting, joking, and relaxing at the Seward residence, Lincoln needed the strength of a best friend.[7]

As Lincoln gave so much time to Seward (much more than he gave to any other cabinet member during his administration), Seward learned firsthand about who Lincoln was and what his mission was all about. Perhaps the most important thing he learned about Lincoln was that he was a man whom God could trust, for he was sensitive and humble. Indeed, God could use such a man to fix a nation and a world.

Seward could easily attest to the fact that Lincoln was a man who (much to the annoyance of Seward and others in his official circle) maintained the most accessible executive branch in American history, even receiving uninvited visits from the lowliest and commonest of solicitors. Lincoln claimed that he allowed these "public opinion baths" so that he might remember that it was "that great popular assemblage out of which I sprung."[8] It was the same humble Lincoln who readily and characteristically

Lincoln and McClellan.

apologized to General Ulysses S. Grant, after a disagreement over military strategy, simply writing him, "I now wish to make the personal acknowledgement that you were right and I was wrong."[9] And it was Lincoln who, after helping to prepare a short biographical sketch of his life to be published to the nation, commented that there was not much of it because "there is not much of me."[10]

And consider how he dealt with the Union commander, General George McClellan! A constant thorn in his side, this young (young enough to be Lincoln's son) and arrogant soldier believed himself to be the national savior, as he himself noted on several occasions. Yet he described Lincoln as "the original gorilla"

WAITING ON McCLELLAN—
THE HUMILITY OF ABRAHAM LINCOLN

On November 13, 1861, President Lincoln, along with Seward and Lincoln's secretary, John Hay, visited the home of General George McClellan to discuss important war business. McClellan was out when the trio stopped by. They patiently waited an hour for his return. Upon arriving, McClellan was told that the president had been waiting in the parlor for some time. McClellan did not greet the visitors, but instead retired to his private chambers. After thirty more minutes, the guests still waiting patiently, McClellan sent word that he would not be meeting with them, as he was going to bed. John Hay was outraged and told Lincoln that, as president, he too should be outraged. Hay could not understand why Lincoln acted as though he didn't even notice the snub. The president then calmly told Hay that "it was better at this time not to be making points of etiquette and personal dignity."[11]

General George B. McClellan.

and Seward as "a meddling, officious, incompetent little puppy." His utter and open disrespect of Lincoln, and his insubordination toward almost all others over him, led the cabinet to seek his ouster. Yet Lincoln, knowing McClellan's popularity among the men of the Union army, simply rebuffed them all, smiled calmly, then humbly admitted that he would hold the general's horse if that meant victory would be achieved.[12] An amazing soul!

The humble spirit that filled Abraham Lincoln may seem to be a side note at first. But it is not. Having to deal humbly with McClellan was nothing compared to the coming challenges that would require even more magnanimity from the president. Events would soon fall upon him that would cause him to have to do something he had promised not to do. He would be asked of God Almighty to dramatically change the national course—a change that everybody, himself included, believed would be his political suicide. But God needed it done, and Lincoln was one of the few prepared to do it. "Whatever shall appear to be God's will," declared Lincoln, "I will do!"[13]

The witness William H. Seward saw this first and foremost. We will periodically revisit Seward throughout this historical examination. Remember his name. For there is a reason he was struck down along with Lincoln on Good Friday, 1865. By the end of this book, you will know that reason, and you will see how it leads us to powerful conclusions about the Civil War and the Restoration of the gospel.

CHAPTER 3

The Covenant Day

One reason Abraham Lincoln has often been misunderstood—the reason his story has rarely, if ever, been fully fleshed out—is because historians begin the narrative in the wrong place. They begin it in 1809, when he was born, or in 1860, when he won the presidency. I believe the story actually begins long before—it begins on April 30, 1789.

"The propitious smiles of Heaven, can never be expected on a nation that disregards the eternal rules of order and right, which Heaven itself has ordained."[1] With independence secured, George Washington stood in Federal Hall, New York City, and declared those covenant words while being inaugurated as the first president of the United States. The date was April 30, 1789—the day the Constitution came into being, a document that, according to our religion, was based in "holy principles" established to protect "moral agency" for "all flesh" (D&C 101:77–80). But this event was clearly much more than an inauguration. It was the day that a covenant between God and America was officially invoked over all the land. *I will be your God,* the Almighty had declared. *Will you be my people?* This covenant—and its power to heal the land—is the secret Lincoln learned and employed to save America.

Just before Washington invoked the national covenant through his "Smiles of Heaven" speech, he was sworn in as the

Washington's inauguration, April 30, 1789.

first president of the United States. The details of this ceremony were profound. He called for a Bible. He raised his right arm to the square (making the sign of an oath or covenant) while placing his left hand upon the sacred book. After repeating the constitutional oath, he declared, "So help me God," then bowed down reverently and kissed the Bible. He then joined the throngs of people cheering below in the street. He led them in a procession through the city and right into a beautiful house of worship—St. Paul's Chapel. He gathered the newly elected senators and representatives of the new nation. What might be called the first joint session of Congress in the United States then commenced. It consisted of a prayer in a church.[2] The covenant was sealed upon the land. America had responded to God: *Yes, we will be your people.*

Now, Washington did not learn of this covenant all at once. No, this theology had grown in him over the almost decade-long war for independence. You might be familiar with some of the stories that make up the pattern of American victory. Washington and/or Congress would invoke this covenant, pleading for the soldiers and the nation to fast, pray, and repent. Then the miracles followed. Are you familiar with the Battle of Long Island, one of the first major battles of the Revolutionary War? It occurred during the summer of 1776. Congress and Washington had promised miracles if the people would but repent. And the people did. Then, at the crucial point, when all seemed lost for the Americans, when they found themselves trapped on the shore of Long Island, the Lord entered the scene. He sent a devastating windstorm to push the British fleet out of the way, allowing Washington and his army to escape across the East River. Then the Lord dropped a heavenly fog to conceal Washington's evacuation route from the British eye. When the fog lifted, the British were dumbfounded to see that the Americans had vanished, as it were, into thin air. Dashed was the British belief that the war would be over that day. Instead, America would live to fight another battle; the Revolution would live on!

I love that story! It's like a page out of the Old Testament. And similar miracles occurred at the siege of Boston, at the camp in Valley Forge, and at the crucial battles of Trenton, Princeton, and Yorktown. There is a reason Washington insisted that "Providence has heretofore saved us in remarkable manner and on this we must principally rely."[3]

William Seward loved General Washington; he loved what Washington had done to create one nation under God. It was his deep fondness for Washington that caused him such pain when Washington's words were once used against him. You might have

MIRACLE AT YORKTOWN

By 1781, the Revolutionary War found itself in a stalemate of sorts. Both sides were seeking the knockout blow. Washington ultimately decided against his initial plan to assault the British at New York. Instead he would take aim at the British Southern Command led by Lord Charles Cornwallis, who had set up camp at the sleepy port town of Yorktown, Virginia. As best-selling author and historian Thomas Fleming explained, "Washington marched south [to Yorktown] and a series of miracles occurred."[4]

First, when the British fleet out of New York set sail for Yorktown to gather Cornwallis and his troops and bring them to safety, they unexpectedly ran into a French fleet, which had barely arrived at the Chesapeake Bay, off the coast of Yorktown, in support of the American effort to trap Cornwallis. On September 5, 1781, the French ships turned on the incoming British and defeated them in what became known as the Battle of the Capes. As author William Bennett explains, between the years 1588 and 1941, the British "'ruled the waves' . . . with one important local exception . . . in the waters off Yorktown, Virginia, in 1781."[5] This one exception in over 350 years of British naval warfare history would directly contribute to the final battlefield victory that sealed American independence. This was no coincidence.

On October 10, having gathered many troops from around the country, Washington directed a young Alexander Hamilton to lead an eastward charge on Cornwallis's position on the Yorktown peninsula. Hamilton obeyed the orders and subsequently pushed the British right up against the Atlantic Coast, capturing British fortifications along the way. This put the Americans in an ideal position.[6]

Having regrouped after their unlikely naval defeat at the hands of the French, the British fleet at last prepared once again to move out of New York to rescue the ailing Cornwallis. Then the Lord stepped in once again. As Fleming explains: "On October 13, the fleet was supposed to sail—when a tremendous thunderstorm swept over New York harbor. Terrific gusts of wind snapped the anchor cable on one of the ships of the line, smashing her

The French overcame the renowned British navy in the Battle of the Capes.

into another ship and damaging both of them. . . . [The British] could not leave until the damage was repaired."[7]

Under severe fire, and having lost faith that his navy would be coming to the rescue, Cornwallis resorted to his desperate contingency plan—evacuate the Yorktown peninsula by ferrying his men northward over the York River and then march toward the British-friendly New York. In a plan that resembled that of Washington at Long Island years earlier, Cornwallis would attempt the crossing on October 16, under cover of night. The only difference, of course, was that when Washington had attempted such an escape, he had been acting under a covenant with God. Not so for Cornwallis. Fleming explains: "About ten minutes [after midnight] a tremendous storm broke over the river. Within five minutes, there was a full gale blowing, as violent, from the descriptions in various diaries, as the storm that had damaged the British fleet in New York. Shivering in the bitter wind, soaked to the skin, the exhausted soldiers and sailors returned to the Yorktown shore. Not until two a.m. did the wind moderate. It was much too late to get the rest of the army across the river. Glumly, Cornwallis ordered the guards and the light infantry to return."[8]

With no other option available, Cornwallis was forced to surrender to Washington on October 19, 1781. This final blow was enough to convince the British to terminate their war efforts (though the peace treaty signed at Paris, which officially ended the war, would not be realized until 1783). America was at last free.

In emphasizing the significance of the details of the Battle at Yorktown, Fleming offers the following insight: "A Cornwallis getaway would have left the French and Americans frustrated and hopeless, facing a stalemated war they no longer had the money or will to fight. American independence—or a large chunk of it—might have been traded away in the peace conference. . . . Instead the Allies had landed the knockout blow."[9]

Though Fleming's analysis is no doubt a sound one, Washington might take issue with one point from his conclusion. The "knockout blow" was first and foremost landed not by the Allies, but by the Lord. "I take particular pleasure," Washington would explain in reference to his Yorktown victory, "in acknowledging that the interposing hand of Heaven, in various instances of our preparations for this operation, has been most conspicuous and remarkable."[10]

On October 20, 1781, only one day after Cornwallis surrendered, Washington directed yet another General Order to recommend "that the troops not on duty should universally attend with that seriousness of Deportment and gratitude of Heart which the recognition of such reiterated and astonishing interpositions of Providence demand of us."[11]

heard of "Seward's Folly," right? Yes, that was the same Seward. As secretary of state, he was responsible for America's purchase of Alaska from Russia. He was severely criticized at the time. (Only later would the nation realize what a blessing this acquisition would be, but that is a story for a different book.) Seward was told by a fellow cabinet member that his constant efforts to secure America's place in the world through negotiating deals with foreign governments and seeking to expand America's interests abroad showed utter disregard for Washington's warning, given in his farewell address, about avoiding "entangling alliances." Though he knew the accusation was unfair and misapplied, the suggestion "vexed" him deeply.[12]

The point I'm trying to make is that Seward greatly revered Washington. You must understand this so that you will understand the power of the following statements our principal witness made in mortality about his friend Abraham. He once declared to the nation that "Abraham Lincoln would take his place with Washington, Jefferson and Adams, among the benefactors of his country and the human race." (A risky prediction about one who was still living and working—but he *was* right!) He even went so far as to prophesy that "Washington is the great man of the era of the Revolution.

> Seward was constantly seeking to extend American power overseas. In 1856, Senator Seward introduced the Guano Bill, which he successfully passed through Congress. The new law authorized America to claim possession of uninhabited islands in the Caribbean and the Pacific that possessed a rich supply of guano, or dried seabird dung, which was utilized for fertilizer. As with his purchase of Alaska, the greatest benefits of these acquisitions were not discovered until years later. Two of the islands claimed under Seward's guano law were Johnson and Midway— both of which became crucial U.S. military bases during World War II.[13]

So Lincoln will be of this [era], but Lincoln will reach a higher position in history."[14] (Now, this was *extremely* risky to say.) You see, both men were asked to fulfill God's will through the same national covenant. However, no national leader was ever made to endure the fires of hell like Lincoln was. He *had* to in order to save the country. And he was willing as few would be willing. For this, I esteem no American leader more highly than him.

Now, back to the great Washington. I told you that his experiences seem to me like something I have read in the Old Testament: the story of Joshua, or perhaps that of Gideon. But as Latter-day Saints, we know the Old Testament is not the only place to find such stories. There is a much better source that is corroborated by the experience of the Revolution—a source that places the covenant right in America. Does our Book of Mormon not declare this? I quote that ancient American founder, Lehi: "Yea, the Lord hath covenanted this land unto me, and to my children forever, and also all those who should be led out of other countries by the hand of the Lord. . . . And if it so be that they shall serve him according to the commandments which he hath given, it shall be a land of liberty unto them; wherefore, they shall never be brought down into captivity" (2 Nephi 1:5, 7).

Does this not apply to the American revolutionaries? If you have any doubt, then I turn you to Lehi's son, who had a vision of the Founding Fathers of the United States. "I, Nephi, beheld that the Gentiles who had gone forth out of captivity did humble themselves before the Lord; and the power of the Lord was with them. And I beheld that their mother Gentiles were gathered together upon the waters, and upon the land also, to battle against them. And I beheld that the power of God was with them" (1 Nephi 13:16–18). Astonishing! Especially as we read Washington's words. He invoked the same covenant—the same

WERE AMERICAN SETTLERS THE LORD'S COVENANT PEOPLE?

As the Puritans arrived upon the shores of the New World, their leader John Winthrop shared words that sounded a lot like those declared by Father Lehi when he brought his people to the same land. Said Winthrop: "Thus stands the cause between God and us, we are entered into Covenant with

The Puritans relied on their covenant with God to sustain them in the New World.

Him for this work. . . . If we shall deal falsely with our God in this work we have undertaken and so cause Him to withdraw His present help from us, we shall be made a story and a byword through the world." Winthrop called upon his people to live the commandments, that God might make them a "City upon a Hill."[15] The prophet Nephi saw the early American settlers in vision and described them appropriately: "And it came to pass that I, Nephi, beheld that they did prosper in the land; and I beheld a book, and it was carried forth among them . . . , which contains the covenants of the Lord, which he hath made unto the house of Israel" (1 Nephi 13:20, 23).

divine rules upon the land—as Lehi, Nephi, and the others did. Is this not powerful corroboration? The covenant is on our land. This idea would have powerful consequences in Lincoln's day, for it was this concept that would begin to define Lincoln and make him the indispensable servant of God.

As I have pondered the concept of this covenant on the land, I can't help but go back to that first national covenant as it was delivered to the Old Testament prophet Abraham. In addition to the spiritual blessings that Abraham's covenant would offer the world, it should be remembered that special lands—lands of the covenant—were also part of the promise. Abraham was to be "a father of *many nations*" (Genesis 17:4; emphasis added). "I will make thee exceeding fruitful, and I will make *nations* of thee" (Genesis 17:6; emphasis added), declared God to Father Abraham.

And here is the kicker for us: America itself was always intended to be one of those nations. You will recall that Abraham's grandson Jacob (later called Israel), who carried the covenant, placed his hands upon his son Joseph and bequeathed this distant promised land:

> Joseph is a fruitful bough, even a fruitful bough by a well; whose branches run over the wall:
>
> The archers have sorely grieved him, and shot at him, and hated him:
>
> But his bow abode in strength, and the arms of his hands were made strong by the hands of the mighty God of Jacob. . . .
>
> The Almighty . . . shall bless thee with blessings of heaven above, blessings of the deep that lieth under, blessings of the breasts, and of the womb:

The blessings of thy father have prevailed above the blessings of my progenitors unto the utmost bound of the everlasting hills: they shall be on the head of Joseph, and on the crown of the head of him that was separate from his brethren. (Genesis 49:22–26; see also Deuteronomy 33:13–17; D&C 133:26–34)

We read here of a blessed land, over the wall (the ocean?), which is more blessed and protected than any other. According to Latter-day Saint doctrine, this was America. Indeed, our instructional manuals state this point clearly.[16] In confirmation, Lehi and his posterity continually claimed they had descended from Joseph: "I am a descendant of Joseph who was carried captive into Egypt," declared Lehi. "And great were the covenants of the Lord which he made unto Joseph" (2 Nephi 3:4). These ancient characters took that concept a step further by continuously invoking the Abrahamic covenant over the land: "Inasmuch as ye shall keep my commandments ye shall prosper in the land" (2 Nephi 1:20).[17] It all comes full circle. It all begins to make sense.

As I have pondered this, and as I have applied it to the American Civil War, the concept of a national covenant has become clearer and clearer. It has dawned on me that almost every time the Lord has initiated a restoration of His kingdom on the earth—think Adam, Noah, Abraham, Moses, Lehi, and Joseph Smith—He has delivered along with it a covenant land, a protected place. And why protected? Because there is an evil one whose goal from the beginning has been to take liberty away. Of course, our adversary would seek this. Liberty, after all, is essential for salvation. Nobody can be forced into exaltation; they must choose for themselves. They must be free to choose. Satan's libertyless, choiceless plan put forth in the beginning was, therefore, always designed to halt progression. In the end, his proposed "plan of salvation" was really not a plan of salvation at all, because exaltation does not work without liberty. He happily sought to eradicate liberty because he did not want anybody to threaten what he saw as his elevated position.

Satan was so passionate about his liberty-eradicating plan that he even fought a war in heaven over it. The scriptures explain that "Michael and his angels fought against the dragon; and the dragon fought and his angels, and prevailed not" (Revelation 12:7–8). "Wherefore," stated the Lord, "because that Satan rebelled against me, and sought to *destroy the agency of man, . . .* I caused that he should be cast down" (Moses 4:3; emphasis added). Fortunately, Satan lost that great war in heaven, but he is on earth today. And he still seeks to thwart our liberty—to buy up armies and navies, to raise up tyrants who will oppress the children of God. He knows now, as he knew then, that liberty is a necessary part of eternal progression and salvation. So he seeks to destroy liberty still.

Now we see the need for national covenants. They exist so God can contend with evil, so He can push darkness and oppression away when necessary, even with righteous armies (like Washington's) who were placed under the covenant. Remember God's promise to Joseph's seed: "The archers have sorely grieved him, and shot at him, and hated him: But his bow abode in strength, and the arms of his hands were made strong by the hands of the mighty God of Jacob" (Genesis 49:23–24). Indeed, God will preserve liberty in the promised land and thus ensure that His gospel remains. What a perfect plan.

And what is the essential part of the gospel worth preserving? What is worth facing evil over and fighting wars over? What is worth dying for? Temples are! They are the portals to heaven. It is there where families are sealed for eternity. It is there where covenants that bring eternal life are made. It is there where God's plan of happiness is realized. I have concluded from my reading of the scriptures that temples are always the purpose of the promised land. Is this not why Moses led the children of Israel out of Egypt, that they might build their tabernacle, then their temple? Is it not why Lehi was taken from the evils of the Old World, where the temple had been desecrated? Did he not come to America to build the temple? And what of Joseph Smith?

And so you see, this whole story—the purpose for this book—revolves around the temple. What do you think happens when evil creeps into the promised land and begins destroying temples and obstructing their development? How far will God go to defend His temple? Americans living in the nineteenth century learned firsthand how far He would go. They lived through the devastations that fall on a covenant people, in a covenant land, who make sport of mocking and destroying God's temple. Perhaps you think my suggestion here—that a major purpose of the Civil War was to cleanse the land so that temples could be built and maintained unmolested by evil—is too bold? I would have thought so too, before I learned what I did, which I will continue to share with you in this book.

For now, I must return to that covenant day of April 30, 1789. For I have failed to tell you the crucial mystery of that day that sheds eternal light on Abraham Lincoln and the national crisis he would inherit. I told you how, before taking his oath, Washington called for a Bible to place his hand upon. Well, he did not just place his hand upon that Bible; he placed it inside. Most commentators downplay or ignore the verses whereupon Washington laid his hand. It seems like Old Testament gibberish to them. In their defense, most of these commentators have not read Mormon doctrine, and therefore do not see the miracle in all this.

The miracle is that George Washington had his hand directly upon Genesis 49—*Joseph is a fruitful bough, . . . whose branches run over the wall. . . .* It is perhaps the most powerful declaration of America and her covenant found in the Bible (and one that really did not come to light until the Book of Mormon and the Restoration revealed it).[18]

A while back, I had the opportunity to lay my eyes on the very Bible that Washington placed his hand inside. I had come to New York City to be filmed for an American history documentary to be shot outside Federal Hall, where Washington had taken his oath using that Bible. Though I had studied and written at length about the events of April 30, 1789, I had never visited Federal Hall before, so I was very excited about the opportunity. On the night before the shoot, I checked into my hotel, which was a couple of miles away from Federal Hall. It was around midnight by the time I had unpacked and settled in. I was restless. I did not want to wait until morning. Notwithstanding the hour, I left my hotel, determined to walk all the way to the sacred site.

Federal Hall is located in a unique place in the city, right next to the renowned New York Stock Exchange. In fact, the two edifices face each other. To access the Hall, one must walk the length of the Stock Exchange, following the famous little road (surprisingly narrow and alley-like) called Wall Street. As I walked down Wall Street, the noise in the city behind me faded. I emerged onto the open square that is bordered by the entrance to the Stock Exchange on one side and the entrance to Federal Hall on the other. And there I saw it. Perched high upon the Hall's grand cement stairway leading to its entrance was a large statue of George Washington with his palm facing downward as if he were placing it upon or inside something. I was spiritually filled as I looked upon him and pondered the marvelous events that had occurred on this sacred ground.

I was somewhat jolted from my spiritual trance when I heard the sound of whipping fabric above and behind me. I turned around quickly and looked up at the other grand edifice that shares the square—the Stock Exchange. The noise I was hearing came from a series of Israeli flags lining the base of the grand pillars high above the doors to the Stock Exchange building. Apparently, I had arrived during New York City's Jewish Appreciation Week, which explained the flags. But they meant more to me than that. Those flags represented the biblical covenant God made with His chosen nation—the same covenant that extended to America. I looked back to the Washington statue and thought how his eyes appeared fixed on that ancient symbol directly before him. How fitting. For that is exactly where Washington's eyes (albeit his spiritual ones) had been fixed while standing on that very spot over two hundred years earlier.

I then followed Washington's procession route, back down Wall Street and into the busyness of the city. A few blocks later, I arrived at that old procession's destination—St. Paul's Chapel. It looked exactly as it would have in Washington's day. Again, the sounds of the city seemed to fade away as I looked upon the sacred edifice and pondered upon the prayer that Washington had led his people to offer there—the prayer that built the United States. Again, I was overcome.

The next morning, I was up early and eager to return to my new favorite spot in the city. After walking up the stairs past the Washington statue, I entered the interior of Federal Hall. The photojournalist who had brought me to New York City was following closely behind. Upon entering, we were immediately drawn to a small room just off the main lobby. As I poked my head in, I received one of the greatest shocks of my life. I could not believe what I was looking at. I'd had no idea it was here; why had I never seen anything printed or published about its resting place? Secure in its own glass case was the very Bible Washington had used to invoke the covenant. I became misty-eyed as I looked upon it, though I tried to conceal this fact from the stoic photojournalist.

A docent soon entered the small room and declared simply, "Do you know how lucky you are to see this Bible?" Of course I knew. I opened my mouth to explain how much I knew, but she excitedly cut me off. Then another shock. "This Bible," she said, "has been in private storage for years. It was only recently brought to rest here at Federal Hall." Before I could ask how recently, the docent, apparently reading my mind, blurted out with a smile, "Yesterday!" I could not believe it. The Bible had returned to Federal Hall the same day I had arrived in the city. I looked at the photojournalist. I could no longer hide my emotion—but I did not have to. He too had tears streaming down his cheeks.

April 30, 1789, was indeed a covenant day, and one that would have awesome consequences (great or terrible) for all inhabitants of the land. The covenant had been reinvoked upon America. The Book of Mormon stories, therefore, would play out all over again in this everlasting promised land. Lincoln and his nation would know, for they lived through some of the most important ones.

CHAPTER 4

Joseph, Abraham, and the Breach

I have told you the story of Abraham of old and Joseph of old, and how they set the foundation for the American covenant. But when Americans of the nineteenth century failed to keep that covenant (and oh, how they failed!), God would call two others. He would call Abraham "of new." He would call Joseph "of new." I submit that names are not always coincidences. As you shall see, God Almighty called two witnesses and holy men of the American covenant. Born within a few years of each other and laid to rest in neighboring cities (each man dying prematurely by an assassin's bullet), Joseph Smith and Abraham Lincoln would be called to save the nation and her covenant.

Read carefully the words of the two witnesses. They were given at about the same time. They were both "broadcasting" (again, perhaps not coincidentally) from the heartland of America, near the precise location of Zion, or the land of the New Jerusalem. America could have listened and staved off the impending doom that was to befall it.

In 1838, a young Abraham Lincoln (in his early thirties) declared the following before an audience at Springfield, Illinois: "Whenever the vicious portion of the population shall be permitted to gather in bands of hundreds and thousands, and burn churches, ravage and rob provision-stores, throw printing presses into rivers, shoot editors, and hang and burn obnoxious persons at pleasure, and with impunity; depend on it, . . . *this Government cannot last.*"[1]

A few years later, standing not far from where Lincoln had spoken, Joseph Smith (also in his thirties) declared:

> I prophesy in the name of the Lord God of Israel, unless the United States redress the wrongs committed upon the Saints in the state of Missouri and punish the crimes committed by her officers that in a few years the government will be utterly overthrown and wasted, and there will not be so much as a potsherd left for their wickedness in permitting the murder of men, women and children, and the wholesale plunder and extermination of thousands of her citizens to go unpunished, thereby perpetuating a foul and corroding blot upon the fair fame of this great republic.[2]

"Oh that I could snatch [the people of the United States] from the vortex of misery, into which I behold them plunging themselves," Joseph wrote on another occasion, "that might be enabled by the warning voice, to be an instrument of bringing them to unfeigned repentance."[3]

In that same 1838 speech already mentioned, Abraham turned his audience to the Founders of the nation: "As the patriots of seventy-six did to the support of the Declaration of Independence, so to the support of the Constitution and Laws, let every American pledge his life, his property, and his sacred honor;—let every man remember that to violate the law, is to trample on the blood of his father, and to tear the character of his own, and his children's liberty."[4]

Yes, Abraham pled with the people to consider the Founders and their great cause—what he called "the noblest cause—that of establishing and maintaining civil and religious liberty." He described the Founders as "the pillars of the temple of liberty."[5] He feared their grand dream was being lost. Joseph concurred when he stated that "the very thought of [America's sins] would have caused the high-minded and patriotic framers of the Constitution of the United States to hide their faces with shame."[6] Another time, Joseph wrote, "Were the venerable fathers of our independence permitted to revisit the earth, how would they frown with indignation at the disgrace of their country."[7]

What American sins, which would lead to America's destruction, were these two young witnesses referring to? And why did they both want to turn the national heart to the Founders? I will get to the sins in a moment. First, I want to address the references to the Founders of the republic. As I pointed out earlier, these Founders understood the covenant upon the land. They understood that their ultimate success as a nation was wholly contingent upon their ability to live the covenant—to obey God's commands. They truly saw and even designated themselves as the "New Israel,"[9] and they wanted to live by those biblical rules. The kind of sin Joseph Smith and Abraham Lincoln identified was just the sort of thing that would lead to national destruction—at least in a promised land like America. As in biblical Israel, there is a particular set of rules in a covenant land.

> "Washington desired the millennial peace in the world that had been promised to Israel."
>
> —Washington scholar Peter Lillback [8]

After witnessing the powerful covenant blessings bestowed upon the colonists fighting on the battlefields of the Revolution, Washington would never forget God's hand in the country's victory. And so, as I already pointed out, upon taking his presidential oath, he made the covenant the principal theme of the day.

THE MOST QUOTED BOOK

That the Founders took seriously their connection to the biblical covenant, particularly in relation to their building the nation and its Constitution, is evidenced in the findings of a 1973 study directed by political scientist Donald Lutz. Dr. Lutz and his team set out to evaluate everything published in America during the time of nation-building (between 1760 and 1805). They sought to settle the long-standing debate about which of the Enlightenment writers most influenced the creation of America. (Was it Montesquieu? Locke? Hume? Hobbes? Or perhaps it was the more ancient writers, such as Plutarch or Cicero.) The answer stunned them all. It was, overwhelmingly, the writers of the biblical covenant. More particularly, the Founders most quoted book was Deuteronomy, which arguably does more than any book to define the covenant relationship between God and a nation.[10]

What I did not tell you is a separate warning Washington penned during his preparations for the grand inauguration. During the same month he officially placed America under covenant with God, he declared:

> If the blessings of Heaven showered thick around us should be spilled on the ground or converted to curses, through the fault of those for whom they were intended, it would not be the first instance of folly or perverseness in short-sighted mortals. The blessed Religion revealed in the word of God will remain an eternal and awful monument to prove that the best Institutions may be abused by human depravity; and that they may even, in some instances be made subservient to the vilest purposes.[11]

Washington concluded that the twin evils that would breach this covenant and bring the nation to its knees were "the sweeping torrent of boundless ambition on the one side, aided by the sapping current of corrupted morals on the other."[12]

He read the biblical accounts. He knew the sure and horrific fate of any nation under God that violates the rules of heaven. Read for yourself! You might start with Leviticus 26 and Deuteronomy 4–6; 28–29. Or read about the curses that fell upon the wicked nations that were under covenant in the Book of Mormon. Father Lehi was not joking when he declared that this land of America "shall never be brought down into captivity; if so, it shall be because of iniquity; for if iniquity shall abound cursed shall be the land for their sakes" (2 Nephi 1:7).

All of this raises the question: Did America violate the covenant? Did it do anything that might provoke heaven to allow the curses to fall, just as the Bible and the Book of Mormon suggest, and as Washington warned might happen? From the day the

Pilgrims invoked the covenant on the land, there is no doubt that God did honor it. But during this otherwise enlightened and miraculous period of American history, spanning from discovery to settlement to independence to nation building, was there a dark side? Was Washington justified in worrying so much about the sustainability of the covenant?

The answer is more tragic than most of us would like to know. It is deeply depressing to learn about the evil works that were being performed in the name of America. Lincoln and his people witnessed much of it in their day and learned very well how easy it is to turn a blind eye to national horrors and thus commit grand sins of omission. Americans today must remember what happened to their nineteenth-century countrymen because of this. We must remember what national sin can lead to. Because history is beginning to repeat itself.

I don't believe most of us can even imagine the horror on the innocent faces of victims of American sin. Catholic convents burned to the ground by angry mobs; Baptist preachers beaten and jailed for nothing more than preaching their religion; Jews stripped of all civil rights; and peaceful Native Americans driven from their own lands and made to suffer and die. In each of these cases, the Constitution of the United States—though present—did not

> "And it shall come to pass, if thou shalt hearken diligently unto the voice of the Lord thy God, to observe and to do all his commandments which I command thee this day, that the Lord thy God will set thee on high above all the nations of the earth."
>
> —Deuteronomy 28:1
>
> "If then their uncircumcised hearts be humbled, . . . then will I remember my covenant with Jacob, and also my covenant with Isaac, and also my covenant with Abraham will I remember; and I will remember the land."
>
> —Leviticus 26:41–42

come to the rescue. In fact, the custodian of that great document, even the government itself, was all too often the offending party in these cases.

I could write volumes on the atrocities leveled against these people. But, because I am writing to a Mormon audience, I choose to focus on two specific groups who found themselves at the tip of this oppressive sword—a sword being arrogantly wielded by the American people and their government.

North Carolina–1828

Harriet Jacobs's precious grandmother had taught her biblical principles as a young child. Harriet wanted so badly to live a righteous life. But the freedom to do so was not granted her—for she was a slave.

When she was but a young teenage girl, Harriet's master demanded that she give up any hope of an unsullied relationship with a man she loved, though that was Harriett's dream. She was to serve as an object of lust for the master. She was forced out of living her religious convictions of virginity, marriage, and family. "He tried his utmost to corrupt the pure principles my grandmother instilled," wrote Harriet. "He peopled my young mind with unclean images, such as only a vile monster could think of. . . . I was compelled to live under the same roof with him—where I saw a man forty years my senior daily violating the most sacred commandments of nature."[13]

Hope entered in one day when Harriet learned that the plantation owners had decided to at last allow their slaves to attend Christian worship services. Would Harriet get to live the religion she had loved as a child? She hurried to the service but sat aghast in the pew when the preacher, brought in by the masters, opened his mouth. "Servants, be obedient to them that are your masters

A family of slaves.

according to the flesh, with fear and trembling, in singleness of your heart, as unto Christ" (Ephesians 6:5). This was not true religion, and Harriet knew it. The preacher continued: "If you disobey your earthly master, you offend your heavenly Master. You must obey God's commandments."

Harriet later documented her thoughts on the preachers of religion: "What does *he* know of the half-starved wretches toiling from dawn till dark on the plantations? of mothers shrieking for their children, torn from their arms by slave traders? of young girls dragged down into moral filth? of pools of blood around the whipping posts?"[14]

Harriet pled with the readers of her memoir not to judge her heart in matters of her personal religion:

O, ye happy women, whose purity has been sheltered from childhood, who have been free to choose the objects of your affection, whose homes are protected by law, do not judge the poor desolate slave girl too severely! . . . I wanted to keep myself pure; and, under the most adverse circumstances, I tried hard to preserve my self-respect; but I was struggling alone in the powerful grasp of the demon Slavery; and the monster proved too strong for me. I felt as if I was forsaken by God and man.[15]

Ultimately, this beautiful soul, this victim of religious persecution in its cruelest form, summed up her only hope by quoting from a spiritual song popular with her oppressed people: "Ole Satan's church is here below; Up to God's free church I hope to go."[16]

Missouri–1838

Bullets were flying all around the young mother, Amanda Smith. She had only recently arrived with her family at the small Mormon settlement called Haun's Mill—though she never would have come had she known she would be a target in a bloody massacre. She grabbed her two small children and made her way, as fast as possible, across the millpond in search of safety. She noticed bullets ripping through her dress. She thought only of her children, doing her best to move with them while simultaneously blocking them from the onslaught of rounds. Another woman, Mary Stedwell, was running beside her. She was hit and dropped to the ground. Before fleeing farther, Amanda managed to find Mary cover behind a log, and not a second too soon. Within moments, more than twenty rounds were caught by the log, saving Mary's life.[17]

"Sardius! . . . Alma!" Amanda yelled with all her might, trying to compete with the blaring blasts of the gunfire. Though she knew her young boys (ten-year-old Sardius and seven-year-old Alma) would never be able to hear her over the cries, screams, and explosions consuming the once peaceful hamlet, she refused to do nothing. So she yelled their names again. She prayed that her husband, Warren, had snagged the boys before the angry mob had surprised the settlers with hellfire in their wake. She found guarded comfort in the mental picture of Sardius and Alma huddled close to their father, perhaps in the safety of the mill or the blacksmith shop. She had no idea that her husband already lay dead on the ground—a victim of religious persecution. She also had no idea that her baby boy Alma had seen his hip shot off and was suffering alone on the cold, hard dirt. And she would wish to God that she never learned the sad truth about what had happened to her little Sardius.[18]

Three days before the massacre, Missouri Governor Lilburn Boggs had issued an extermination order aimed at all Mormons in the state. *Leave or die* was the clarion call. For years, the Mormons had been driven from state to state by mobs backed by local governments. No exception to this rule was granted at Haun's Mill. Some of the men of the mob were even compensated by the state for their services rendered in the "Mormon War." Amanda and her small community, however, were profoundly confused. Nobody in their peaceful settlement had been involved in any past fighting, and the mobbers hailed from an adjacent county where no fighting with Mormons had *ever* occurred. Furthermore, the Mormon settlers had only barely entered into a peace treaty with their neighbors. As the mob entered, the Mormons raised a white flag and called for peace. They were ignored. Why this senseless attack was happening was a mystery to them—and it is a mystery even today.[19]

In the end, members of the mob were called heroic by their communities. Not a single man was arrested. Amidst complaints by the Mormon community, the Missouri legislature first considered, then officially shut down any talk of an investigation into what had actually happened.[20]

The massacre—roughly 240 angry men pitted against perhaps 30 Mormon men in the assaulted village, which was full of women and children—was exactly that. It was a massacre. And the right to practice religion free and unmolested was at the center of it all.[21]

After the mob departed, Amanda came out from hiding and reentered the village. She described it as "an awful sight. Oh Horrible!" Young mothers found themselves instantly widowed, sobbing over the corpses of their husbands. At least forty children, now fatherless, wandered aimlessly and in emotional shambles through the once happy hamlet. Amanda stumbled upon her dead husband and her suffering little Alma (who miraculously survived). At last she came upon Sardius—or what was left of him. It was too much for any mother to bear.[22]

Witnesses described the death scene. Upon hearing the initial gunfire, ten-year-old Sardius and his friend, nine-year-old Charley Merrick, crawled under the blacksmith's bellows, fearful for their lives. A member of the mob, William Reynolds, saw Sardius and dragged him out. Without thinking twice, he placed the muzzle of his gun against the boy's forehead and blew off the top of his head. Reynolds then remarked, "Nits will make lice, and if he had lived, he would have become a Mormon." Overcome by it all, Charley ran out of the shop only to run into two members of the mob. They both leveled their guns at little Charley and shot him dead—one with a rifle ball, the other with buckshot. Charley's last words as he confronted his assailants were a final plea for his life. The words the lad chose should have worked for him; in light of what was happening, they were at once tragic, stunning, hopeful, telling, and most profoundly ironic: "I am an American boy!"[23]

At the moment Sardius and Charley fell to their tragic and premature deaths, the Constitution of the United States had been the law of the land for almost *fifty years.*

◆　◆　◆

These stories (which represent only a fraction of the terror that visited these poor victims) are difficult to digest, especially in light of the fact that so few were willing to stand up for the innocent. Instead, the majority chose to ignore the injustice. But certain people would not ignore it. They would fight and die to bring liberty to all. The two servants chosen to lead this cause of restoring the purposes of America were among these great defenders. They were raised up by God Almighty and given the attributes necessary to make the sacrifice. Joseph Smith and Abraham Lincoln were many things to many people. But above all, they loved.

"And if a stranger sojourn with thee in your land, ye shall not vex him. But the stranger that dwelleth with you shall be unto you as one born among you, and thou shalt love him as thyself; for ye were strangers in the land of Egypt: I am the Lord your God."
—*Leviticus 19:33–34; see also Leviticus 24:22; 25:35; Deuteronomy 10:16–19; 14:29*

They reached out to uplift the sick and afflicted. They refused to ignore them. This is why God could use them in His cause of liberty and salvation.

Lincoln's friends were regularly astonished at the compassion he showed for others. Often they were shocked at the amount of time he would spend as president dealing with the most mundane and seemingly unimportant requests from the lowliest of solicitors. And frankly, many of his closest advisors were annoyed at his constant efforts to find any justification for pardoning young soldiers—Northern and Southern—whose acts of cowardice or treason justified their execution. Yet he could not turn his back—ever. He would spend countless hours at military hospitals, shaking every hand and conversing with every suffering individual.[24] He was, as one good friend declared, "always on the side of the weak."[25]

One story that sums up Lincoln's compassion (a compassion some called "sensitive almost to a fault") is that of the hog. While riding with a group of men through a prairie, Lincoln passed a hog deeply mired in thick mud. The men went on by without giving much notice. After moving on some distance, Lincoln stopped his horse. He told his companions that he could not stop thinking about the poor animal. He said he imagined it had said to itself, as the men passed by: "There now! My last hope is gone." Lincoln returned, crawled through the mud, and saved the poor creature.[26]

And what about Joseph Smith? When it comes to compassion, the Prophet indeed shared this attribute. The stories that prove his character, as documented in Church history, are abundant. One that I recently came across touched me deeply.

Jane Manning (born in the early 1800s) was a young black woman who had accepted the gospel in Connecticut at the hands of two Mormon missionaries. She was baptized along with family members to whom she had taught the gospel. Desiring to travel to Nauvoo to be with the Saints, she purchased a steamboat ticket. After her luggage had already been loaded onto the boat, she was refused passage because she was black. Then the captain refused to return her luggage. And so she began the long walk all the way to Nauvoo without a penny in her pocket. After a journey that almost did her in (between the winter storms, lack of proper clothing and food, and slaveholders wanting to kidnap her), she

A SYMPATHETIC HEART

"Lincoln, man and boy, had unusually intense sympathy with the suffering of his fellow creatures: for lost cats, mired-down hogs, birds fallen out of the nest, [etc.]. This sympathy extended also, as is not always the case with animal lovers, to his fellow human beings: to the old Indian who wandered into the camp; the woman whose drunken husband beat her; the farm boy who is going to be shot for falling asleep on sentry duty; the coffle of slaves on the boat in Ohio, chained together like fish on a line. This natural human fellow-feeling he found in himself must have been part of the reason he [had] . . . sympathy for the slave. . . . That, he affirmed, would still be there even if the Declaration of Independence had not been written."

—*William Lee Miller, Lincoln biographer*[27]

Abraham Lincoln and Tad Lincoln.

arrived at Nauvoo. She was shocked and saddened to find that many Saints there rebuffed her because of the color of her skin.

After several days, Jane had still not found employment. She sat weeping. It was then that Joseph Smith approached her and asked why she was crying.

"The folks have all gone and got themselves homes, and I have got none," was her reply.

"Yes, you have," replied Joseph. "You have a home right here." He left briefly and brought Emma back with him, introducing her to poor Jane. "Sister Emma," asked Joseph with a smile on his face, "here is a girl that says she has no home, haven't you a home for her?" Emma opened her arms and home to Jane. She lived with the Smiths as a sister and family member. She died at the age of eighty-six in Salt Lake City as an active and faithful Latter-day Saint.[28]

Indeed, Joseph and Abraham shared many characteristics that made them chosen servants of God. But in the battle over national sin, and in the struggle to elevate all God's children as joint-heirs of the American covenant, their shared attributes of deep sympathy and compassion would be paramount. Their sentiments on the matter ran so deep that they would sacrifice everything before relinquishing this noble trait. This is who the Lord needed.

Knowing the covenant was in severe breach, and not wanting the adversary to undo all that had been done for the salvation of mankind, God would not let evil be. He would fight back. And His battle plan called for two of the greatest men of the nineteenth century. He called on Joseph and Abraham!

PROPHETIC WORDS TRAGICALLY FULFILLED

President-elect Lincoln declared that the bonds of "Christianity" and "patriotism" and "liberty" and "equality" for all, as incorporated in the Declaration and the Constitution were worth fighting for. "I would rather be assassinated on this spot than to surrender it."[29]

The Prophet Joseph boldly declared, "The Saints can testify whether I am willing to lay down my life for my brethren. If it has been demonstrated that I have been willing to die for a 'Mormon.' I am bold to declare before Heaven that I am just as ready to die in defending the rights of a Presbyterian, a Baptist, or a good man of any other denomination; for the same principle which would trample upon the rights of the Latter-day Saints would trample upon the rights of the Roman Catholics, or of any other denomination who may be unpopular and too weak to defend themselves."[30]

CHAPTER 5

The Prophet for President

Two significant years in the life of William Seward were 1820 and 1830. In 1820, he graduated from Union College with high honors. And 1830 marked the year he was first elected to public office; it was the year that launched his long career in politics.[1] It is interesting how those two years—as important as they were for our primary witness—were everlastingly more important for the world. For they were the years that marked, respectively, Joseph's grand vision of the Almighty and the establishment of The Church of Jesus Christ of Latter-day Saints. Those events meant little or nothing to the likes of Seward or Lincoln or almost anybody living in that generation. But that would not always be the case.

If only they could have known how tightly connected those events were to their work in America during that awful fraternal conflict we call the Civil War! If only they could have turned back the clocks of time and been given another chance to listen to the words of Joseph Smith, a man they thought in mortality to be a wild-eyed religious fanatic. If only they had known just a fraction of what he knew—of what he pled for the nation to learn. That would have made all the difference.

Many people then (and even now) were perplexed by Joseph's decision to run for the office of president of the United States in 1844. *What is he thinking?* is what they declared at the time.

Shall I tell you what I believe he was thinking? Would you believe me if I told you that Joseph Smith knew the Civil War was coming? Not only that, he knew *why* it was coming. It was a consequence of national sin and a broken covenant. But it gets even more profound. Joseph knew the precise solution to heal the land—he called for a specific national policy that would represent the restitution phase of America's repentance. If he could get the nation to listen and comply, then the United States would be spared from that awful war.

But in the end, they did not listen to the prophet-candidate. The war came. And it would not end until Abraham Lincoln and his nation applied the *precise* solution prescribed by the Prophet Joseph. But I'm getting ahead of myself.

Let me take you back to 1833. While Seward was going about as a New York state senator, working on improving the prison system and trying to galvanize the national bank, the Mormon people were suffering as few in America were. American

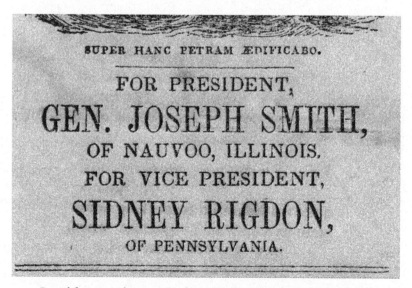

SUPER HANC PETRAM ÆDIFICABO.

FOR PRESIDENT,
GEN. JOSEPH SMITH,
OF NAUVOO, ILLINOIS.
FOR VICE PRESIDENT,
SIDNEY RIGDON,
OF PENNSYLVANIA.

Detail from an advertisement for Joseph Smith's presidential candidacy.

politicians, and the people they represented, turned a blind eye as the Latter-day Saints were completely denied the promises of the Constitution. They were run out, smoked out, pillaged, trampled upon, and murdered.

Joseph dropped to his knees. *Why, God?* was his question, his plea to heaven. Like many of you, I have participated in a number of LDS-sponsored patriotic programs. Almost always, during these services, we hear a famous Mormon doctrine. Said the Lord, "I established the Constitution of this land, by the hands of wise men whom I raised up" (D&C 101:80). A happy verse, it would seem. But on second thought, maybe it was not so happy after all. You see, this verse was the answer given to the heartbroken prophet. It was an attempt to comfort him with the knowledge that America was in fact a promised land, despite evidence to the contrary—evidence manifested by the broken countenances of Mormon men, women, and children.

The point the Lord was making directly follows this more popular verse. What comes next is a call to action. *Joseph,* the Lord was saying, in essence, *go out and save the promised land. Bring it back!* We must understand that the way things were going for Joseph and the Saints, the temples of God could not stand. They had been, and would be, continually obstructed, confiscated, and burned if the national status quo remained. Again I ask, what is the purpose of a promised land if you can't have a temple therein? You see the desperate situation here.

And so, after claiming America as His design (verse 80), the Lord declared to His prophet and church, "Let them importune at the feet of the judge; and if he heed them not, let them importune at the feet of the governor; and if the governor heed them not, let them importune at the feet of the president" (D&C 101:86–88). Joseph was to seek the solution. He was to exhaust every effort, at every level of government, to redress the national calamities. And he tried! He went to the judge. He went to the governor. Nothing but further abuse from the state.

But the revelation told him to also go to the federal government for help. A novel idea—perhaps one supported by the Book of Mormon. You see, some individual states (such as New York, Ohio, Missouri, and Illinois) proved severely abusive to the Saints. The states represented American factions—the lesser part of the people. The Constitution, however, even that document that was based in "holy principles" and made to maintain the "rights and protection of all flesh" (D&C 101:77) had created another government. It created a government that included all the states—all the people. Perhaps this new national or federal government that represented the voice of everybody in America would come to the rescue. For, though "it is common for the lesser part of the people [for example, the state of Missouri] to desire that which is not right . . . it is not common that the voice of the people [the national government, or all the states combined] desireth anything contrary to that which is right . . . therefore this shall ye observe and make it your law—to do your business by the voice of the people" (Mosiah 29:26). (This, of course, only works when the people stay alert and maintain their constitutional power and influence over the federal government.) There was indeed a reason Joseph was specifically called upon to seek help from the federal government.

Within months of the revelation, an appeal for redress had been made to President Andrew Jackson. But the Prophet was turned down.[2] A later appeal in person to President Martin Van Buren produced the same results: though the president agreed the Mormon cause was "just," he told Joseph that the federal government could not intervene in matters pertaining to the states. His federal authority was too limited.[3] Joseph even secured an audience with prominent members of Congress, but their response did not vary from that of the White House.[4]

Is this to be believed? If state governments decided to deny any group of people basic First Amendment rights, they could do so? Unfortunately, yes. This is the dirty little secret of nineteenth-century America. That grand Bill of Rights pertained only to the federal government. In other words, only the federal government had to respect those precious rights. The states could do what they wanted. They could apply those sacred rights, or they could deny them. Too often, they chose the latter. And the federal government, agreeing with the constitutional interpretation of the states, would not come to the rescue. As a result, the Latter-day Saints and other minorities suffered dearly.

> States like Connecticut and Massachusetts maintained state-sponsored religions well after the U.S. Constitution had been ratified. When members of non–state-sponsored religions refused to pay church taxes, they were penalized by the state. As un-American as such a practice may seem to us today, at that time it was deemed constitutional.[5]

Now, I could get into a legal debate about whether the Constitution encouraged the federal government to enforce the Bill of Rights for all Americans, even if it meant coming to blows with the oppressive state governments that denied certain groups these rights. But suffice it to say for now that, according to our own scripture, God had sent Joseph Smith to ask for federal intervention in the matter. In wanting the federal government to intervene in the states, was God seeking to break the rules of that Constitution He Himself claimed to have influenced?

Joseph didn't think so. He refused to accept the explanation

The Constitution of the United States.

coming from the government. He believed the Constitution was not being carried out appropriately. He demanded federal intervention. "If the General Government [federal government] has no power, to re-instate expelled citizens to their rights," complained the Prophet to Congress, "there is a monstrous hypocrite fed and fostered from the hard earnings of the people!" Joseph marveled at the irony of the fact that the federal government professed the constitutional power to "protect the nation against foreign in-vasion and internal broil," and yet the Saints—who were being hounded, robbed, raped, and killed by raging mobs supported and enabled by the state—were not protected by the same power.[6] The Prophet laid out his feelings plainly to Congress, declaring that "all men who say the [federal] Congress has no power to . . . defend the rights of her citizens have not the love of truth in them."[7]

Joseph saw the federal government—even that body that rep-resented the voice of all Americans—as the solution to the crisis. And if the federal government would not change its mind, he was determined to become, in essence, the federal government him-self, then appropriately carry out the duty of delivering full liberty to all. Declared Joseph, "When we have petitioned those in power for assistance, they have always told us they had no power to help us. Damn such traitors! When they give me the power to protect the innocent, I will never say I can do nothing for their good: I will exercise that power, so help me God."[8] Hence, his run for the presidency. You see, he took that revelation to engage the federal government very seriously.

Now, here is the key question. What did he call for? What was his national solution, his political platform? To understand Abraham Lincoln and the Civil War, you must understand this part. Just before announcing his candidacy, Joseph Smith pro-claimed the following:

> It is one of the first principles of my life, and one that I have cultivated from my childhood, having been taught it by my father, to allow every one the liberty of conscience. I am the greatest advocate of the Constitution of the United States there is on earth. In my feelings I am always ready to die for the protection of the weak and

oppressed in their just rights. The only fault I find with the Constitution is, it is not broad enough to cover the whole ground.

Although it provides that all men shall enjoy religious freedom, yet it does not provide the manner by which that freedom can be preserved, nor for the punishment of Government officers who refuse to protect the people in their religious rights, or punish the mobs, states, or communities who interfere with the rights of the people on account of their religion. Its sentiments are good, but it provides no means of enforcing them. It has but this one fault. Under its provision, a man or a people who are able to protect themselves can get along well enough; but those who have the misfortune to be weak or unpopular are left to the merciless rage of popular fury.

The Constitution should contain a provision that every officer of the Government who should neglect or refuse to extend the protection guaranteed in the Constitution should be subject to capital punishment; and then the president of the United States would not say, *"Your cause is just, but I can do nothing for you,"* a governor issue exterminating orders, or judges say, "The men ought to have the protection of law, but it won't please the mob; the men must die, anyhow, to satisfy the clamor of the rabble; they must be hung, or Missouri be damned to all eternity." Executive writs could be issued when they ought to be, and not be made instruments of cruelty to oppress the innocent, and persecute men whose religion is unpopular.[9]

And so we come to what Joseph called *the provision:* an amendment to the Constitution that would bring consequences to state governments that denied the constitutional rights of the people. This provision has since been achieved. Indeed, we no longer face the challenges of the early Saints. Why? Because Joseph's provision is here! We call it the Fourteenth Amendment. It simply proclaims that all Americans are heirs to the blessings of the Constitution. All are citizens of America! And if Missouri or any other state tries to take away our First Amendment rights (or any other rights protected by the Constitution), then the federal government will intervene on our behalf. The national government will, as Joseph demanded, "punish the mobs, states, or communities who interfere with the rights of the people on account of their religion."[10]

The federal government eventually proved what a power for good this amendment could be. When states continued to abuse black minorities, at last there was reprieve in the land. Who sent the U.S. Marshals to accompany the innocent black child to her public elementary school, a right being denied to her by the racist majority supported by the state? Who sent the U.S. military to do the same for black students being persecuted by their state for wanting to attend the public university? It was the federal government, backed by the Fourteenth Amendment. States have since complied; they have decided that the best route to take is to behave and protect God-given liberty and equality under the law. But the check and balance is, and has been, the Fourteenth Amendment enforced by the national government.

Interestingly, the father of the Constitution seems to have had the intuition of Joseph Smith. Yes, James Madison, who was a principal author of the Bill of Rights, called for the very same provision to be added to the Constitution. He knew the states were abusing religious minorities; he saw it happening in his own beloved Virginia. The Constitution was his chance to stop it. He

JAMES MADISON AND THE BILL OF RIGHTS

During the creation of the Bill of Rights, James Madison, the "father of the Constitution," proposed the following amendment: "*No state* shall violate the equal rights of conscience, or the freedom of the press, or the trial by jury in criminal cases."[11] His colleagues balked. They refused. The states would not be told what to do. In the end, the First Amendment would apply only to the federal government. Only the federal government would have to uphold these constitutional blessings. The states could continue their abuse against the innocent, if they so desired.

James Madison.

Madison was outraged. He shot off a dispatch to Thomas Jefferson, telling him that without his proposed amendment, the Constitution would "neither effectually answer its national object nor prevent the local mischiefs which every where excite disgusts [at] the state governments."[12] He practically screamed to the House of Representatives, which was considering his added amendment, telling them that his proposal was "the most valuable amendment in the whole list." Madison added, "If there was any reason to restrain the Government of the United States from infringing upon these essential rights, it was equally necessary that they should be secured against the State Governments."[13]

Much to the dismay of minorities, both racial and religious, his plea fell on deaf ears.

wanted to use the Constitution to influence the new national government to block the oppression.[14] Sadly, he was denied. So Joseph would pick up the torch.

I know that today we Americans face a different set of challenges. Many of us believe the federal government intervenes too much over the states. But please, try to read nineteenth-century American history through nineteenth-century lenses—not through twenty-first-century lenses. If the states had behaved themselves, the Fourteenth Amendment would not have been required. But how long could they have been allowed to oppress, enslave, destroy, kill, and perform the works of the adversary? Perhaps *the provision* was a lesser law, as it opened the door for unrighteous interpretations and allowed the pendulum to swing too far in the opposite direction, causing too much federal intervention. Sometimes lesser laws are required due to the people's disobedience. (Just ask the children of Israel, who because of unrighteousness were given the lesser law we call the law of Moses.) But to say such a provision was not needed is to deny the truth of what was happening to the Mormon people and millions of other suffering Americans.

Joseph Smith saw the truth clearly because he lived it. In his final assessment, he understood what he needed to eradicate. He declared, "The States rights doctrine are what feed mobs. They are a dead carcass, a stink and they shall ascend up as a stink offering in the nose of the Almighty."[15] In the end, Joseph knew that his provision (a provision that would be reflected in the Fourteenth Amendment) would temper the "States rights doctrine," thus ensuring that the blessings of the Constitution would secure God's temples in the land.

Joseph Smith's presidential platform was not limited to *the provision*. There was an even more glaring national ill. As John

Jay (one of the most inspired Founding Fathers of the Revolution and an important proponent of the Constitution) declared, "We have the highest reason to believe that the Almighty will not suffer slavery and the Gospel to go hand in hand. It cannot, it will not be."[16] Joseph knew this as well. Nothing brought America into deeper breach of covenant than this sin. And so Joseph the candidate called for slavery's eradication. He pointed out the great American irony of the Declaration of Independence: that it preached the words and promises of liberty to all, even while "at the same time some two or three millions of people are held as slaves for life, because the spirit in them is covered with a darker skin."[17]

On an earlier occasion, the Prophet had cried: "Break off the shackles from the poor black man, and hire them to labor like other human beings." He demanded, "Set them free, Educate them and give them their equal rights." He explained, "They come into the world slaves, mentally and physically. Change their situation. . . . They have souls and are subjects of salvation."[18] As part of his presidential platform, Joseph even offered a clever solution to freeing the slaves: buy their freedom through sales of public lands and through deductions of pay from members of Congress.[19] Indeed, the nation as a whole, and particularly its representatives who had failed God and country by encouraging or at least tolerating this sin, should have sacrificed in their repentance and restitution.

"It is not right that any man should be in bondage one to another."
—D&C 101:79

Of course, you will recognize that this portion of Joseph Smith's plan was eventually delivered through the Thirteenth Amendment, even that necessary provision that would naturally precede the Fourteenth Amendment. Yes, Joseph called for both!

He wanted so badly for the people to listen. He knew that the adoption of these principles would mean that the nation had repented of sins past, that America had overcome and reset the Constitution to reflect the repentance and restitution phases of national forgiveness. The covenant would be restored. Tyranny would be knocked to the ground, and the temple would take its place. This was the solution he sought. It was the Prophet's response to God's mandate to engage America and make it the promised land it was intended to be.

But what if the nation did not listen? Would God's justice sleep forever? Joseph knew the answer to this as well. He knew that God would have His American people experience the national humility and repentance that would by necessity support and be reflected in these amendments. The nation could choose repentance and righteousness on its own, or God could help it by sending a heavenly judgment—a judgment so severe that humility and repentance (and those inspired amendments) would become the only way out. Read your Civil War history. Ask yourself, what ended the war? What was the ultimate fruit of that awful calamity? The answer: It was precisely what Joseph Smith had prescribed for the nation. It was the Thirteenth and Fourteenth Amendments. Quite astonishing. In the end, it was Joseph's deeper understanding that led him to publicly (and quite boldly) describe his presidential bid as the "last effort which is enjoined upon us by our Heavenly Father before the whole nation may be left without excuse and He can send forth the power of His mighty arm."[21]

Can you guess which way the country went? Can you guess

> "God will have a humble people. Either we can choose to be humble or we can be compelled to be humble."
>
> —*Ezra Taft Benson*[20]

IF THE NATION HAD HEEDED

Years after the Civil War, the renowned politician and one-time mayor of Boston, Josiah Quincy, recognized how things might have been different had the nation heeded the Prophet. Quincy had visited Joseph Smith during the Prophet's 1844 run for the presidency, and therefore knew something about his politics. Based on this knowledge, Quincy made a most astonishing statement about Joseph Smith and the Civil War. While discussing the merits of a certain Christian scholar, who had developed a plan in 1855 that, if implemented, might have spared the nation any civil war, Quincy said this in the 1880s:

"We, who can look back upon the terrible cost of fratricidal war which put an end to slavery, now say that such a solution of the difficulty would have been worthy a Christian statesman. But if the retired scholar was in advance of his time when he advocated this disposition . . . in 1855, what shall I say of the political and religious leader [Joseph Smith] who had committed himself, in print, as well as in conversation, to the same course in 1844?"[22]

Josiah Quincy.

what they chose? Here is a hint: if they had listened to the Prophet, I would not be writing this book and Abraham Lincoln would not have been called upon to clean up the greatest disaster in American history. Do you still wonder what they chose?

One more hint: On June 27, 1844, at five o'clock p.m., while in the middle of his presidential candidacy—indeed, at the height of his warnings to the nation— Joseph Smith was killed. Not only was he martyred but, as a budding politician entering the national stage, he was assassinated. The murder was followed by silence from the state and the nation. Shortly thereafter, the temple was burned to the ground. Again, silence and apathy followed. As was its right, America had chosen how to respond to God's prophet. As was *His* right, God would then invoke the consequences of that decision.

> "Certain it is that had Joseph Smith been elected President of the United States and had been sustained by Congress in his policies, this land would have been spared the desolating war which filled its hamlets and fields with carnage and its homes with sobbing widows and orphans."
> —*George Q. Cannon*[23]

Those constitutional amendments were too important for the salvation of the nation and for the kingdom of God Almighty; they could no longer be neglected. They would be born one way or another: either through the gentle promptings of God and His prophet, or through the fires of hell and humiliation, even through the heavenly punishment of civil war. Oh, that His people had listened!

CHAPTER 6

The Civil War Prophecies

As the idea may have been new to you, I'm wondering if maybe you are not yet convinced that God Himself was directing Joseph Smith in his presidential candidacy and his efforts to save the nation. Perhaps you believe, as many do, that Joseph's bid for the presidency and his message to the nation were merely reflections of Joseph the man, not Joseph the Prophet.

Many find it odd, if not a bit presumptuous and extreme, that Joseph called his presidential bid the "last effort which is enjoined upon us by our Heavenly Father before the whole nation may be left without excuse and He can send forth the power of His mighty arm."[1] That was not all he said. The year before his candidacy, he warned Congress that if they refused to "hear our petition and grant us protection, *they shall be broken up as a government.*"[2] One historian declared that, during this time, Joseph believed it was "his duty as a prophet of God to warn his nation, even as Isaiah of old had warned the nation of Israelites, of impending doom and destruction."[3]

"Oh that I could snatch them [the people of the United States] from the vortex of misery, into which I behold them plunging themselves . . . ," cried the prophet-candidate, "that I might be enabled by the warning voice, to be an instrument of bringing them to unfeigned repentance."[4]

Was Joseph really stating, or at least implying, that if his warnings went unheeded, a punishment (like a civil war) would befall the nation? It seems to fit. Since the kingdom of God was at stake, certainly such drastic measures were justified in the Prophet's mind.

To fully answer these inquiries, however, we must return to the Doctrine and Covenants.

In the preceding chapter, I wrote about that grand revelation on the Constitution found in Doctrine and Covenants 101. After acknowledging the divine hand over the document and the nation (verses 76–80), the Lord commanded Joseph to fix the national crisis before him. He was told to importune at the feet of the judge (verse 86), and if the judge ignored him, to importune at the feet of the governor (verse 87), and if the governor ignored him, to importune at the feet of the president (verse 88). But the Lord had one more contingency, should the president (the last hope, representing all the people) also ignore the desperate pleas. In the very next verse, things really heat up:

"And if the president heed them not, then will the Lord arise and come forth out of his hiding place, and in his fury vex the nation; and in his hot displeasure, and in his fierce anger, in his time, will cut off those wicked, unfaithful, and unjust stewards, and appoint them their portion among hypocrites, and unbelievers" (D&C 101:89–90).

Think about this in context. Joseph was told to act on behalf of the broken Constitution. He presented (in essence) the Thirteenth and Fourteenth Amendments, even running for president in order to bring about these powerful solutions. God told Joseph that if the nation rejected his efforts, then He Himself would bring to pass the solution. But His way would not be pretty, for it would be delivered in "fierce anger" and "hot displeasure." He would "vex the nation." Now, I don't know what the word *vex* means to you, but in the dictionary it is defined as follows: "to bring trouble, distress, or agitations to; to bring physical distress to; to shake or toss about."[5]

After Joseph, following God's command, had engaged every level of government and been rejected outright by each, only one event in history fits the scriptural description of what was supposed to happen next. There has been one (and only one) furious act that vexed the nation so severely that, through the humbling effects it had upon the people, it produced Joseph Smith's provisions. It was the Civil War.

Nobody wanted this to happen. After announcing His intention to bring the calamity, the Lord declared, "Pray ye, therefore, that their ears may be opened unto your cries, that I may be merciful unto them, that these things may not come upon them" (D&C 101:92). But what was He to do? Again, if the promised land rejects the temples of God, not allowing them to stand, what is the point of the promised land? God loves His children, and so He will go to great lengths to ensure their happiness in the gospel. He does this not only for His living children but for the dead, who were also looking with great anticipation for temples to dot the earth and who were also devastated when the temple efforts were thwarted again and again. As Elder Dallin H. Oaks has said, "God's anger and His wrath are not a *contradiction* of His love but an *evidence* of His love."[6]

Indeed, the Lord could not have been clearer about why He would deliver the national scourge. In the next verses, He explained: "What I have said unto you must needs be, that all men may be left without excuse; that wise men and rulers may hear and know that which they have never considered; that I may proceed to bring to pass my act, my strange act, and perform my work, my strange work, that men may discern between the righteous and the wicked, saith your God" (D&C 101:93–95).

The terms *strange act* and *strange work* are used by God to describe the fulness of His gospel (see Isaiah 28:21; D&C 95:4). And so now we see definitively what this was really all about. The Restoration. The gathering of Israel. This was the reason for it all. A just cause, don't you think?

At last, Joseph's overzealousness and extreme behavior (that is, warning the nation of destruction and running for the presidency) do not seem so overzealous or extreme after all. Joseph saw the whole picture. He knew the plan. He knew what the nation would have to endure should they continue down the path of sin. And so he fought tooth and nail, literally running himself into the ground, to get those provisions (those powerful amendments) on the national table. As he himself lamented, by denying his petitions, Americans were "plunging themselves" into "the vortex of misery."[7] Anyone who lived through the Civil War could tell you that Joseph's description was spot-on. More than six hundred thousand dead. Pain. Loneliness. Thousands of young widows. Tens of thousands of children crying for their dead fathers, brothers, uncles, loved ones, and friends. Not a family went unaffected. Words can't describe what Joseph saw—what those poor Americans went through. But it was the final contingency. And it worked. For, through it, God was able to bring about Joseph's constitutional provisions (what Lincoln would describe in his Gettysburg Address as "under God . . . a new birth of freedom"), and as a result temples would begin to dot the land at long last.

Are you convinced yet that God, and His prophecies delivered through His Prophet, were behind the Civil War? If not, the fulness of Abraham Lincoln—his thoughts, words, acts, and deeds—will never be completely understood.

In case you are not yet persuaded, I have found a few additional wonders I would like to share with you. Back to the scriptures. As early as 1831, the Lord revealed that a war connected to His efforts to bring forth the gospel might be expected to hit the very American generation from which had sprung the early Church. "And when the times of the Gentiles is come in, a light shall break forth among them that sit in darkness, and it shall be the fulness of my gospel; but they receive it not; for they perceive not the light, and they turn their hearts from me because of the precepts of men. . . . And there shall be men standing in that generation, that shall not pass until they shall see an over-

> As the war began and raged on, Brigham Young declared: "God has come out of his hiding-place and has commenced to vex the nation that has rejected us, and he will vex it with a sore vexation."
>
> A few years later, he said, "[Joseph's] prediction is being fulfilled, and we cannot help it."[8]

flowing scourge; for a desolating sickness shall cover the land." The Lord then describes this scourge in part, leaving little doubt as to what He is referring to: " . . . and they will take up the sword, one against another, and they will kill one another" (D&C 45:28–33). Considering the time frame and description of this imminent scourge, and considering it was given in response to the general disobedience of the people, does the Civil War not fit the bill?

In 1832, over thirty years before it began, the Lord revealed to the Prophet Joseph the coming of the Civil War, even revealing the very state where it would commence:

"Verily, thus saith the Lord concerning the wars that will shortly come to pass, beginning at the rebellion of South Carolina, which will eventually terminate in the death and misery of many souls; . . . for behold, the Southern States shall be divided against the Northern States. . . . And it shall come to pass, after many days, slaves shall rise up against their masters, who shall be marshaled and disciplined for war. And it shall come to pass also that the remnants who are left of the land will marshal themselves, and shall become exceedingly angry, and shall vex the Gentiles with a sore vexation" (D&C 87:1–5).

This prophecy was fulfilled, as the first shots fired in the Civil War were at the Southern invasion of Fort Sumter, South Carolina, in April 1861. The scripture also states that the "Southern States will call on . . . Great Britain" (verse 3). This part of the prophecy was certainly fulfilled when, at the beginning of the conflict, a Southern delegation was dispatched to Great Britain in hopes of obtaining recognition and aid for the new Southern Confederacy.[9]

It is fascinating to see that such specific prophecy was, during the years leading up to the Civil War, streaming out of

The Confederacy fires on Fort Sumter, South Carolina.

EARLY WARNINGS OF THE CIVIL WAR

Joseph Smith was not the only one to prophesy concerning the war. Some of the first founders of America also knew. During the creation of the Constitution, one of the delegates at the convention, George Mason, warned his countrymen of what God would do if America continued to permit the sin of slavery in the land. Such national sin, he predicted, would "bring the judgment of heaven on a Country. As nations can not be rewarded or punished in the next world they must be in this. By an inevitable chain of causes & effects providence punishes national sins, by national calamities."[10] Thomas Jefferson had also uttered such a prophecy a few years earlier, warning, "There must doubtless be an unhappy influence on the manners of our people produced by the existence of slavery among us. . . . Indeed I tremble for my country when I reflect that God is just: that his justice cannot sleep for ever." He then described "a revolution" over the

Thomas Jefferson warned of the possible conflict over slavery.

conflict as being "among possible events" and that such an event would be administered by "supernatural interference! The Almighty has no attribute which can take side with us in such a contest."[11] These men understood the national covenant—and they understood the consequences should that covenant be broken by the people.

that obscure little band of people called Mormons. It's incredible! While hundreds of thousands were living and sweating out this horrific vexation in the land, others, who were shunned and ignored at the time, actually (ironically) knew the secret of why it was occurring. Notwithstanding this incredible fact, it has occurred to me that so many later generations of Mormons today do not know this secret that their pioneer forebears possessed. I fear too many do not fully grasp the magnitude of what was happening. And we must! For if we don't, nobody will. And if nobody will, then America is likely to fall into the same destructive cycle.

One other Civil War prophecy that helps make my point is as follows. It was uttered by Joseph Smith in 1843, just months before he announced his presidential candidacy:

> I prophesy in the name of the Lord God of Israel, unless the United States redress the wrongs committed upon the Saints in the state of Missouri and punish the crimes committed by her officers that in a few years the government will be utterly overthrown and wasted, and there will not be so much as a potsherd left, for their wickedness in permitting the murder of men, women and children, and the wholesale plunder and extermination of thousands of her citizens to go unpunished, thereby perpetrating a foul and corroding blot upon the fair fame of this great republic, the very thought of which would have caused the high-minded and patriotic framers of the Constitution of the United States to hide their faces with shame.[12]

I have observed how many make a fuss over this prophecy—both Mormons and non-Mormons. Why? Because it is said that it was a "false prophecy." The wrongs against the Mormons were never redressed, they say, yet Missouri remained unmolested and unchanged. Joseph's words never came to pass. Mormons get concerned. Anti-Mormons get giddy.

My response is, *How can anyone think this prophecy was not fulfilled to the letter?* When Joseph's political provision was rejected, this prophecy was in fact shortly thereafter fulfilled. The Civil War not only physically destroyed America—especially Missouri (more on that later)—but the old government was in fact "overthrown" in a way that at last made it unconstitutional for the "murder of men, women and children" and for the "wholesale plunder and extermination" of the Saints. Indeed, the advent of the Fourteenth Amendment—even that direct fruit of the Civil War—changed the government forever, leaving the old government dead and "wasted." A new government—a clarified version of the Constitution—had been employed. And this new government at last would deliver the God-given civil rights to all the people and would empower the national government to enforce such rights in the face of wicked state governments.

> "And now, we can behold the decrees of God concerning this land, that it is a land of promise; and whatsoever nation shall possess it shall serve God, or they shall be swept off when the fulness of his wrath shall come upon them . . . ; for it is the everlasting decree of God."
> —Ether 2:9–10

This prophecy perhaps sheds further light on why Joseph Smith included in the conclusion of his presidential platform publication—offered just months later—a singular description of God. Of the many defining characteristics of God that he could have given, Joseph chose this one: "God, who once cleansed the violence of the earth with flood."[13]

Unfortunately, all these astonishing prophecies did not result

BRIGHAM YOUNG PROPHESIES OF JUDGMENTS TO COME

Brigham Young knew the time of the foretold national vexation was very close at hand. In a revelation received by Brigham on the heels of Joseph's martyrdom, still some fifteen years before the Civil War, the Lord, after calling for the Saints' preparation to move westward, declared: "Thy brethren have rejected you and your testimony, even *the nation* that has driven you out; and now cometh the day of their calamity, even the days of sorrow, like a woman that is taken in travail; and their sorrow shall be great unless they speedily repent, yea, very speed-ily. For they killed the prophets, and them that were sent unto them; and they have shed in-nocent blood, which crieth from the ground against them" (D&C 136:34–36; emphasis added).

Brigham Young added his prophecy about the pending calamities.

Commenting upon this "sor-row" that was shortly to come upon the nation, Brigham de-clared that it would come be-cause they "reject the servants of God; they reject the Gospel of salvation; turn away from the principles of truth and righ-teousness . . . [and] they are sinking in their own sins and corruptions. . . . What will be their condition when the Spirit of the Lord is withdrawn? They will whet the knife to cut each other's throats, and . . . [will] try to make Mason and Dixon's the dividing line; but that will not remain, for they will cross it to destroy each other, and the sword and fire will be prevalent in the land."[14]

in the national righteousness they meant to produce. Instead, the nation crossed the line. It passed the point that finally forced the Lord's hand, compelling Him to activate the frightening prophecies. With a prophet murdered in the land, and the last temple left in ashes, that was it. Think about it! At that point, God Almighty picked up His Saints and placed them outside of the United States. Then He unleashed the prophesied hell. He would now fix the nation in order to make it the vehicle for the gospel that it was destined to become.

His first order of business, before realizing the prophecies, was to place a driver in that vehicle—one who could ensure that the vexation resulted in His divine intent. He needed a humble servant who would see the vexation for what it was—a punishment from above—and then guide the nation to adopt the necessary solutions.

Before I introduce you to the national leader God would call to fill this divine mandate, I will first tell you about a little-known connection this leader's election had to yet another Joseph Smith prophecy. You see, it appears that Joseph initially might have had another man identified in his mind as the leader God might use to save the country and help protect the Church. Joseph once dined with this man and extended a powerful and prophetic warning to him. The man was Stephen Douglas.

On May 18, 1843, the Prophet Joseph had dinner with Illinois Supreme Court Justice Stephen A. Douglas. Joseph, turning to Douglas, prophesied to him, "Judge, you will aspire to the presidency of the United States; and if you ever turn your hand against me or the Latter-day Saints, you will feel the weight of the hand of the Almighty upon you; and you will live to see and know that I have testified the truth to you."[15] Thirteen years later, Douglas turned against the Saints, declaring in a speech delivered in June 1857 that "the knife must be applied to this pestiferous, disgusting cancer [meaning Mormonism] which is gnawing into the very vitals of the body politic."[16] Months later, the *Deseret News* published Joseph's prophecy regarding Douglas and—in a most powerful reminder—addressed the column directly to Douglas.

Three years after the prophecy was published, Douglas indeed aspired to the presidency and was expected by many to win it. Notwithstanding such expectations, however, as the prophecy declared, Douglas would feel the *weight of the hand of the Almighty.* And he no doubt felt it when his political nemesis was chosen to be president instead. During the same year he lost his bid for the presidency, the forty-eight-year-old Stephen A. Douglas suddenly died, "a broken-hearted man."[17]

Douglas proved unworthy, and the prophecy was activated. So, who was the national leader chosen instead to take the presidency in that election, which was perhaps the most important election in American history? It is my pleasure to now introduce you to the miracle that was Abraham Lincoln!

CHAPTER 7

Lincoln's First Holy Field: Willie and the Divine

Everyone who visited the White House (known as the Executive Mansion in those days) with any regularity knew the boy Willie Lincoln, Abraham's beloved child. The eleven-year-old lad was indeed special. The father of Willie's best friend called him a "good-hearted boy" possessing "more judgment and foresight than any boy of his age that I have ever known."[1] His babysitter called him "the most lovable boy I ever knew, bright, sensible, sweet-tempered and gentle-mannered."[2] Seward would recall the day he came riding up to the Executive Mansion with a prince of France. Seeing Willie playing on the lawn, Seward saluted the boy. Willie then turned to Seward and his party and, without a thought, straightened his body, removed the hat from his head, and offered a gracious and formal bow. As one Lincoln biographer so appropriately declared, Willie "was the sort of child people imagine their children will be, before they have any."[3]

I recently came across a sweet poem written by young Willie. It

Young Willie Lincoln.

was a tribute to his father's friend Edward Baker, who had been killed in battle. Baker had been with the president the day before he rode off to battle to meet his tragic fate. Willie remembered that day. Before Baker had left for the battlefield, he had lifted Willie in his arms and hugged him good-bye.[4]

> *There was no patriot like Baker*
> *So noble and so true;*
> *He fell as a soldier on the field,*
> *His face to the sky of blue.*[5]

There is a reason I begin this chapter with this poem. The last two phrases—"on the field" and "His face to the sky of blue"— have great meaning now as we look back upon the war that inspired these words. They relate to Lincoln, America, and the fate of the Latter-day Saints in powerful ways. You see, Lincoln would pass through sacrificial "fields"—both literal and metaphorical— in order to come to his most important decisions, in order to gain his testimony of the American covenant. And the fact that these words came from the precious mind of Willie makes them all the more potent, for it was Willie who first brought Lincoln to the knowledge of who he was and what he must do to fulfill the will of God.

I will get to the holy "fields" of Abraham Lincoln (I propose three specific ones), but first I must have you understand why these "fields" were necessary in the first place—why Lincoln or any of his people needed to be converted to a new, even spiritual, way of thinking.

The Northern faithful applauded vigorously when President Lincoln declared in his first inaugural address that he had "no purpose, directly or indirectly, to interfere with the institution of slavery in the States where it exists."[6] His early position on slavery was further confirmed when, even as the Civil War began, he made it clear that he "had no intention of making emancipation the war aim, nor is it likely he could have persuaded his troops to fight to free blacks."[7] This is not to say Lincoln did not hate slavery—he had stated his personal disdain for the institution many times before. The problem was that the South had already begun to secede from the Union in fear that the new Republican party, led by Lincoln, would take their slavery from them. Lincoln feared war so much, he was unwilling to see that perhaps the looming catastrophe was God's judgment on America. He was unwilling to understand the deep sin that penetrated the land— slavery representing just the tip of the iceberg. He did not see that this Civil War was to be a purging, a tool of national repentance to bring restitution—to bring emancipation and those amendments called for by the Prophet. He and his administration wanted everything to return to the way it was before the great secession began. The problem was that everything prewar was not as it should have been. And God knew it. God needed Abraham to know it as well if he were to be a tool in heaven's hand.

And so God led Lincoln into his first "field." He led him into the darkest place imaginable so that he would have nowhere else to turn but to God Himself. Only then would the revelations arrive.

As if it were not already the most difficult of times for Lincoln—losing so many battles in a war he had thought he would win, being hated on all sides, being questioned and betrayed by friends, and knowing his decision to stay in the war was leading to tens of thousands of deaths—on top of it all, he had the ultimate parental nightmare thrown upon him.

He never realized how much he loved that boy until that moment on February 20, 1862.

Memories flooded his mind of the countless times he would sprawl his elongated body out on the floor as he playfully wrestled with Willie and the boys. He thought of how he would regularly indulge them, allowing them unfettered access to his office and encouraging them to ride their pet ponies and goats throughout the mansion—all to the chagrin of his staff. Once, when the president was busy in his office, Willie and his beloved little brother, Tad, barged in to tell their father that he needed to grant a pardon to their misbehaving toy soldier, Jack. Instead of turning them out, Lincoln played along as if it were the most important thing in the world to him. In the end, the president drafted a letter for his boys: "The Doll Jack is pardoned by order of the President. A. Lincoln." On another occasion (this one, I admit, was quite funny) the boys snuck up into the attic and managed to sabotage the network of bells used to summon the servants. All at once, every bell rang throughout the mansion, causing great confusion and concern among the staff. Lincoln wasn't upset; rather, he was amused. Instead of issuing punishments, he just laughed along with his boys.[8]

Having witnessed all this, Lincoln's closest advisers would have to agree with the notion put forth by a friend of the family: "His children literally ran all over him, and he was powerless to withstand their importunities." Lincoln chuckled at this criticism, simply reciting his favorite maxim: "Love is the chain whereby to lock a child to its parent." And no child was ever locked to a parent as strongly as Willie was to Lincoln. A close friend of the president once admitted that Lincoln was "fonder of that boy than he was of anything else."[9]

Why Willie? Why Willie! On February 20, 1862, this was all the president could think as he looked upon the lifeless body of the boy who had, rather suddenly, contracted typhoid fever

Mary Todd Lincoln in 1860.

and died. This was *his* boy. Of all his children, it was Willie who looked like Lincoln (tall and thin) and who thought like Lincoln (pensive and analytical). Willie was his father's constant companion. Now what would he do? Upon the moment of Willie's death, Lincoln felt instantly lost. He stumbled, almost aimlessly, into his secretary's office and declared, "My boy is gone—he is actually gone!" He then began to sob. When he later entered the room where Willie's body was laid, Lincoln stopped and looked at his child's face. He then "buried his head in his hands, and his tall frame was convulsed with emotion."[10] To make matters worse, after the boy's death, Mary Lincoln became inconsolable and would never recover.[11] The Lincolns had already lost their three-year-old Eddie a few years earlier. To have to also give up their Willie was unbearable. Upon looking at Willie's lifeless body, Lincoln exclaimed, "My poor boy, he was too good for this earth. God has called him home. I know that he is much better off in heaven, but then we loved him so. It is hard, hard to have him die."[12]

For weeks after the boy's death, Lincoln would just disappear every Thursday (the day Willie had died). He would go to the quiet, lonely room where Willie had passed away. He went to grieve and weep in solitude.[13] To a friend, Lincoln confided, "Ever since Willie's death, I catch myself involuntarily talking to him, as if he were with me, and I feel he is."[14]

Lincoln found some comfort in Shakespeare's *King John,* particularly in Constance's lamentation over her lost boy. He would be in the middle of a meeting or riding in a carriage with friends when, completely out of the blue, he would begin reciting from his memory the lines from the lamentation, tears always forming in his eyes:

> *And, father cardinal, I have heard you say*
> *That we shall see and know our friends in heaven:*
> *If that be true, I shall see my boy again.*[15]

During these dark days, Lincoln was appropriately described by an eyewitness as a tormented soul, sleepless and pacing the halls of the Executive Mansion, "his hands behind him, great black rings under his eyes, his head bent forward upon his breast,—altogether such a picture of the effects of sorrow, care, and anxiety as would have melted the hearts of the worst of his adversaries."[16] Noah Brooks was surprised to see how the once "happy-faced lawyer" had by 1862 become sad and stooped, with "a sunken deathly look about the large, cavernous eyes."[17] Lincoln would try at times to self-medicate with his relentless storytelling and humor, but he admitted that "nothing could touch the tired spot within, which was all tired."[18] On one occasion during the

Abraham Lincoln learned to turn to God in his sorrow.

difficult days of 1862, an intolerant senator rebuked Lincoln for attempting a little humor, to which the president replied, "I say to you now, that were it not for this occasional *vent,* I should die."[19]

As difficult as this was, perhaps it was a reflection of God's will at last being done. Sometimes heaven's medicine is not pleasant, but if it is given, it is necessary. You see, it was precisely during these trying months that Lincoln, not knowing what else to do, turned to God like never before. As he would later admit: "I have been driven many times upon my knees by the overwhelming conviction that I had nowhere else to go."[20]

According to the government printer, John DeFrees, Lincoln (though always a God-fearing man) became much more of a religionist "about the time of the death of his son Willie," which had provoked in Lincoln a desire to expound and converse "on the subject of religion."[21] Mary Lincoln implied that as the war became increasingly intense, so did the president's reading of the scriptures. In fact, several witnesses during this time commented on how they had stumbled in upon the president—whether in his office or in an obscure corner of a steamboat transport—"reading a dog eared *pocket* copy of the New Testament." Lincoln's long-time friend Joshua Speed noted that, though Lincoln had been somewhat of a religious skeptic in his more youthful days, he had now "sought to become a believer."[22]

With Mary devastated, Lincoln needed help to care for his other boy, Tad, just younger than Willie. God sent a nurse, the widow Rebecca Pomroy. And, as it turns out, she may have been sent to administer to Lincoln as much as she was sent to Tad. Rebecca Pomroy was an especially interesting woman. Having lost her husband and two of her three children (her third and last was fighting in the war), she still exuded a peace and happiness that was surprising to others. Not least among those others was Abraham Lincoln.

Lincoln, completely unrecovered from his own loss, needed to know how she did it. How did she find happiness with such misery around her? He needed a way out—perhaps Nurse Pomroy had the key. She did. Lincoln asked her, and she shared it. "God met me," she told the president simply enough. His response was tearful: "This is the hardest trial of my life." But he was willing to be "met" as well. The nurse later recalled how Lincoln, on the next three nights, pleaded with her to teach him "the secret of placing myself in the Divine hands."[23]

Over the next weeks, Nurse Pomroy would witness the president during his lunchtime, his eyes fixed on the Bible. He would often seek out the nurse to discuss a particular passage. His conversion was taking place. The nurse witnessed the fruits of it all on a particularly stormy day in Washington, D.C. At the end of her workday, Lincoln insisted on calling for his carriage to take her home, that she might not hazard the storm by foot. He went with her. When they got to Fourteenth Street, the carriage became bogged down in rain and mud. Lincoln ordered his footmen to hold the horses steady while he jumped down, placed three large stones aside the carriage, then took the widow's hands and guided her over his makeshift bridge to the safety of the sidewalk. As he so often did, he found a teaching opportunity in the ordeal. Looking back and forth between the nurse and the bridge of stones he was guiding her over, and with a glimmer in his eye that had been absent for so many weeks, he declared: "All through life, be sure to put your feet in the right place, and then *stand firm.*"[24]

Lincoln was at last on firmer ground than ever before in his life. He was prepared to be what he often claimed he wanted to be: "a humble instrument in the hands of our Heavenly Father."[25] Willie's poem seemed written for this moment: for his father, after forging through the difficult *field,* was at last looking heavenward, *His face to the sky of blue.* He would take his newfound spiritual power and apply it to his national calling. Speaking to a group during those days and weeks of spiritual enlightenment, the president declared: "Whatever shall appear to be God's will, I will do."[26]

Lincoln had made it through the first and most heart wrenching of his "holy fields"—the one that broke him to pieces but led him to his God. He was now ready for the next one. Indeed, God was preparing a second "holy field" for Abraham—the one that would reveal to him the next step he needed to take in order to fulfill the prophecies as received and recorded by the Prophet Joseph.

This time it would fall upon William Seward to lead him into it.

CHAPTER 8

Lincoln's Second Holy Field: The Grassy Meadow of Frederick

The question: What was to be Lincoln's next step? The answer was the Emancipation Proclamation: Free the slaves! Many think this was an easy and obvious decision. It was not. It never was. Few wanted this, even in the North. Union soldiers had signed up to preserve the Union; they, like Lincoln, were fighting because the Southern states had attacked federal property—forts and ports—that belonged to *all* the people of *all* the states. This was unacceptable. It represented an internal invasion. Of course, they were willing to fight back to defend their country.

But they did *not* sign up to rescue enslaved people! Most Northerners had never even seen a black person, nor did they care to. Lincoln himself had pledged not to pursue emancipation. What might happen if he did it now? The few slave states loyal to the Union might join the secessionist movement, landing a solid blow—maybe the knockout blow—to the Northern cause. The better part of the Union army, Lincoln feared, would pack up and go home. They would not fight and die for a principle they did not care for. The administration would be ruined.

Only God (and Joseph Smith, I suppose) saw the whole picture. Freeing the slaves meant eradicating national sin in a promised land that would not tolerate it. The Emancipation Proclamation, of course, did not free all slaves, but it began the process. It paved the way for the Thirteenth Amendment (which did free them all) and for the Fourteenth Amendment, which would usher in an era in which state governments could no longer deny their own people the God-given rights offered in the Constitution. It would mean black freedom! It would mean freedom for religious minorities as well! Freedom for the Mormons—something they had yet to fully experience. Temples would, at last, be able to be built unobstructed by the state! When Lincoln finally learned what far-reaching consequences for good the Emancipation Proclamation would bring, he was able to bear witness of it before Congress, saying: "In *giving* freedom to the *slave*, we *assure* freedom to the *free*."[1]

We must understand how important this decision would be—this decision to swim against the current and ignite the flame that would end in national repentance, restitution, and the restoration of the American covenant. This is what Lincoln was being prepared for. But only he could pull the lever on this one.

Of course, it had to be Lincoln. As William Seward stated, in some ways he was "superhuman" and proved to be "the best of us."[2] He was a pure vessel. Perhaps his humility and purity were the most important qualities for a person in his position. His neighbors and friends likely sensed those traits in a speech he gave on the station platform in Illinois as he was about to board the train for Washington, D.C., and his presidency: "I now leave, not knowing when, or whether ever, I may return, with a task before me greater than that which rested upon Washington. Without the assistance of that Divine Being, who ever attended him, I cannot succeed. With that assistance I cannot fail. Trusting in Him, who can go with me, and remain with you and be everywhere for good, let us confidently hope that all will yet be well. To His care commending you, as I hope in your prayers you will commend me, I bid you an affectionate farewell."[3]

And there was a sign and symbol of his purity that Latter-day Saints will appreciate. Lincoln lived the Word of Wisdom. Indeed, it was a matter of personal policy for him to refrain completely from alcohol and tobacco.[4] Upon winning the Republican nomination for president in 1860, Lincoln was told that a delegation from the party was on its way to officially provide him the good news. Mary, ever the socialite, insisted they serve alcohol to the delegation. She became irate when Lincoln refused. "Having kept house for sixteen years, and having never held the 'cup' to the lips of my friends," explained Lincoln, "then my judgment was that I should not, in my new position, change my habit in this respect." He served them water.[5]

His purity no doubt thrived under his study of the Bible. "All the good Savior gave to the world was communicated through this book," he said of the Bible. "All things most desirable for man's welfare, here and hereafter, are to be found portrayed in it."[6] He further declared that "this great book . . . is the best book God has given to man. . . . But for it we could not know right from wrong."[7]

The point is that Lincoln was already predisposed to attend to God's revelations. The tragic events of 1862, which included Willie's death, among other things, simply enhanced his spirituality and prepared him to make the most difficult decision of his life. He openly declared, "I talk to God," and admitted the following to General Dan Sickles: "When I could not see any other resort, I would place my whole reliance in God, knowing that all would be well, and that He would decide for the right."[8]

Throughout 1862, Lincoln began to recognize like never before that he was being called to commune with God, not just over Willie, but over the plight of the nation. "It has pleased Almighty God to put me in my present position," Lincoln told one friend in the spring of 1862, "and looking up to him for divine guidance, I must work out my destiny as best I can." Similarly, he told another group that "it is my earnest desire to know the will of Providence in this matter [of emancipation]. *And if I can learn what it is I will do it.*"[9] In September 1862, after being pressed by those seeking clarification of his intention over emancipation, he would only say that the subject was "on my mind, by day and night, more than any other. Whatever shall appear to be God's will, I will do."[10]

The God-fearing population in America began rallying around their president. During those dark and confusing months of 1862, a friend and Baptist minister, Noyes Miner, told Lincoln that "Christian people all over the country are praying for you as they never prayed for a mortal man before," to which Lincoln responded: "This is an encouraging thought to me. If I were not sustained by the prayers of God's people I could not endure this constant pressure."[11]

The events leading up to and through 1862 ultimately provided what Lincoln sought. Revelations began arriving; his conversion began solidifying. Lincoln described it as "a process of crystallization" during which he "constantly prayed."[12]

And then he said it: *I think I should free the slaves.* He told Seward first, very quietly. It was during the summer of 1862 while they rode together in a carriage on their way to a funeral. The funeral was for the small child of Secretary of War Edwin Stanton.[13] Perhaps this event reminded him of Willie and caused him to express what the Almighty had been trying to tell him. He knew he could trust Seward and reveal to him what was on his mind, though it seems he was not completely sure about the decision yet. But the answer was becoming clearer.

Seward's response would lead Lincoln to the second holy field on this spiritual journey. *Wait!* Seward told him. He told him to wait until after a Union military victory. Otherwise, he said, it would seem like a "last measure of an exhausted government, . . . our last *shriek,* on the retreat."[14] Lincoln did as his friend suggested. And what followed was one of the great miracles of American history.

A few months passed, and summer had turned to fall. It was September 1862, and Lincoln was done waiting. He fell to his knees once again. He knew something was about to happen. He picked up a pen and a piece of paper. He then wrote something unbelievable. "In the present civil war it is quite possible that God's purpose is something different from the purpose of either party. . . . I am almost ready to say this is probably true—that *God wills this contest,* and wills that it shall not end yet."[15] He could not believe he was having this thought—much less that he was actually writing it down on paper. He read the statement he had just penned, the ink still wet. Could his life and perspective get any more bizarre? Throughout the history of the world, what commander-in-chief would dare say such a thing? Yes, it is easy to argue that your enemy is wrong—but to suggest that your own side is also wrong? To suggest that God is doing this awful thing to both sides for some purpose heretofore unknown? It was like something out of the biblical account of ancient Israel or the Book of Mormon. What was he thinking?

Of course, he was not about to share this message with anyone. He would have sounded like he was morphing into a prophet—not a safe move for the president of the United States. And so, he tucked the memo away; it was, after all, not intended for anyone to see. In fact, it would not be discovered among the Lincoln papers for years. When Lincoln's secretary happened upon it one day, he was moved. He later explained that the note was "not written to be seen of men. It was penned in the awful sincerity of a perfectly honest soul trying to bring itself into closer communion with its Maker."[16]

Having hid the memo—which was titled "Meditation on the Divine Will"—Lincoln found himself again on his knees. Reports were coming in: a fierce battle at Antietam was looming large. Lincoln knew he had been very clear to the nation the previous year during his First Inaugural Address—*I will not touch slavery in the South* was the take-home message. Indeed, this war had never been about some moral crusade; it had never been a religious movement. Lincoln now recognized he had been wrong. The nation had been mired in sin for too long, slavery representing just one of many national ills. And now God was purging the land—both North and South—of the iniquity. Lincoln was trying to get in line with "the Divine Will."

As he prayed during the days and hours before that September battle, one thought prevailed above the others. Lincoln later testified to his colleagues that, at that moment, "he had made a vow, *a covenant,* that if God gave us victory in the approaching battle, he would consider it an indication of the Divine will, and that it was his duty to move forward in the cause of emancipation."[17] This was the battle he was waiting for—the one Seward had asked him to wait for.

If Lincoln was expecting divine intervention, then the miraculous events directly contributing to the Union victory at Antietam do not disappoint. As it had been for General Washington, so it would be for Lincoln—the prayer was answered, the covenant was honored, and God entered the battlefields of America once again.

And how would God enter? At about the same time Lincoln was writing his memo-to-self and making his covenant, a young

Lincoln at Antietam.

Union soldier, Corporal Barton W. Mitchell, was walking through an empty field near Frederick, Maryland (not far from where the Battle of Antietam would shortly take place). This would be Lincoln's second "holy field" (this time it was literally a field). And this is why it was holy:

Days before Corporal Mitchell found himself in this field, Confederate General Robert E. Lee had convened a war council near that very spot. During the meeting, Lee announced a daring plan that would culminate in the Battle of Antietam. If his secret plan were executed correctly, he would score his first real victory in Northern territory, and nothing would then stop him from marching into Washington, D.C., and destroying the Union forever. His secret plan called for his army to divide into several parts, then converge upon the Northern troops. The plan was extremely risky because it would leave several Confederate divisions isolated and exposed. And so extreme care was taken to account for the few written copies of the plan, which Lee called Special Order #191. Lee insisted that the copies remain secured.

Having left that field to execute their daring plan, no Confederate officer at that secret meeting would ever be able to explain what happened days later to Union Corporal Mitchell in that sacred field. In fact, up until the present day, *nobody* has been able to explain it. As he walked through that field, he stumbled upon something. It was an envelope wrapped around three cigars that had apparently been abandoned. Pulling the envelope off the cigars, Corporal Mitchell opened it and read the profound message—it was a copy of Lee's Special Order #191!

Mitchell knew what he needed to do. The battle plans were immediately sent up the chain of command. Before long, they found their way into the hands of the Union commander, General George McClellan. Then, in a second miracle, McClellan was able to immediately verify the order's authenticity because his aide had been close friends in the prewar U.S. Army with Lee's adjutant, Robert Chilton. The Union aide quickly recognized his old Southern friend's handwriting. "Here is a paper," McClellan then declared, "with which if I cannot whip 'Bobbie Lee,' I will be willing to go home."[18]

Thanks to the miraculously delivered military intelligence, the Union pulled off a narrow victory at Antietam. In such a close battle, which could have gone either way, without that piece of intelligence, the North could easily have lost the battle. Such a loss may have ended the entire war in favor of the South.[19] The Union cause was miraculously saved!

I was reading about this miracle in a piece by the Pulitzer Prize-winning historian James McPherson, a renowned expert on Antietam. He concluded that "the odds against the sequence of

A copy of Lee's Special Order #191.

events that led to the loss and finding and verification of these orders must have been a million to one."[20]

But did McPherson, or any other Civil War scholar, ever put that miracle together with the fact that Lincoln had, in the days leading up to this battle, been praying and covenanting over it? I could not find any writings on this amazing connection. I needed to go to this field; I knew it had a story to tell. It was a lost gem in the history of America. And so I jumped on an airplane and went there.

Upon arriving at Frederick, Maryland, I stopped in at a local museum in town. The curator of the museum was very aware of the story and the field, and he pointed me in the right direction. He told me that the reason Lee had been in that field was because it was adjacent to the property of farmer John Best. The Southern soldiers could lean on the farm for provisions, and so they made camp around that field. He told me that if I traveled a few miles south of Frederick, I would soon find myself in empty farmland. Then I would see the old abandoned Best farm—the forgotten field sitting just to the north of it.

I did as he told me, and moments later I was pulling into a scene right out of the nineteenth century. The two-story farmhouse, flanked by a barn and a few small outbuildings, had faded white walls and a red roof. It looked exactly as I imagined it might have during the Civil War. As I parked and exited my rental car near the completely abandoned farmhouse, I looked northward and saw the very large, upward-sloping field. As I looked, two thoughts simultaneously entered my mind. I remember feeling that I was indeed standing on holy ground. But the joy of being there was slightly diminished by my second impression: the sense of overwhelming abandonment. I did identify a small marker on the edge of the field, which read "Lee's Lost Order" and briefly told the story. But how many knew about this place? How many ever visited it? By the looks of things, very few. And if they did come here, would they know the entire miraculous story? Would they recognize Lincoln's spiritual role and what it all really meant in the grand plan God had for America and His gospel?

I pondered these things as I walked through the field. Then I looked up to my right and saw a curious building, perhaps a half mile away. The building looked like a museum of sorts; it sat upon a hill across the small highway that had led me to the farm. Almost as lonely looking as the Best farm, the museum sat by itself in a large, empty field, with no visible cars or people around it. I went there in search of more answers.

As it turned out, years after Antietam, another Civil War

The two-story farmhouse at the Best farm.

battle had been fought near the Best farm—the Battle of
Monocacy. The lonely museum, owned by the U.S. National
Park Service, was the visitors' center built to commemorate that
battle. As I entered the building, I immediately realized I was the
only one there. I looked around at some of the memorabilia that
told the Monocacy story. But I could not focus on that battle.
All I could think about was the field and Lee's lost orders. Before
long I found myself standing at a large window with a full and
beautiful view of the Best farm and the sacred field.

"Do you know what happened out there?" someone said behind me. As I had not yet seen another soul in the museum, I
was slightly startled. I turned around and was happy to see it was
a national park historian. *Perfect,* I thought to myself. I simply
said, "Lee's lost order." She smiled. I asked, "If so much care had
been taken to conceal the battle plan, how did this happen?" The

historian seemed overjoyed, not only that someone had actually come to her visitors' center but that someone was asking about the mystery she had clearly studied in depth.

As we looked out over the field together, she pointed out where each of the Southern generals had set up camp with their armies before they met with Lee to receive their copies of the secret order. Then she provided some incredible insight. She explained that during the meeting, everyone noticed that both of Lee's hands were in splints. He had recently taken a fall off his horse. Therefore, it was left to Lee's adjutant Robert Chilton to write the orders. "And this," I added excitedly, "would be paramount days later, when Chilton's good friend, who just *happened* to be Union General McClellan's aide, authenticated the lost order by recognizing the handwriting."

She nodded and smiled. "Exactly! But that's not all," she continued. "The generals had been given strict instructions to conceal their copies of the plan at all costs. Two of them sewed their copies into the lining of their jackets. Another memorized the order, then chewed it up and ate it." The historian added, "When orders such as these went out, records were kept to account for how many copies were made and who exactly received them. After their defeat at Antietam, and after they had learned that the Union had found a copy of the orders just prior to the battle, Southern leaders called for an investigation. Records were checked, and Chilton was interviewed. But the South could not crack it, nor has any historian today been able to. Nobody remembered anything, and no record or witness could account for how that copy ended up in that field."

I added, "Nor can anyone account for how Union Corporal Barton Mitchell just *happened* upon that *very* place in that *very* field."

The first reading of the Emancipation Proclamation.

"So, to answer your question," she said, "it is simply a mystery."

No, I thought to myself, *it is a miracle.* I suspect Lincoln would agree with me.

Days after the news of the Union victory at Antietam arrived at the capital, Lincoln called an emergency cabinet meeting. He knew what he now needed to do. He had covenanted with God, and God had responded. It was September 22, 1862. The president marched into that meeting and boldly declared that "his mind was fixed, his decision made." It was clear to all present that any objection to his call for emancipation would be immediately dismissed. The president told his cabinet *not* to bother him over "the main matter—for that I have determined for myself." [21] He then laid upon the table a sacred document: the preliminary draft of the Emancipation Proclamation. His cabinet read the document, which concluded most appropriately with the words, "I invoke the considerate judgment of mankind, and the gracious favor of Almighty God."[22]

In an emotional state, Lincoln then declared unequivocally that "God had decided this question in favor of the slaves." He continued, saying that he would keep "the promise to myself, and [he paused here] to my Maker."[23] The secretary of the navy took notes on what he had witnessed during this sacred cabinet meeting. He wrote that Lincoln had, at that moment, made a "covenant" with the Almighty.[24] Referring to Lincoln's newfound belief that emancipation was the *real* purpose of the war, one prominent historian stated, "Truly, it was a 'Damascus Road' experience for the president."[25]

At this point in the war, it could be said, in a very real sense, that God's truth was at last marching on!

◆　◆　◆

As I drove my rental car away from the field at Frederick, I was on a spiritual high. I could not stop pondering these events: the praying Lincoln, the covenant, the miracle on that field, the powerful cabinet meeting that followed. I felt like I was floating. Then, all of a sudden, my cell phone rang and brought me back to earth. I looked at my phone and noted it was a foreign number. I knew the number. It was a child trafficker I had been negotiating with. He was calling to close a huge deal. It hit me that I was in the middle of a miraculous event right then and there not unlike what had occurred with President Lincoln, Corporal Barton Mitchell, and the rest of the players during that providential month of September 1862. I realized that I was smack-dab in yet another miracle that proves what Lincoln had learned—that the cause of liberty is the cause of God. Indeed, the Almighty will work wonders to liberate His enslaved children.

This particular phone call was the result of inexplicable events that had occurred in the weeks prior to my visit to Frederick. Before my trip, I had received a phone call from an informant, Scott, who was working in Guatemala. (Names of people and places have been changed to protect those involved.) Scott and his wife are good Christian people who run a rehabilitation center in Guatemala for child-trafficking victims. A mother had recently brought her daughter, Liliana, to Scott's facility. The child was in complete shambles. She told of how she had been kidnapped from her home in Guatemala weeks earlier and smuggled into Mexico, where she was forced into sex slavery. After weeks of severe abuse, according to Liliana, a woman she had never seen before walked into the cell she was being kept in and opened a window that Liliana had never seen before. The woman told her, "Jump out of this window and run. And don't stop running." She did as she was told.

Days before this angel-woman had appeared to her, Liliana had smartly taken advantage of a fortuitous opportunity. While one of the male clients who had been forced upon her was drunk and sleeping, she used his cell phone to call her mother. She told her mother that she did not know where she was, but that she believed it was a certain port town in Mexico. The mother, who had a truck-driver friend, asked him to please travel to that port town and snoop around. He did. And as it happened, when Liliana was running with all her might after having jumped through the miracle window, she ran right into her mother's trucker friend. He scooped her up and took her back to Guatemala.

As Scott was telling me this story over the phone just before I left for Frederick, I could hardly believe it. But I should have immediately believed, as this was not the first time I had seen angels working on behalf of these enslaved children. Scott said that the child's heart was broken in half knowing that there were several other children being held as sex slaves in that Mexican brothel. "Tim, can you send some folks into the town to check things out?" he asked. I explained that it would be better if we had more detailed intelligence on the trafficking ring, but that I would do what I could.

I then called down to the U.S. consulate closest to the Mexican town. It seemed to me a good omen when the U.S. agent who answered the phone was an LDS coworker named Chuck whom I had heard about before. I asked Chuck if he could snoop around the area. He told me that the consulate was very poorly staffed and the town in question was several hours away. He was also discouraged by the fact that I had so little information for him to go on—just the name of a town. But he said he would do what he could.

Then something incredible happened a few hours after my phone call with Chuck: he received a call from *another* law-enforcement agency in the United States, an agency that was far from my home office. Chuck was told by the U.S. officials on the other end of the line that a Mexican national living in the United States had just walked into their office to report a suspicious phone call he had received from an acquaintance in Mexico. The acquaintance had told the Mexican national that he had a stable of children, ages eleven to fourteen, whom he wanted to sell to U.S. nightclub owners to work in the sex industry. The Mexican national had had the presence of mind to play along, then had immediately reported the event to the U.S. officials. Those officials then naturally called the U.S. consulate nearest to the town where the trafficker claimed to be holding the children. It was Chuck's consulate. And which Mexican town was it where the children were being held? The *same* little town that Liliana had recently escaped from. When Chuck heard this, he naturally thought that these U.S. officials were working with me and that there had simply been a miscommunication between me and them about who would report to the consulate. "Oh, you must be working with Ballard, right?" Chuck asked. He almost dropped the phone when he heard them say, "Who the heck is Ballard?"

I received a phone call from Mexico late that afternoon. "Tim, you won't believe this!" I heard Chuck say. He explained what he had just learned. "Could it possibly be the same brothel Liliana fled from?" Chuck asked in amazement. "Could we possibly be talking about the same captive children Scott reported? What are the chances?" *About the same,* I thought to myself, *as the probability that Corporal Barton Mitchell would have stumbled upon those lost orders, which nobody even knew were lost. About a million to one.*

Chuck gave me the number of the U.S. officials, and I called them right away. After introducing myself, I blurted out: "Tell the Mexican national to call the trafficker in Mexico. Have him tell the trafficker that he has his nightclub owner . . . have him tell the dirtbag that it's me!" I provided my undercover phone number. Then I waited.

The next morning the call came in. I could not believe I was quite possibly speaking directly to Liliana's captor, whom I had just learned about the day before. Hours earlier, all I had was a vague story (almost too amazing to believe) and the name of a little Mexican town. I had no idea at that point how I could possibly identify, much less infiltrate, the ghost criminal organization. And now, here I was receiving a phone call from the likely perpetrator. No earthly explanation could ever account for this.

The phone call shortly turned into Facebook communications, which gave me the desired photos of the alleged captors. I immediately sent the photos to Scott, who I knew was still caring for the child victim in his Guatemala shelter. Five minutes later Scott called me. "I showed Liliana the picture, Tim, and she immediately fell to her knees and began to vomit. The man you spoke with was the same man who kidnapped our precious child."

At that point, I knew it was on. But more important, I knew that God was orchestrating the entire thing.

Over the next several days, I began negotiating the deal via phone with the monster in Mexico. He told me he would make arrangements for me to come down and check out his "product." I told him that I would come the moment he called. Shortly thereafter, I jumped on the plane for my already scheduled trip to Frederick, knowing all along that when the call came in, I would drop everything and head south. That call was the call I received as I drove out of Frederick. I knew I would not even need to pack my bags. I was already on my way to the Baltimore-Washington International Airport.

Before long, I found myself sitting at a small bar in a small hotel in the small Mexican port town I had spent hours every day (over the last several days) thinking about and strategizing over. I sat at the bar in prayer—thanking God for the miracle that had brought me there and pleading for the safe rescue of His children. The monster and his minions soon arrived. I was already in character, ready for them. I stood up, smiled, and gave them big hugs, as if they were my best friends in the world. After some small talk (and after I had spent several minutes struggling to not break role and reach out for their throats), a few of them left to pick up the children. Apparently I had convinced them sufficiently that I was the real deal.

When they returned with the children, I really had to focus to stay in role. This was always the most difficult part. I immediately counted five little girls. I looked into their shattered eyes as they looked into mine. I wanted to cry, knowing that they were looking at *me* thinking that I was to be the next monster in their lives. I wanted so badly to proclaim to them, *No! I'm the good guy. And your long night of hell has come to an end!* But I could not. I had yet to finish my work with the monsters.

After pretending to "check the girls out" as they sat at a table near the bar, I nodded to the monsters. We then went into a private room to finish our negotiations as the girls were shepherded into respective bedrooms to await the "clients" whom the monsters believed I had brought with me as part of the "product research trip." During our private meeting, we discussed how we would smuggle the girls into the United States, and I made a handsome down payment. My stomach began to ache and I became nauseous as I was forced to listen to the monsters describe these poor children as objects of lust that my clients would be enjoying soon. I can't even repeat the words they said. I somehow managed to smile and act thoroughly pleased with their abhorrent and perverse reports.

The only satisfaction I had left was my knowledge that in a few short minutes, life as those monsters knew it would be over for good. A most deserved punishment was on its way—a punishment with hellfire in its wake.

As we exited the room and entered the courtyard of the hotel, I gave the inconspicuous sign that the deal was complete. I knew the Mexican special operations strike team was watching me from the shadows, anxiously awaiting the preplanned signal. Seconds later, it was as if lightning and thunder had struck that little hotel dead-on. The monsters were tackled to the ground, with assault rifles smashed into their faces. As was the routine, I went down as hard as they did (a ruse to keep my undercover status uncompromised).

It was over. Six arrested, and five precious children of God rescued—emancipated from the worst form of slavery that has ever existed on this earth.

I was again reminded of the fact that the cause of liberty is the cause of God. I once again had gained a deep respect for the darkness of slavery, while simultaneously gaining an even deeper respect for my heroes, like Abraham Lincoln, who had taught me how to tap into heavenly powers to rescue the most oppressed beings on earth.

This experience added more personal insight than I can possibly describe concerning the covenant, Lincoln, and the war. Because of this experience, and others like it, somehow I knew more than ever that the spiritual conclusions I was coming to as a result of my historical investigation into the people and events of the Civil War were true and righteous altogether.

CHAPTER 9

Lincoln's Third Holy Field: The Book of Mormon

Think on Willie's poem. *He fell as a soldier on the field, His face to the sky of blue.* These words are so fitting for Abraham Lincoln. His many "fields" of sacrifice and conversion indeed directed his attention to heaven. And heaven smiled down.

His final field, albeit a literary or metaphorical one, was perhaps the most stunning of them all—it was the Book of Mormon. Yes, for many months, Lincoln was in possession of a copy of the Book of Mormon, which he himself signed for in November 1861. I've included a copy of the actual signed ledger from the Library of Congress, which proves this little-known fact of history.

But so what if he had the book? Perhaps he was just curious about the Mormons. Perhaps he just wanted some information for devising policy for the Utah territory. Many, of course, will make little of Lincoln's Book of Mormon. But they should look deeper. Admittedly, we do not know exactly why he initially checked out the book, but that's not the point. It's what he ended up doing with it; that is what I want to discuss.

Let us start with the timing. Lincoln had the book from November 1861 to July 1862. According to the ledger, the book was out for more than eight months. Why did he keep it so long? Well, we should ask ourselves what was going on in Lincoln's life during those eight months. Those very months marked what he

*Entry in the Library of Congress ledger showing that
Lincoln checked out a copy of the Book of Mormon.*

called his "process of crystallization," even those months of his life that have been described as his "Damascus Road Experience." He had the book when Willie died, when he met Nurse Pomroy—*yes,* he had it precisely when he found God and turned the nation over to Him. Now get this: he turned the very overdue book back to the Library of Congress on July 29, 1862, a mere *seven days* after he submitted the first draft of his Emancipation Proclamation to his cabinet. A mere seven days after our first indication that his conversion had finally congealed.[1] Perhaps he had, at last, learned the lesson he needed to learn and so could finally relinquish the tool that was guiding him.

And what was the lesson he may have derived from the Book of Mormon? For starters, the entire story confirms that there is a covenant on this land. This is the doctrine. America is a promised land, and the behavior of its people induces consequences from heaven, either for good or for ill. "This is a choice land, and whatsoever nation shall possess it shall be free from bondage, and from captivity, . . . if they will but serve the God of the land" (Ether 2:12). And consider how many times the following promise is repeated throughout the account: "Inasmuch as ye shall keep my commandments ye shall prosper in the land" (2 Nephi 1:20). When grappling with issues like slavery, minority rights, and the systematic, state-sponsored abuse of God's children in America, are these lessons not relevant? Is this not exactly what Lincoln needed to understand in order to frame the Civil War in its proper context? Might this have been the final push he needed to make his difficult decision regarding emancipation? Is this not the perfect answer from heaven to a pleading, desperate president presiding over a promised land?

That Lincoln read the Book of Mormon is almost certain. As perhaps our most well-read president, it is doubtful he checked out books for eight months only to let them sit on a shelf and collect dust. But did he apply the book's message? Did he internalize these Book of Mormon principles and encourage them to take hold in the land and change the course of American history?

To answer that, let me take you to a momentous day: Lincoln's 1865 second presidential inauguration. In his famous Second Inaugural Address, he declared, "The Almighty has his own purposes." He boldly stated, "Woe unto the world because of offenses! for it must needs be that offenses come; but woe to that man by whom the offense cometh." The president then asserted that God "now wills to remove" slavery from the land and He is doing so through hurling the devastations of "this terrible war" to affect "both North and South." Unless and until the nation as a whole rejects sin, he suggests, the fires of national refinement will continue. "Fondly do we hope—fervently do we pray—that this mighty scourge of war may speedily pass away," declared Lincoln. He then concluded: "Yet, if God wills that it continue until all the wealth piled by the bondman's two hundred and fifty years of unrequited toil shall be sunk, and until every drop of blood drawn with the lash shall be paid by another drawn with the sword, as was said three thousand years ago, so still it must be said, 'The judgments of the Lord are true and righteous altogether.'"[2]

Let us not take this most unusual address for granted. It is difficult to imagine that a national leader would stand before his people in the middle of a bloodbath of a war and tell them, in essence, that God was punishing them. Not only the South but the North also, according to Lincoln, was to blame. It seems to me that one must go to the Old Testament or to the Book of Mormon to find a national leader willing to take such a prophet-like stand. And yet Lincoln did it.

This is national covenant language. It is Book of Mormon language. "Except the Lord doth chasten his people with many afflictions, yea, except he doth visit them with death and with terror, . . . they will not remember him" (Helaman 12:3). In a very real way, Lincoln would have understood these words he read from his copy of the book.

But, wasn't it likely just a coincidence that Lincoln's words reflected those of the Book of Mormon? Or is there additional evidence that the Book or Mormon actually influenced this profound speech? The answer may surprise you. Please follow me now as we discover the scriptural mysteries of that inaugural day.

Before his speech, Lincoln raised his right arm to the square and placed his left hand in the Bible to take his oath. Following Washington's example, Lincoln did what many presidents have done throughout history: he honored the inauguration day tradition of taking the oath while placing a hand upon a favorite biblical chapter or verse. The scripture Lincoln chose was Isaiah, chapter 5.[3] Isaiah, chapter 5! Do you see the relevance? Isaiah 5 ends with a prophecy regarding the gathering of Israel and the Restoration of the gospel in latter-day America. You will recognize it from your Sunday School classes: "And he will lift up an ensign to the nations from far, and will hiss unto them from the end of the earth: and, behold, they shall come with speed swiftly" (verse 26). That this *ensign* is latter-day Zion is corroborated in Doctrine and Covenants 64:42 and 113:6.

Furthermore, these verses are immediately followed by a description of what Isaiah saw as the great gathering of latter-day Israel—the elders of the Church flowing out of the promised land to gather the elect of God. Isaiah described (in verses 27–30) great vehicles to assist in the work, to include vehicles that "roar like young lions" and have "wheels like a whirlwind." These vehicles would allow travelers to move without "slumber nor sleep; neither shall the girdle of their loins be loosed, nor the latchet of their shoes be broken [they would travel far distances without having to sleep or change clothes]." Elder LeGrand Richards explained that these words represent (in the best words Isaiah could find to describe them) visions of trains and airplanes supporting the work of LDS missionaries. "With this manner of transportation," said Elder Richards, "the Lord can really 'hiss [signal] unto them from the end of the earth,' that 'they shall come with speed swiftly.'"[4]

So, why would Lincoln care to make reference to this great event? That is the question with a most exciting answer. You see, before describing the wonderful events of the Restoration, Isaiah saw that something terrible must first hit the land: a scourge, a purge, a refiner's fire. Isaiah described a war in the land as a result of national sin.

LDS Church manuals interpret verse 8 of Isaiah 5 as indicating that the unworthy nation had "built up great estates through wickedness."[5] Isaiah further identifies how the unrighteous people call "evil good, and good evil" (verse 20). And finally, the people "justify the wicked for reward" (verse 23), which, according to LDS manuals, means that "those who were guilty of crimes were declared innocent by bribed judges and other officials, whereas the innocent were found guilty so that

> "The war now raging in our nation is in the providence of God, and was told us years and years ago by the Prophet Joseph; and what we are now coming to was foreseen by him, and no power can hinder. Can the inhabitants of our once beautiful, delightful and happy country avert the horrors and evils that are now upon them? Only by turning from their wickedness, and calling upon the Lord. If they will turn unto the Lord and seek after Him, they will avert this terrible calamity, otherwise it cannot be averted."
>
> —Brigham Young, 1864[6]

they could be silenced or their property exploited."[7] These crimes against man and God, which Isaiah saw among the people of his day, were clearly being projected for latter-day America. And sure enough, these sins describe the very thing that brought America under condemnation—they describe in detail what the nation did to both black Americans and Mormon Americans.

The prophesied consequences from the Lord for these sins further match what occurred in the Civil War. We are told that "therefore hell hath enlarged herself, and opened her mouth without measure: and their glory, and their multitude, and their pomp . . . shall descend into it" (verse 14). Isaiah experts interpret the Hebrew word for *hell* used in this verse (*sheol*) to mean *spirit world* (not necessarily eternal punishment), which indicates that God's vexation, in this case, would result in countless deaths.[8]

After Lincoln completed his oath of office, he bent down to kiss the Bible. Chief Justice Salmon Chase, who had administered the oath, later commented that Lincoln seemed to intentionally kiss two particular verses from Isaiah chapter 5—verses 25 and 26.[9] Verse 24, leading into these verses, discusses the destruction to come "because they have cast away the law of the Lord of hosts, and despised the word of the Holy One of Israel." Verse 25 goes on to explain the consequences of this rebellion: "Therefore is the anger of the Lord kindled against his people, and he hath stretched forth his hand against them, and hath smitten them: and the hills did tremble, and their carcases were torn in the midst of the streets. For all this his anger is not turned away, but his hand is outstretched still."

Consider what this revelation provides as the reason for the Lord's anger: they had "cast away the law" and had "despised the word of the Holy One of Israel." Is this not a perfect ful-fillment of the Civil War prophecies we discussed earlier? Isaiah had just declared that, in the latter days, "out of Zion shall go forth the law" (Isaiah 2:3). President Harold B. Lee stated that what Isaiah foresaw here as "Zion" was in fact America, and that what he called "the law" was in actuality the U.S. Constitution.[10] If "the law" in this Isaiah 5 prophecy was also in reference to the Constitution, which had been "cast away," then indeed this prophecy was fittingly chosen by the president of the United States.

Then, after having cast away the law, Isaiah says that they "despised the word of the Holy One of Israel." Indeed, after having spit upon the Constitution, the wicked nation *despised the word* (and warnings) of the Holy One's prophet—they despised and even killed the Prophet Joseph. And so the war came, as mandated by the prophecies we discussed earlier, and as prophesied in Isaiah 5:25 (the very verse Lincoln kissed): "the hills did tremble, and their carcases were torn in the midst of the streets."

But there is good news here too. According to Isaiah, the war ends in gospel fruit. In the very next verse, which Lincoln also kissed, is the prophecy we have already discussed: "And he will lift up an ensign to the nations from far, and will hiss unto them from the end of the earth: and, behold, they shall come with speed swiftly" (Isaiah 5:26). Isaiah then proceeds with his detailed description (recited above) of the traveling missionaries leaving from Zion to gather Israel and bring about the Restoration.

And this is my point! These were the two verses Lincoln kissed—the war followed by the Restoration! Do you see how amazing this is? It seems clear that this Isaiah prophecy, which he referenced during his oath, was the inspiration behind that great speech, a speech that reflects this same spirit of judgment followed by repentance, mercy, and ultimate light.

Yes, you say, but how would Lincoln have had any idea that

Isaiah might have been referencing America and her spiritual battles? This is where his reading of the Book of Mormon comes in.

During his prophetic statements about latter-day America, the prophet Nephi quotes chapter 5 of Isaiah in its entirety. In the second book of Nephi, Nephi spends a significant amount of time commenting on latter-day America and her national covenant. He quotes his father, Lehi, declaring that latter-day America will be a land of liberty (see 2 Nephi 1); he foresees the coming of the Prophet Joseph Smith (see 2 Nephi 3); he quotes Isaiah about the gathering of latter-day Israel (see 2 Nephi 8); he quotes his brother, Jacob, who speaks directly about the latter-day American covenant (see 2 Nephi 10); and then he again quotes an Isaiah prophecy—found in Isaiah 2—about the latter-day gathering of Israel and the building of latter-day temples (see 2 Nephi 12). It is within this latter-day American context that we get to Nephi's recitation of Isaiah 5 (found in 2 Nephi 15), even the words Lincoln chose during his inaugural ceremony.

If Lincoln read these chapters and verses in 2 Nephi, when he came to the recitation of Isaiah 5, he would have known definitively that Nephi was declaring that Isaiah 5 was about latter-day America. Indeed, the Book of Mormon places Isaiah 5 in its proper context. It seems logical that Lincoln's questions would then begin to formulate in his mind and heart. *Is this me? Is this my America? My presidency? Is this my war that Isaiah saw?* If Lincoln did seek answers to these questions, then it appears this book of scripture might have guided him to his ultimate decision. For it was at this point, right after his reading of the book, that he began to place the Civil War in the context of a holy war—a judgment from God to bring about national repentance.

Don't believe me? Let's reflect upon the words Lincoln

invoked precisely at the time he presumably finished his reading of the Book of Mormon and sent it back to the library. We already discussed the memo he wrote to himself in September 1862, in which he bore witness that *"God wills this contest,* and wills that it shall not end yet."[11] He continued to develop these thoughts, eventually finding the courage to come out and declare his profound message to the public. A few months after issuing the Emancipation Proclamation (our first sign of his conversion), he declared to the nation: "And insomuch as we know that by his divine law nations, like individuals, are subjected to punishments and chastisements in this world, may we not justly fear that the awful calamity of civil war which now desolates the land may be but a punishment inflicted upon us for our presumptuous sins, to the needful end of our national reformation as a whole people?"[12]

Indeed, it was at this point that Lincoln began calling the people to repentance like some Nephite prophet of old who understood the consequences of sin in the promised land. As Lincoln stated, "If we do right God will be with us, and if God is with us we cannot fail."[13]

All these thoughts, testimonies, exhortations, and prophecies culminated in that Second Inaugural Address and that powerful reference to Isaiah 5 (and/or 2 Nephi 15).

But there is something else I need to share with you about that copy of the Book of Mormon that Lincoln had. Did you know that, apparently, it still exists today in the rare books collection of the Library of Congress? According to the Library, there is record of only one copy of the Book of Mormon that might have been available to Lincoln during 1862—and they still have it!

Not long ago, I made a trip to the Library. After a security vetting process (which took almost an hour), I was granted permission to enter the Library of Congress Rare Books Reading

LINCOLN: PRESIDENT OR PROPHET?

"It is the duty of nations as well as of men to own their dependence upon the overruling power of God; to confess their sins and transgressions in humble sorrow, yet with assured hope that genuine repentance will lead to mercy and pardon; and to recognize the sublime truth, announced in the Holy Scriptures and proven by all history, that those nations only are blessed whose God is the Lord. . . .

"We have been the recipients of the choicest bounties of Heaven. We have been preserved, these many years, in peace and prosperity. We have grown in numbers, wealth and power as no other nation has ever grown; but we have forgotten God. We have forgotten the gracious hand which preserved us in peace, and multiplied and enriched and strengthened us; and we have vainly imagined, in the deceitfulness of our hearts, that all these blessings were produced by some superior wisdom and virtue of our own. Intoxicated with unbroken success, we have become too self-sufficient to feel the necessity of redeeming and preserving grace, too proud to pray to the God that made us.

"It behooves us, then, to humble ourselves before the offended Power, to confess our national sins, and to pray for clemency and forgiveness. . . .

"Let us then rest humbly in the hope authorized by the Divine teachings, that the united cry of the nation will be heard on high, and answered with blessings no less than the pardon of our national sins, and the restoration of our now divided and suffering country."

—*"A Proclamation by the President of the United States of America,"*
March 30, 1863[14]

The Library of Congress in Washington, D.C.

Room. The Library itself is one of the most beautiful buildings in the city, with its highly decorative and ornamental architecture. It is situated just to the west of the U.S. Capitol Building and just to the south of the U.S. Supreme Court Building. When I entered, I was given somewhat complex instructions—go down this entranceway; walk through the long, narrow, winding corridor; go up the second bank of elevators; turn left; take the second corridor on your right; and so on. The Rare Books Reading Room was clearly not placed in a very accessible part of the building, and for good reason. But having to walk the labyrinth only intensified the anticipation I already felt, as my heart beat faster and faster with every awkward twist and turn. *What would I find in the book?*

After having to stop and ask for directions a few times, at last I found the large doors to the Reading Room. Upon opening the tall and heavy doors, I found myself in a small reception area that looked directly into a large, ornately decorated room. The large room was separated from the reception area by stunning arches and pillars that reached to the top of the very high ceiling. The room had several large tables that were neatly lined across the red velvet carpet. Each table was adorned with matching lamps. A large chandelier hung from the ceiling, which complemented the wall lamps hanging throughout the room. I remember thinking that the lighting appeared to have been designed for oil lamps. In fact, the entire room looked like something right out of Abe Lincoln's day.

My thoughts were quickly interrupted by the female librarian behind the counter. "You must exit immediately," she said. "No backpacks are permitted in here. You may have paper and pencil only if you want to enter the Reading Room." I had forgotten these instructions, which I had been given earlier. I stepped out, stashed my backpack in one of the lockers that lined the corridor outside the room, then reentered.

When I approached the librarian behind the counter again, I told her that I had been in contact with a Rare Books reference librarian and that I had come to see the first-edition copy of the Book of Mormon. After checking my I.D. and verifying with her computer system, she told me to enter the large room and have a seat. Though I had managed to stay calm in many stressful situations in my work, this experience was killing me. I felt that my heart might jump out of my chest.

The front door opened, and I saw my good friend and publicist walk in. I had asked him to meet me there, as I wanted to have a witness verify whatever we might find. He sat down next to me and explained how he had, like me, gotten lost in the maze of the massive building.

Before I knew it, a heavyset, middle-aged male librarian approached us and placed the first-edition copy of the Book of Mormon in front of me. He also brought a second first-edition copy of the book, but explained that the second one had been donated to the Library during the mid-twentieth century. The first book—the one in front of me—was the only candidate to be the Lincoln Book of Mormon. I could not believe I was actually seeing this book. Its very worn cover gave it immense character. I instantly felt that it would provide the answer I had come for.

I reached out carefully to touch the book, after which the librarian immediately moved it away from my reaching hand. "You must pass a test before you can open this book," he said.

Puzzled, I responded, "Okay, let's have it."

"What are the first words printed in the book?" he asked.

I was not feeling patient enough for a quirky joke. I rapidly blurted out, "I, Nephi, having been born of goodly parents."

"Correct!" he said boldly with a proud smile, as if I had accomplished some amazing feat. I reached out for the book again, only to have the librarian push it, once again, away from my hand. I glared at him with the most impatient look I could muster. "Did you know that these Book of Mormon copies are the most frequently checked out books in my Reading Room?" he asked.

"No, I did not," I replied, trying to pretend I was interested in the factoid, but not really caring at all and not able to keep my eyes off the book for more than a few seconds.

"Did you further know," he said without skipping a beat, "that first-edition copies of the Book of Mormon are the most stolen books in the world?"

"I promise I will not steal them," I said smugly. *Now leave me alone!* I thought (but dared not say). Perhaps he read my mind, because at that moment he promptly turned and walked away.

I carefully took the book in my hands. I was determined to study every single page of the book, starting at the beginning. "Turn it to the Isaiah 5 reference!" my publicist blurted out. I told him to hush, that I was going to scan every page in turn. After some back and forth between me and my friend, I heard a voice: "You gentlemen need to be quiet!" The voice came from right behind me. It was another male librarian. Embarrassed, I apologized (I had not realized how loud we were being). The only thing more embarrassing that occurred that day was when that same librarian returned a few moments later and again told us (demanded of us!) to hush our tones, and this time offered a warning that we might be asked to leave if we could not control our volume. I apologized once again and immediately felt like I was back in grade school. Our excitement was simply overtaking us.

As I went through the book, I noticed no markings or writing, but I did note that there were exactly twenty-four places where someone had dog-eared the corners of the pages. (In contrast, the other first-edition copy had no dog-eared pages whatsoever). Twenty-four dog-ears are not that many in a book that is almost six hundred pages long. I recognized, of course (as you should) that this copy of the Book of Mormon likely went through countless hands, and its pages could have been dog-eared by any of those hands. That said, I was still undeterred from looking for clues.

Of the dog-eared pages, I noticed that one stood out among the others. For one of the pages was dog-eared three times on the same corner. Yes, some person or persons had folded that same corner three times in three different places. Apparently, someone was very interested in referencing that page and/or that chapter. Can you guess what chapter was triple dog-eared? It was the 2 Nephi chapter that constituted the full recitation of Isaiah 5! I could not believe it; yet at the same time I had always been expecting it.

I immediately thought of something. During Lincoln's months of conversion, eyewitnesses testified that they had seen him—whether in his office or in an obscure corner of a steamboat transport—"reading a dog-eared pocket copy of the New Testament." *He did dog-ear his pages!* I thought to myself. I wonder if any of these witnesses looked carefully enough at the books he was reading; perhaps it was not only the New Testament he was engrossed in.[15]

My mind also recalled the true account of one witness who might have seen the president during the thick of his "process of crystallization"—a witness who might have stumbled in upon Lincoln and his Book of Mormon experience. Exactly eight days before issuing his first draft of the Emancipation Proclamation and exactly fifteen days before returning his Book of Mormon to the Library, Lincoln had one of the longest nights of his life. He locked himself in his study and asked not to be disturbed. He was evidently reading and studying something until daybreak. That morning, he received a knock on the door of his study. When he realized it was his friend Orville Browning, he made a brief exception to his earlier order to be left alone and permitted him to come in. Browning was alarmed when he saw Lincoln's appearance. According to Browning, "He looked weary, care-worn and troubled. I shook hands with him and asked how he was. He said 'tolerably well.'" Browning told the president he must take better care of himself. Lincoln would not release the powerful grip he had formed with Browning—his huge hand enveloping the hand of his friend. Then, according to Browning, Lincoln replied "in a very tender and touching tone—'Browning, I must die some-time.' . . . He looked very sad, and there was a cadence of deep sadness in his voice. We parted . . . both of us with tears in our eyes."[16]

Whatever this event may or may not have meant, one thing is certain: by late 1862, it was decided. He had submitted, and he would not look back. He once told a friend, "The purposes of the Almighty are perfect, and must prevail, though we erring mortals may fail to accurately perceive them in advance. We hoped for a happy termination of this terrible war long before this; but God knows best, and has ruled otherwise. We shall yet acknowledge His wisdom and our own error therein. Meanwhile we must work earnestly in the best light He gives us, trusting that so working still conduces to the great end He ordains. *Surely He intends some great good to follow this mighty convulsion,* which no mortal could make, and no mortal could stay."[17]

He followed up these brave words with a request to his friend for "earnest prayers to our Father in Heaven."[18]

After Lincoln had made his decision on emancipation, even his own wife questioned this profound change in his early policies and promises. She asked, *Will you really go through with it?* With a glance to heaven, then back to Mary, he simply replied: "I am a man under orders; I cannot do otherwise."[19] By that time, his closest friends, as well as a growing number of the general popu-lace, would have agreed with a Chicago city lawyer who declared, "*You may depend upon it, the Lord runs Lincoln,*" to which a local Methodist preacher responded, calling that statement "the true theory & solution of this 'terrible war.'"[20] And this, I believe, was likely due (in no small degree) to the Book of Mormon.

All of this spiritual power culminated in that Book of

Lincoln's inauguration for his second term as president.

Mormon-like speech the president delivered during his Second Inaugural. Which is why I want to share with you the bookends of that speech. What I'm about to tell you about this speech is true; several credible firsthand witnesses testified that it was. The entire inaugural celebration that morning, leading up to the president's address, had been plagued by terrible winds and thunderstorms, prompting a general advisory to women and children to stay indoors for their protection. But at the very moment Lincoln approached the podium, as explained by the prominent journalist Noah Brooks, who was there, something strange occurred. "Just at that moment," recalled Brooks, "the sun, which had been obscured all day, burst forth in its unclouded meridian splendor, and flooded the spectacle with glory and light. Every heart beat quicker at the unexpected omen . . . so might the darkness which had obscured the past four years be now dissipated."[21] Lincoln later said to a friend who had been present, "Did you notice that sunburst? It made my heart jump."[22] Chief Justice Chase called it "an auspicious omen of the dispersion of the clouds of war and the restoration of the clear sun light of prosperous peace."[23]

Now I will end this chapter with the second bookend about the address. It is so telling of what Lincoln had learned and what he had passed on to the nation. Commenting on the strong language he had used in his Second Inaugural Address, particularly regarding his assertion that heavenly punishments would continue as God saw fit, Lincoln admitted that his speech would not be "immediately popular." He explained, "Men are not flattered by being shown that there has been a difference of purpose between the Almighty and them. To deny it, however, in this case, is to deny that there is a God governing the world. It is a truth which I thought needed to be told."[24]

CHAPTER 10

National Repentance

I love the Book of Mormon! It is so helpful in understanding the Civil War. I recently reread the account of the great Nephite leader Mormon. Lincoln, once converted to the covenant, had much in common with General Mormon. Both leaders knew the truth: that their respective American nations were under condemnation and needed to repent. And both understood that their respective civil wars represented God's final warning and contingency. Unfortunately for those ancient Americans, it did not work. They fell. As Mormon lamented, "Notwithstanding the great destruction which hung over my people, they did not repent of their evil doings" (Mormon 2:8). It was not enough for Mormon or Lincoln to believe and turn to God. Their nations would have to follow suit. So, would Lincoln be forced to conclude the same thing about his modern America as Mormon did about his ancient version of the same covenant land? Or could the United States turn things around? This would be one of the most important questions of the nineteenth century. Everything hung on the answer.

It is a difficult thing to believe God would punish a people with such a miserable punishment. He Himself instructed the Prophet Joseph, in the midst of the Civil War warnings and revelations, "Pray ye, therefore, that their ears may be opened unto your cries, that I may be merciful unto them, that these things may not come upon them" (D&C 101:92). But mankind's eternal salvation was at stake. God needed a repentant America in order to bring to pass His plan, in order to create the fertile ground for temples to stand unmolested on this earth. The humbling effects of war represented the last hope that America would fall to its knees and turn to the light. "Except the Lord doth chasten his people with many afflictions, yea, except he doth visit them with death and with terror, . . . they will not remember him" (Helaman 12:3).

Notwithstanding the light at the end of the dark tunnel, I still say, *poor Lincoln!* Of any prominent person in history whom I have studied, he was the one who hated violence the most. He even refused to participate in the great sport of hunting because he felt so tenderhearted toward his would-be prey. Once, while riding through the capital, past medical camps and ambulances, he became overwhelmingly emotional. Turning to his traveling companion, he cried out with tears in his eyes, "Look yonder at those poor fellows. I cannot bear it. This suffering, this loss of life is dreadful."[1] He once sadly confessed to a congressman: "Doesn't it seem strange to you that I should be here? Doesn't it strike you as queer that I, who couldn't cut the head off a chicken, and who was sick at the sight of blood, should be cast into the middle of a great war, with blood flowing all about me?"[2] But what was he to do? Like the Prophet Joseph, he had pled with the nation for a peaceful resolution. He had asked them to make the change of heart on their own; he even offered a plan for the government to buy human freedom instead of killing for it.[3] But they would not listen. Then it grew too late. The frightening prophecies were activated. God had spoken, and Abraham knew it.

Yes, God had spoken on this again and again, even long before the war had crashed down upon the land. I reviewed many of these prophecies from the Prophet Joseph in an earlier chapter. As early as 1833 God had told him that the war must come, that He "may proceed to bring to pass my act, my strange act, and perform my work, my strange work"—referring to the Restoration (see D&C 101:93–95). Years later, things had not improved for the Prophet and the Church. Joseph found himself unjustly imprisoned at Liberty Jail in the spring of 1839, and as he pled with the Lord to understand the terrible persecutions being suffered by his people, the Lord again echoed the national warning. The message was clear: something would hit the nation very hard as a consequence of the unrelenting national sin. This prophetic response is recorded in section 121 of the Doctrine and Covenants.

God revealed to the Prophet that the enemies of righteousness "shall melt away as the hoar frost melteth before the burning rays of the rising sun," that "their hopes may be cut off," that in "not many years hence . . . they and their posterity shall be swept from under heaven," that these "children of disobedience" who "swear falsely against my servants, that they might bring them into bondage and death" will surely suffer and "their basket shall not be full," and "their houses and their barns shall perish." The revelation continues, "Wo unto all those that discomfort my people, and drive, and murder, and testify against them, saith the Lord of Hosts; a generation of vipers shall not escape the damnation of hell." And finally, the Lord assured the Prophet, "I have in reserve a swift judgment in the season thereof, for them all" (D&C 121:11–24).

Some may argue that these verses apply to broader events, and that confining them to a Civil War prophecy is overly presumptuous. However, this Liberty Jail prophecy, like the other proposed Civil War prophecies I wrote about earlier, is directed at the very generation that attacked the Church, and the punishments refer to mortal events like the burning of houses and barns. When else, if not during the Civil War, could these prophecies have been fulfilled?

But God was not doing this because He is mean and full of vengeance. No, there is always purpose. Just like in the Book of Mormon, He let these things fall to cause a change in the heart of the nation, to turn the people to goodness and righteousness and light. In fact, the Lord said as much in this very revelation. He declared that these devastating acts would allow Him to "set his hand and seal to change the times and seasons" (D&C 121:12). Reference to such powerful change is completely consistent with the ultimate fruits of the Civil War, as discussed in an earlier chapter and as defined in D&C 101:93–95. That is, the result of the calamity would be a national change that would amend the Constitution to protect God's kingdom on the earth.

Interestingly, in the middle of this D&C 121 warning, the Lord stated that while this punishment was being carried out, the Lord would "blind their minds, that they may not understand his marvelous workings" (D&C 121:12). This became significant in the days of the Civil War when Abraham Lincoln pointed out on several occasions that the nation did not know what spiritual meaning and overall purpose were *really* behind the war. Note how Lincoln suggested in 1862 that "God's purpose [for the war] is something different from the purpose of either party."[4] In 1864 he declared: "The purposes of the Almighty are perfect, and must prevail, though we erring mortals may fail to accurately perceive them in advance. . . . Surely He intends some great good to follow this mighty convulsion, which no mortal could make, and no mortal could stay."[5] And in 1865, he emphasized it again, declaring that "the Almighty has his own purposes" for the war.[6]

Of course, Lincoln grew to understand what that purpose

was. It was exactly what the Lord declared it to be: a vexation and scourge to "set his hand and seal to change the times and seasons" (D&C 121:12). Or, in Lincoln's own words, the war came from God for "the needful end of our national reformation as a whole people."[7]

It all fits so perfectly! History corroborates our scripture! Now it was Lincoln's job to apply the message—to ensure that his America did not walk the dark path of General Mormon's America.

So, what happened? Well, since freedom rings in our America (unlike when the early Mormon settlers resided on the land), and since slavery no longer exists (unlike what the Saints witnessed in mortality), and since temples dot the land at last (a seemingly impossible feat in Joseph Smith's day), the answer is obvious. The people did change. They repented. But this repentance phase of the war has not been emphasized in our current history books, and it needs to be. For this change was the fruit of the war. It was the key to America's salvation in the nineteenth century—and it's the key to our salvation today. So we must pay attention!

Just as many of us Americans too often believe of ourselves today, the North believed from day one that they were right. They signed up for the war—soldiers and politicians—to defeat the South, to fix the South. However, Lincoln and many in the North began to think twice about this original belief as the vexation of war continued to thrash them. The truth is, the North should have won this war in the first year. Its advantage was stunning. Union troops numbered two million, while Southern troops topped off at eight hundred thousand (the desertion rate was also significantly higher among Southern troops). Additionally, the North had twenty thousand miles of railroad track (much of which ran north-south, facilitating the moving of supplies to the

RELYING ON GOD'S GUIDANCE

After a congressional delegation visited Lincoln during the war and pressed him to make sure slavery would be cast away forever, Lincoln made a most astonishing comment. First, he echoed the principles behind the American covenant—that national salvation was dependent upon doing right, and so slavery's eradication would be paramount. But then he went further, testifying that perhaps there was even more to it. His words had a powerful effect upon Congressman James Wilson (who recorded Lincoln's statement). Wilson noted that as the president spoke these words with his right arm outstretched, "his face [was] aglow like the face of a prophet."[8] Lincoln's full response was as follows:

"My faith is greater than yours. I not only believe that Providence is not unmindful of the struggle in which this nation is engaged; that if we do not do right, God will let us go our own way to ruin; *and* that if we do right, He will lead us safely out of this wilderness, crown our arms with victory, and restore our dissevered union, as you expressed your belief; but I also believe that He will *compel us* to do right in order that He may do these things, not so much because we desire them as that they accord with His plans of dealing with this nation, in the midst of which He means to estab-

lish justice. *I think He means that we shall do more than we have yet done in furtherance of His plans,* and He will open the way for our doing it. I have felt His hand upon me in great trials and submitted to His guidance, and I trust that as He shall further open the way I will be ready to walk therein, relying on His help and trusting in His goodness and wisdom."[9]

battlefront), while the South had perhaps ten thousand miles of track (much of which went east-west, unable to supply the frontlines). Furthermore, the North dominated the South in other areas: 32 to 1 in firearm production, 14 to 1 in merchant shipping, 3 to 1 in agricultural acreage, and 412 to 1 in wheat. The North also controlled over 90 percent of the cotton cloth industry and the boot and shoe industry, and it maintained almost all of the iron furnaces needed for arms manufacturing.[10]

As the war produced Union defeat after Union defeat, what else could be said except that, as Lincoln increasingly began to point out, "the North as well as . . . the South, shall pay fairly for our complicity in that wrong [the national sin]."[11] The North and the federal government had, after all, watched and done nothing as the sins of oppression hit the innocent minorities—from black slaves to Mormon settlers (not to mention the many other oppressed minorities). It became every day clearer to the North that it too needed fixing. For if the war had ended early—with either Southern subjugation (a quick Union victory) or Southern independence (a quick Southern victory)—the North would have remained unchanged. The United States would have remained unchanged. The kingdom of God would have been left with the same weak application of the Constitution, which weak application was responsible for the Church's frustrated growth and ultimate exile. And so, God would make sure that—notwithstanding Northern advantage—the war would go on until the vexation ran its course, until North as well as South repented and fixed the covenant for the kingdom of God on earth.

It is here where Lincoln's and the North's conversion to the idea of *national repentance* comes strongly into play. For if *national repentance* was God's purpose, then He would be sure they all got the message. We already know that Lincoln got it. But what about the rest of the nation?

When the war started, the North (generally) did not believe that heaven was behind it, or that it was about repentance or even about slavery. Then came the great change of heart. Some two years into the war, the message that slavery was, as one soldier put it, a "curse" that "hung like an incubus to tarnish" the very soul of America, began flowing out of Union camps.[12] One soldier newspaper attributed the ruined cities of war to the biblical promise that "thy sin will find thee out," further declaring that the ash heap of death and destruction in the wake of battle was proof positive that "on their sin has the punishment fallen." Another soldier recognized that "the nation is passing through a terrible revolution, such a one as she doubtless needs to purge" her sins. Assistant Union surgeon John Moore wrote his wife that he was happy to see that Northerners were "beginning to see that slavery is and has been a national evil" and that "God will not bless a nation who are guilty of such gross evil."[13] "Any country that allows the curse of Slavery and Amalgamation as this has done, should be cursed," according to another Illinois soldier, "and I believe in my soul that God allowed this war for the very purpose of clearing out the evil and punishing us as a nation for allowing it."[14]

Removing this evil, according to Private Orra Baily, would require a powerful event to "shake the nation and our institutions to the very center."[15] Lieutenant Quincy Campbell agreed that the sin was so deeply rooted that the Lord's purging would not be brief or easy. Even after the North had accepted and had begun enforcing emancipation, and even after the Union victories at Vicksburg and Gettysburg in the summer of 1863 turned the tide in favor of the North, Campbell declared that "the chastisements of the Almighty are not yet ended. . . . The Almighty has taken up the cause of the oppressed and . . . will deny us peace until we 'break every yoke' and sweep every vestige of the cursed institution from our land."[16]

Many perceived the punishment of God through war as purging not only slavery but, as one soldier put it, "the enormity of [the nation's] crimes" to include bias and discrimination of all kinds, and that until the nation repented of such crimes it could never "enjoy that peace which the nation has so long lost, and will never again have until made to know that God's image, of whatever hue, is worthy of respect, liberty, and equality."[17]

This soldier understood, along with his fellow soldiers, his president, and a growing segment of Northern society, what the *New York Daily Tribune* captured early on in the conflict: that the United States was "engaged in trying a great experiment, involving not merely the future fate and welfare of this Western

Civil War soldiers join in prayer.

continent, but the hopes and prospects of the whole human race." Union victory would mean "the democratic principle of equal rights [and] general suffrage . . . [was] capable of being carried into practical operation," while its defeat would be seen by the world "as the first step toward the entire breakdown of our whole system of republican government."[18]

America was the first to attempt a republic on such a large scale. The rest of the world watched. If it failed, the nations of the world would most likely abandon democratic ideals and maintain their despotic ways, which at least (they thought) would offer security. If the American republic survived, however, then democracy would be deemed a viable option, and others would attempt it. So much hung in the balance: the survival or destruction of human liberty the world over.

Something else also hung in the balance—the Restoration. The Church would need liberty to usher the gospel in to every corner of the earth. If America had failed here, if it had proved that a republic could not survive in the end, then budding republics the world over might have lost hope. Tyranny might have gained a stronger foothold throughout

> "But it was not the operation of these evils [of slavery] alone that brought so speedily the fulfillment of [Joseph's] prophecy. . . . It was crime the most gross and terrible in its consequences of any that man can commit. It was the shedding of the blood of innocence—it was the murdering of Prophets and Apostles and Saints. Whenever a man or nation was guilty of this crime in ancient times, the retributive justice of the Almighty speedily followed them, and their downfall was sure. Who can behold what is now taking place in [America] and not feel that the Lord's hand is in the events that have transpired? What power but His could so signally have brought to pass his word spoken by his Prophets."
> —Millennial Star, 1861[19]

the nations of the world, and the proliferation of the Restoration might have been stymied. Lincoln himself declared as much:

> [This civil war is] an important crisis which involves, in my judgment, not only the civil and religious liberties of our own dear land, but in a large degree the civil and religious liberties of mankind in many countries and through many ages. . . . You all may recollect that in taking up the sword thus forced into our hands this Government appealed to the prayers of the pious and the good, and declared that it placed its whole dependence upon the favor of God. I now humbly and reverently, in your presence, reiterate the acknowledgment of that dependence, not doubting that, if it shall please the Divine Being who determines the destinies of nations that this shall remain a united people, they will, humbly seeking the Divine guidance, make their prolonged national existence a source of new benefits to themselves and their successors, and to all classes and conditions of mankind.[20]

Yes, so much was hanging on this war and its final outcome. And so heaven rejoiced as it witnessed Americans recognizing sin and fighting for righteousness as a result of the war. For as the conversion happened, God could honor the covenant and bring victory to the Union, victory to the Republic, victory and liberty over tyranny.

I could go on and on citing evidence that the national heart was changing most penitently, which eventually led to what Lincoln called in his Gettysburg Address "under God . . . a new birth of freedom." But let me just sum it up by citing an exhaustive study conducted a few years ago by Professor Chandra Manning. She collected everything she could find of the remaining notes, letters, camp newspapers, and publications from the North during the war. She wanted to know the motive for fighting. She discovered it. Her conclusion: By the summer of 1863, more than six months after the Emancipation Proclamation, the general feeling among the Union rank and file was that the "North had some real soul-searching to do before it could meet God's demands. Many soldiers felt sure that destroying slavery was necessary to gain God's favor, but . . . emancipation was not, by itself, enough to appease the Almighty."[21]

> The soldiers in this study show that they did feel a strong sense of connection and duty to the United States government [or, as we might insinuate, to the American covenant], which grew in part out of an antebellum millennialist understanding of the United States' unique mission in the world. In the main, Union soldiers cared about the United States government not primarily because it served their families' interests, but because its survival mattered for the survival of ideals like liberty, equality, and self-government for all humanity.[22]

Manning continues—and this is the important point: "By the spring of 1865, the war had created a world almost no American could have recognized in 1861. White Union troops who might once have eschewed radical abolitionism now took pride in fighting to redeem the nation from the sin of slavery, and many took seriously the obligation to make ideals like freedom and equality into realities for black as well as white Americans."[23]

And there it is! Prophecy fulfilled.

Of course, the blessings always follow in a covenant land that decides to repent. Understanding that is the only way to make sense of this little-known fact: "Despite the cataclysmic

A SIGN OF THE REDEEMED COVENANT

On April 22, 1864, Congress passed an act mandating that the U.S. Mint director place the following words on U.S. coins: *IN GOD WE TRUST*. The first appeal to apply such a divine invocation on the currency had come a few years earlier by way of a letter from the Reverend M. R. Watkinson to Lincoln's secretary of the treasury, Salmon Chase. Reverend Watkinson told Secretary Chase that such an act was needed, as it "would place us openly under the Divine protection we have personally claimed." It would also, he declared, help the nation achieve repentance, as "our national shame in disowning God" was "not the least of our present national disasters." Picking up on the covenant theme issued by the reverend, Secretary Chase perpetuated it with a statement of his own to the director of the U.S. Mint at Philadelphia: "Dear Sir: No nation can be strong except in the strength of God, or safe except in His defense. The trust of our people in God should be declared on our national coins." And so it was by 1864. *IN GOD WE TRUST* was later made, by an act of Congress, the national motto of the United States.[24] The covenant had been invoked once again.

The 1864 two-cent coin.

destruction caused by the Civil War, the reunited states, North and South, would be far richer in 1870 than in 1860. During the same period, the nation's population would rise by more than 20 percent, and its gross domestic product would nearly double."[25] How do you explain this? More prosperity just after the greatest scourge ever to hit the land than existed just before it? God is the only explanation. We see how fast the promise is made good: "If my people . . . shall humble themselves, and pray, and seek my face, and turn from their wicked ways; then will I hear from heaven, and will forgive their sin, and will heal their land" (2 Chronicles 7:14). The lesson for America today is clear: no matter how difficult or impossible the challenges may appear (and we have many such challenges), there is always a clear way out, and it always begins with turning the nation back to God. If only our America could learn this lesson and apply it now . . . before it's too late.

In the end, and notwithstanding the easier path not taken, the prophecies and purposes of God's national scourge and vexation were fulfilled. And the American covenant grew stronger in the heart of the nation. Only then did the North begin to fight and die for the very thing called for, through revelation and prophecy, by the Prophet Joseph. Liberty in law! Liberty unto eternal salvation!

CHAPTER 11

A Fight between Heaven and Hell

I feel I need to put a finer point on what I believe the Civil War was all about. Of course, as I have stated, the war was about human freedom and redemption from national sin. But remember why the promised land was created: as a place to build Zion, to build temples, to build the kingdom of God on earth. The broad-brush themes of human freedom and national redemption would naturally support these lofty goals, but it was always these lofty goals that heaven had its eyes on during this great conflict.

Think about this: the Church went from a time when state governments beat, killed, and exiled their people to a time when these same governments formally and officially apologized for their sins and allowed the Saints to rejoin the Union. It went from a time when the federal government sat idly by while Mormons suffered to a time when the federal government awarded one of our prophets the highest honor given to civilians. It went from a time when members of the Church were denied all civil rights to a time when Church members hold the most prominent positions in Congress and are strong candidates for the presidency of the United States. It went from a time when God's temples were allowed to be burned to the ground to a time when the government called on special police forces to protect the temple from the threat of mobs.[1]

No event in recent history illustrates this powerful change

in America better than the events that occurred in Los Angeles, California, on November 6, 2008. In protest over the Church's stance on Proposition 8 (California's marriage amendment), more than one thousand rioters gathered around the Los Angeles Temple, threatening both the sacred edifice and the Saints working therein. Though in days past, the temple might have been left to the will of the mob (as it was with the Kirtland and Nauvoo temples), in this case the American covenant came to the rescue. Police officers in raid gear landed powerfully upon the temple grounds, prepared to defend the building by force if necessary.[2] We should not take this for granted. Joseph Smith would not have. He would have been overjoyed to see such protection. He had pled with all his heart for the apathetic nation to provide this protection to the Church. He was completely ignored. The Los Angeles Temple might have burned if that scene had played out in Joseph's America.

So, what has since happened? How did the Church become elevated from its Nauvoo Temple status (a burned temple) to its Los Angeles Temple status (a rescued temple)? Did America just wake up one day and say, *Let's stop beating up those Mormons; let's stop enslaving black people; let's stop burning temples, convents, and synagogues?* No! That does not happen.

A prominent journalist recently asked on national television: "How do you go from being the ultimate outcast to the embodiment of the mainstream in two generations? It's a breathtaking transformation. . . . [Mormons became] the embodiment of what it means to be America."[3] That is a mystery to many. But not to those who understand the scriptures—for it is all spelled out in the prophecies delivered by Joseph Smith. The Lord warned that if America chose not to fulfill its divine mandate as the protectorate of the gospel, then He would, in "hot displeasure" and in "fierce anger," arise and "come forth out of his hiding place, and in his fury vex the nation;" and "set his hand and seal to change the times and seasons," that He might "bring to pass [His] act, [His] strange act, and perform [His] work, [His] strange work" (D&C 101:89, 90, 95; 121:12). This, in the end, is what caused that "breathtaking transformation." It was the war. The people's unrighteousness pushed God to activate these frightening prophecies for the sake of His kingdom on earth. And the war came. Admittedly, it would take years after the war for the fulness of its fruit to materialize, but the war is what began the process of bringing liberty and salvation to America.

I discussed with you the powerful redemptive change that occurred in the North during those first two years of war. That was Act I of the war. Now, with the Northern heart changed—with its new understanding that this war was a holy war—Act II could begin: the eradication of slavery in all its forms. In hindsight, the plan was perfect. God would convert His army to His cause, then (once they were sufficiently prepared) He would send them to eradicate the evil that persisted in the land. You see, the demon here was *always* slavery. Once eradication of that evil became the goal and intent of Lincoln and the North, the game changed. At that point, the war became what Lincoln's contemporary George Washington Julian rightfully (even prophetically) called "a fight . . . between God and the Devil—between heaven and hell!"[4]

Yes, you say, *but what does slavery have to do with the Restoration?* My answer: *Everything!* Said Lincoln: "Slavery is the evil out of which all our other national evils and dangers have come. It has deceived and led us to the brink of ruin, and it must be stopped."[5] If some atrocious thing could socially and politically be done to blacks, it could conceivably be done to anyone. And it was! (Check your Mormon history.) This is perhaps why Frederick

The institution of slavery had to be abolished.

Douglass so poignantly declared that "the destiny of the colored American . . . is the destiny of America."[6] It is also why Civil War witness and literary great Ralph Waldo Emerson stated, "I think we must get rid of slavery, or we must get rid of freedom."[7]

Once the North began to understand this, the fight with the South was no longer just about saving the Union. It was about eradicating the evil that festered, grew, and proliferated in the Southern system. That said, we should (as Lincoln did) show a degree of sensitivity and compassion toward the South. As in any war, the individual reason each soldier fought varied. For example, many Confederate soldiers fought simply because they were drafted into the fight. Lincoln and his honest friends would allude to the idea that, had they been born in, say, South Carolina, they likely would have worn the gray uniform too. At the same time, however, it feels contrary to history to pretend that the Southern leadership was not fighting to keep slavery intact. The new Republican Party, whose major initiative was antislavery, got one of their own (Lincoln) in the White House. This would scare any society whose lifeblood was slavery. And so the Southern states left. And they fought to preserve a wicked ideal. Once converted to the truth behind the God-ordained mission in the conflict, the North sought to destroy this wicked ideal.[8]

If the North could not emerge victorious, the cause of the Restoration would be severely hampered. And this is why: A people cannot support and love a system that enslaves an entire race and not see the effects of such evil spill out in other areas of life. Yes, Southern intent was even darker than the preservation of slavery. Why? Because the ability for the South to enslave blacks provided the justification to do the same to any other group—and Mormons *were* that other group. The kingdom of God on earth *was* that other group.

Earlier, I mentioned the work of Professor Chandra Manning, one of the first to study the *true intent* of the soldiers fighting in the Civil War. She identified the Northern change of heart in Union letters, newspapers, and other writings. She also analyzed the letters, newspapers, and other published materials of the Confederates. Here is what she found. In fighting for slavery, the South was in fact fighting for

"As a nation we began by declaring that 'all men are created equal.' We now practically read it 'all men are created equal, except Negroes.' When the Know-Nothings [anti-immigrant/anti-minority party] get control, it will read 'all men are created equal, except Negroes and foreigners and Catholics.' When it comes to this, I shall prefer emigrating to some country where they make no pretense of loving liberty—to Russia, for instance, where despotism can be taken pure, and without the base alloy of hypocrisy."

—*Abraham Lincoln*[9]

SOUTHERN INTENT

Why did the South fight? Many students of the war have theories they utilize today in order to push political agendas. We could listen to these theories, or we could simply ask the South why they did what they did. After all, they published their intent for all to see. For example, the president and vice president of the Confederacy spoke frequently about the need for Southern victory in order to preserve slavery; they called slavery the "great truth," the "foundation," and the "cornerstone" of their new government.[10] Before the war, the would-be Confederate president, Jefferson Davis, "had frequently spoken to the United States Senate about the significance of slavery to the South and had threatened secession if what he perceived as Northern threats to the institution continued."[11] At the onset of the war, Confederate Vice President Alexander Stephens stated that slavery was "the proper status of the negro in our civilization" and that the issue of slavery was "the immediate cause of the late rupture and present revolution."[12]

In South Carolina's secession convention (the principal and most important secession convention), the delegates discussed their fears that Lincoln would allow "black Republicans" who were "hostile to slavery" to take positions of leadership in the government.[13] They could not have been any clearer than they were in their own documents: the "Declaration of the Immediate Causes Which Induce and Justify the Secession of South Carolina from the Federal Union" and their "Ordinance of Secession." They printed it in black and white for all to read—their rebellion and secession were due to the "increasing hostility on the part of the non-slave-holding States to the Institution of Slavery."[14]

The Confederate constitution made Southern intent even clearer. Southern leaders believed and declared, "Our new Government is founded . . . upon the great truth that the negro is not the equal of the white man. That slavery—subordination to the superior race, is his natural and normal condition."[15] During the war, Confederate President Jefferson Davis sought to make slaves of all black people in America, even free ones. In response to the Emancipation Proclamation, Davis ordered the following: "On or after February 22, 1863, all free negroes within the limits of the Southern Confederacy shall be placed on slave status, and be deemed to be chattels, they and their issue forever." The order was to be executed even upon free black persons outside Confederate territory. Davis ordered that black people "taken in any of the States in which slavery does not now exist

Confederate President Jefferson Davis.

. . . shall be adjudged . . . to occupy the slave status." Said Davis, the black race is "an inferior race, peaceful and contented laborers in their sphere."[16]

Through the years and into the present day, Southern sympathizers have tried to make the argument that the South was not fighting for slavery, as evidenced by the fact that relatively few Confederates actually owned slaves. These Southern apologists fail to comprehend a slave society. White Southerners saw their slaves as property, just as farmers today view their farm equipment—their tractors, their horses, their cattle. If all the farm equipment and livestock just disappeared in any agricultural economy, *everyone* would be affected, though relatively few actually owned the equipment. Without these tools, the working folks (even those without the equipment) would have nothing to do, nowhere to go. The folks who bought and sold agricultural products (even those without farm equipment) would likewise find themselves jobless. They would all want and need the farm owner to preserve his tools and equipment. Likewise, Southerners (whether slave owners or not) wanted and needed their slavery. They understood what was at stake in this war. So should we.

much more. According to Manning, "losing to the Union was unthinkable, according to Confederate soldiers, because it would mean abolition, and abolition would destroy the southern social order."[17] She continues, "The loss of slavery would call white men's right to rule over blacks into question, and once right to rule in any sphere was weakened, its legitimacy became suspect in every sphere. . . . Black slavery constantly reminded white men that in a society where most residents (African Americans, women, and children) were disenfranchised and subordinate to them, the independence that white men enjoyed as adult white males, and the ability to command . . . set them apart and identified them as men."[18]

To further illustrate how this oppressive ideal readily flowed from the acceptance of slavery to the adoption of other ungodly principles, consider an exhaustive study done by political scholar Richard Bensel. Bensel dug deeply into the Confederacy's handling of "property rights," "control of the railroad," "destruction of property," and "confiscations." He concluded that "the North had a less centralized government and was a much more open society than the South. . . . The Confederacy was far more government-centered and less market-oriented." Agreeing with Dr. Bensel, renowned historians Larry Schweikart and Michael Allen have pointed out how the Confederacy nationalized enormous percentages of private industries. In the end, these two historians concluded that "The Confederacy reached levels of government involvement unmatched until the totalitarian states of the twentieth century."[19]

And there is more. Under the Confederate constitution, the powers of the president were nearly unlimited, as no judicial check against the executive was put into place. The South's constitution further supported censorship, even that killer of democracy. As best-selling author-historians Chris and Ted Stewart pointed out, "The Confederacy was not a clone of the United States with the simple addition of humans being viewed as property. It rejected the American Constitution. It rejected the Bill of Rights. It rejected the very foundation of democracy."[20]

In the end, the war was fought over the existence of a social order. It was a fight to determine whether the promised land of America would or would not continue to maintain a system wherein one group dominated at will any other group it desired to rule. The North was right because (eventually) it began fighting against oppression of the human spirit, and oppression of the human spirit has been Satan's plan from the beginning.

Yes, Satan's plan. And he was winning before the war shook things up. The evidence of the adversary's success is readily apparent in a reading of LDS history. History shows how Satan managed to take the principles of slavery and utilize those principles to attack the Latter-day Saints. The South liked to talk about "states' rights." This was the "noble cause" they claimed to be fighting for. Don't be fooled. Yes, they *were* fighting for "states' rights"—a state's right to own a human being or burn down a Mormon temple or kill a prophet of God without any legal consequence. Remember the problem from the beginning: the states wanted the right to

> Lincoln was particularly concerned about the fact that the Confederacy's founding documents erased any semblance of that American theme of "all men are created equal." Lincoln pointed out that whereas the U.S. Constitution began with "We the People," the Confederate equivalent began with "We, the deputies of the sovereign and independent States."
>
> "Why?" asked Lincoln. "Why this deliberate pressing out of view, the rights of men, and the authority of the people?"[21]

opt out of the Constitution, to deny the Bill of Rights to those
they did not approve of (blacks, Mormons, and so on). They
wanted the right to maintain that social order Professor Manning
identified as the thing festering in their souls. This is what the
North was fighting to change. This is what Joseph Smith sought
to change in his America. It is why he screamed to the nation:
"The States rights doctrine are what feed mobs. They are a dead
carcass, a stink and they shall ascend up as a stink offering in the
nose of the Almighty."[22]

This is why Joseph sought an increase in federal authority—
to quash the states' rights doctrine that was responsible for denying blacks, Mormons, and other racial and religious minorities
the God-given constitutional rights of liberty. It was the basis for
Joseph's political platform; it was the *provision* he claimed should
be *added* to the Constitution. You will recall the important fact
that this was the same solution for religious persecution that
the "Father of the Constitution," James Madison, demanded be
amended into the Constitution (though he was rejected).

Once the North became converted to the covenant, it was
blessed (like Joseph Smith and James Madison were) with this
vision. That is why, again, the war became about bringing forth
the Thirteenth and Fourteenth Amendments—those tools that
represented Joseph's *provision* and eventually relieved the suffering
in America. Once those amendments finally landed, states could
no longer deny the Bill of Rights to America's people; if they did,
the national government would come to the rescue. This deterred
most states from even trying to oppress racial and religious minorities as they had done before. Ultimately, those amendments
provided the difference between burned temples and protected
ones—between living, thriving prophets and murdered ones.

Yes, that evil social order derived from the demon slavery,

and from the nineteenth century's definition of the states' rights doctrine, directly attacked the Latter-day Saints and the great gospel Restoration. We must understand this in order to understand Lincoln, the war, and the Restoration. Beyond the death and destruction of prophet and temple, I have more examples for you. Elder Parley Pratt, an Apostle, was murdered in the South some three years prior to the Civil War after converting a woman to the gospel. Her estranged husband disapproved of the conversion. And in accordance with this accepted and evil social order—which the North had only recently begun to reject and which the South was fighting to preserve—even a world in which the white male controls all in his "dominion," the assailant and his friends caught up with Elder Pratt and killed him in cold blood, stabbing and shooting him in the back.[24] Elder B. H. Roberts recorded the deaths of other LDS missionaries and members in this same general time period: Elder Joseph Standing, killed in Georgia; Elders John Gibbs, William Berry, and others, killed in Tennessee; and up to four hundred additional Saints killed in the border state of Missouri.[25]

> "We have the highest reason to believe that the Almighty will not suffer slavery and the Gospel to go hand in hand. It cannot, it will not be."
>
> —John Jay, an inspired Founding Father[23]

The high number of Mormon casualties in Missouri certainly draws our attention to that state. For all intents and purposes, Missouri most certainly embodied the evil, antigospel political system the South was fighting to preserve. Though the state was technically north of the Mason-Dixon line, the Missouri Compromise of 1820 legalized the already active practice of slavery there, which had unleashed the oppressive culture that hurt the restored gospel. As one political scholar pointed out, "The spirit of mobocracy loosed against the Mormon people, that ignoble spectre of hate, became characteristic of the controversy over slavery and political power and was to bathe in blood . . . Missouri . . . and eventually culminate in Civil War."[26] One Missourian summed up the spirit in that state accurately when he announced that Mormons should not have civil rights, "no more than the negroes."[27] The Missouri mobocrats declared, "Mormonism, emancipation and abolitionism must be driven from the state."[28] This was the Southern cry. It was the opposite of God's designs for America. It countered Lincoln's new intention for the war. It directly challenged the American covenant.

Elder Roberts stated that these murders of the Saints in the South were a direct fulfillment of the Book of Mormon prophecy that the Restoration would come forth "in a day when the blood of saints shall cry unto the Lord" (Mormon 8:27).[29] Indeed, the cries of the Saints would forever endure under the sociopolitical system that the South was fighting for—that the adversary was fighting for. This system above all else, which prevailed in the prehumbled, preconverted North and especially in the South, was drowning the Church. And with slavery on the rise, thus increasing the evil of all that slavery implied, hope grew dimmer. As Satan bought his armies and navies in the South to enforce these evil designs, hope grew dimmer still. You see why the North had to win this fight. You see why Lincoln arrived on the scene when he did.

But most important, you see why it was imperative that the people of the North were able to listen to the converted Lincoln and repent themselves, thus reactivating the American covenant. In the months after the issuance of the Emancipation Proclamation (the first sign of national repentance), we begin to see the change of heart. It was right after the Proclamation went forth, during 1863, that the majority of those Professor Manning documents were produced—proof that the change in the North was taking effect. But the greatest proof that the North had finally crossed over to God's side manifested itself that very summer—the summer of 1863. Two battles occurred that would determine the entire outcome of the war. These battles could have easily gone either way, and whichever side won them was going to win the entire war. They were the battles at Gettysburg and Vicksburg. The Union won both. Though they occurred on opposite sides of the country, both battles culminated on July 4! The North claimed it to be "divine intervention and [it] reawakened Union soldiers' millennial understanding of the war."[30] Sgt. J. G. Nind summed up well such feelings in his own post-Gettysburg/Vicksburg reflections when he stated that now the "nation will be purified" and "God will accomplish his vast designs."[31]

But nobody knew this more than Abraham Lincoln. You see, as the battle at Gettysburg was raging, the president found himself in what may have been the most powerful prayer of his life. In that moment, he made the covenant once again, ushering in the Union victory on his knees. (I will tell you more about that prayer in a later chapter.)

With the covenant at last reactivated, the Lord was able to bring in another miracle in the weeks and months after Gettysburg. It is a hidden gem in Civil War history—*hidden* because without Mormon scripture it means very little, and *a gem* because it manifests what this war was about and bears testimony of the Prophet Joseph.

It began on July 15, 1863 (days after Gettysburg), when Lincoln issued his Proclamation of Thanksgiving. In his proclamation, Lincoln encouraged Americans to pray and give thanks.

In doing so he invoked the "Holy Spirit . . . to change the hearts of the insurgents."[32] And who were the insurgents? Obviously they included the Confederates and those of the proslavery movement in general. And certainly they should have *especially* included anyone who aligned themselves with such oppressive movements *and* had wielded such oppression over God's Church and kingdom. If the many aforementioned gospel prophecies concerning the sociopolitical elevation of the Church were fulfilled through the Civil War, then we should certainly expect to see those enemies of the Church who caused its oppression to be affected, humbled, and positively changed by the war.

In the previous chapter, I pointed out a Joseph Smith prophecy (which he received while imprisoned in Liberty Jail) recorded in section 121 of the Doctrine and Covenants. This is the passage in which God promises to use the national punishment and scourge to "set his hand and seal to change the times and seasons" (verse 12). That prophecy was clear that God's judgment and vexation upon the land would specifically seek out those who had "lift[ed] up the heel against mine anointed" and who had "[sworn] falsely against my servants, that they might bring them into bondage," as well as those who had "driv[en], and murder[ed], and testif[ied] against them." In other words, the punishment would fall upon the people who persecuted the Prophet and the Church. (In this same prophecy the Lord provides further evidence that this same generation would suffer the vexation by stating that in "not many years hence . . . they and their posterity shall be swept from under heaven.") And this punishment and corrective action would fall upon these "children of disobedience," even to the point that "their basket shall not be full," and that "their houses and their barns shall perish" (D&C 121:11–24).

So, we must ask ourselves where these 1830s enemies of the Church found themselves during the 1860s war. We especially wonder about those in Jackson County, Missouri, who so horribly persecuted the Saints. Were these folks especially targeted in the war, as the prophecy indicates? The answer is chilling. The great American historian David McCullough pointed out that the Civil War in Missouri began some seven years before it began in the rest of the country: "It was a war of plunder, ambush and unceasing revenge. Nobody was safe. Defenseless towns were burned. . . . Neither then nor later did the rest of the country realize the extent of the horrors."[33] There is no doubt that Satan had set up camps in Missouri years earlier to stomp out any Mormon efforts to build Zion—certainly the adversary knew it was a promised land designated for Zion. Just because the Mormons left doesn't mean the adversary did. As one eyewitness declared: "The Devil came to the border [state], liked it, and stayed awhile."[34]

The Prophet Joseph, after all, was never shy about expressing his prophecy that Missouri would one day "witness scenes of blood and sorrow."[35] And indeed it did.

But there was one stunning and dramatic event that happened in Missouri within weeks of Lincoln's appeal for corrective action to "change the hearts of the insurgents." It was called General Order #11. It was a Union order to strike at the very heart of the evil brewing in Missouri. By August 1863, the Union army had recognized the mobocracy in Missouri that continually attacked those trying to support the Union and the eradication of slavery. It was this same mobocracy, perpetuated by the same groups of people, against freedom and liberty that had almost snuffed out the Saints years earlier. It was the same evil spirit of oppression introduced by the adversary to limit eternal progression and to impede the gospel plan—and it was this very evil that had therefore become a principal target of God's vexation. This time the evil power was being specifically directed at antislavery supporters, and the Union army had seen enough.

"The depopulation of Jackson . . . is thorough and complete. One may ride for hours without seeing a single inhabitant and deserted houses and farms are everywhere to be seen. The whole is a grand picture of desolation."

—*Excerpt from the* St. Joseph Herald, *October 1863*[36]

And where exactly within Missouri did the Union armies see this spirit of mobocracy and destruction against the innocent? Where did the Union armies direct their attack under General Order #11? The answer is almost too fitting: Jackson County, along with a few other surrounding counties. General Order #11, issued on August 25, 1863, forced these Jackson County residents from their homes.[37] The Doctrine

General Order No. 11 (1863).

and Covenants prophecy that "their houses and their barns shall perish" had been fulfilled to the letter.

Evidence that this corrective action perhaps was successful is seen in General Order #20, issued months later. This order allowed all those who would take an oath of allegiance to the Union, and prove this allegiance, to return to their homes.[38] In light of what we know the Union now stood for, Jackson County residents willing to accept this oath were, in a sense, entering the American covenant. They were promising to at last reject their self-serving ways and embrace the true constitutional principles of liberty and justice for all. I can't help but wonder if, as they took their oaths and returned to their lands, they thought on "old Joe Smith." I wonder if they remembered that he had told them this would happen. Either they could choose the right on their own, or God would vex them and humble them until they did so. Either way, I hope they did think on him; I hope they did realize that they had been caught and pinned in the frightening prophecies of that Mormon prophet whom—though he had sought to save them—they had sought tirelessly to destroy.

> It was Lincoln's policy throughout the war to allow captured rebels to take the "oath of allegiance" to the Union and the Constitution, thereby setting themselves free from Union bondage. Lincoln explained that such oaths embodied "the Christian principle of forgiveness on terms of repentance."[39] Though officials in his administration might have thought this a strange practice, it would not have been strange to one who had read the Book of Mormon. For Captain Moroni did the same.

With this understanding, the purpose of the Civil War becomes clearer than ever. Think about this: America had fallen so low that God literally picked up His Church and dropped it outside U.S. territory (where Utah is today). With the Saints

safely tucked away, the Almighty then unleashed the prophesied scourge upon the land. As a result, Zion was being purged.
As Brigham Young stated during the war, instead of suffering
through the bloodshed and tears of fraternal conflict, the Latter-
day Saints were "comfortab[ly] located in our peaceful dwellings
in these silent, far off mountains and valleys. . . . We are greatly
blessed, greatly favored and greatly exalted, while our enemies,
who sought to destroy us, are being humbled."[40]

Someday, with the purging complete, with the addition of
Joseph's constitutional *provision* (the amendments created in the
wake of the war), and with righteousness restored in the land, the
Mormons would be able to return to Zion, be a part of America
and build their temples and grow their gospel. The promised land
would not be defiled forever. God will not be mocked forever.

Yes, by 1863, the Civil War had indeed become an extension
of that war in heaven. It had transformed into something nobody
understood at the beginning of the conflict. God had kept His
promise to Joseph, and now the Civil War could forevermore be
described as "a fight . . . between God and the Devil—between
heaven and hell!"[41]

CHAPTER 12

Answering the Critics

Having presented this research to thousands of people, the majority of whom agree with me, I am well aware that others do not. I am well aware that I have ruffled the feathers of many a patriot who is far more sympathetic to the South and its cause. These good people have accepted the notion that Lincoln and the North were wrong to pursue the war, and that they should have let the South go as it pleased. They paint the South as noble "separatists" who wanted only to innocently "withdraw from the Union." Lincoln, on the other hand, is painted as a tyrant who "authorized" the death of hundreds of thousands of his own citizens because of an evil intent based in the "love of money and dominion."[1]

These critics also claim that our liberty was lost because of the war. "What the people lost during the Civil War (the Great War of Coercion), we have yet to get back," they argue. They want us to believe that "Lincoln himself became the principal instigator of America's suicide" and that his war "ended the Founders' dreams in America." You see, they are irritated that the Civil War produced the Fourteenth Amendment, which empowered the federal government. They believe that the federal growth caused by the war and the amendment has hurt that thing they hold so dear called "the states' rights doctrine." The South, they claim, in fighting to preserve this noble doctrine, was right. These critics—some of them Latter-day Saints—claim that the amendment was "foist[ed] upon the states."[2] (Definition of *foist:* "to force upon or impose fraudulently or unjustifiably.")

Such ideas, of course, fly in the face of the abundant evidence put forth in this book. Based in the *entire* history—to include the prophecies and revelations streaming into and out of Joseph Smith, Abraham Lincoln, and other inspired ones—this war was not the doing of Lincoln. Though they want to blame him, the evidence points in a very different direction. *It was God.* Lincoln simply became exactly what he had claimed himself to be: "a humble instrument in the hands of our Heavenly Father."[3]

Now, I have much to say in response to the critics. I understand that the vast majority of those reading this book do not and will not agree with their Lincoln assessment. However, I invite you to join the discussion anyway, for it is still relevant to you. Not only will it arm you when they come knocking at your door, but through responding to them we get to some profound truths about how the war was in fact a manifestation of the covenant in the land, and how it really became a fight between good and evil, between light and darkness, between Zion and the demon. Through engaging in this debate, we also learn vital lessons about the importance of giving full consideration to prophecy, scripture, and truths about covenant lands when reading history.

I have made a full response to the critics' arguments in earlier works that are more comprehensive than this rebuttal.[4] Notwithstanding, I will now address a few important things.

To begin with, the North did not want this war and did not start it. The South attacked first at Fort Sumter in South Carolina. Southerners had seized other federal forts and ports before that attack. Those forts and ports did not belong to *them;* they belonged to *all* the people of *all* the states. Of course there was a response. The response was to get that national property back and to force the salvation of the Union. But did the South not have the right to leave and take that national property with them? Lincoln and his people did not think so, but others did. Admittedly, without any clear constitutional mandate or instruction on this issue (only personal interpretations), this part gets controversial. Though I believe there is insufficient evidence in the Constitution to make any definitive claim on the matter, I think it wise to at least listen to the words of the "Father of the Constitution," James Madison. Madison was alive to witness South Carolina's *first* effort in 1832 to leave the Union. Madison's response was as follows: "It is high time that the claim to secede at will should be put down by the public opinion." He declared that a state's proposed twin rights to nullify federal law ["nullification"] and leave the Union ["secession"] are a "colossal heresy."[6] If Lincoln was off base, he was in good company with the "Father of the Constitution."

> According to Brigham Young, "South Carolina committed treason" when it seceded from the Union. Brigham continued, stating that the president should have "hung up the first man who rebelled."[5]

Yes, it was controversial. But this is the point the critics must understand: the controversy flew out the window once the North became converted to the idea that God was behind this war and that He sought a purging of sin, a purging from both North and South. Everything changed at that point. Nobody was going to duck out of God's prophesied judgment on the land, no matter how convincing an argument they made about states' rights or the right of secession. To God, that was never the point. Anyone who reads the Book of Mormon and believes it is applicable to the modern-day covenant land it speaks of should find this concept easy to accept. In fact, if the Book of Mormon teaches us anything about America, it is that fierce judgments will befall the land when its inhabitants choose gross sin. During the nineteenth century, then, we should expect to see such judgments in the land, even if we did not have the Civil War prophecies from Joseph and the historical corroborations from Lincoln and his people.

Let the South go? the Northern leaders say. Let them keep enslaving, persecuting, torturing, raping, and killing minorities, religious and racial? Is that the answer? Is there no responsibility on the part of righteousness to seek out darkness and destroy it, especially when that darkness lurks within our own covenant land?

Think of what would have happened if the South had gained independence. That wicked social order would have remained and haunted all the American continent for years on end. Both independent countries (of the North and South) would have sought the western frontier, fighting for that territory and battling over whether that new territory would become slave-land or free-land. The war would not have ended with Southern independence. More bloodshed would have followed, and the fulness of the Restoration would henceforth have been delayed until peace and security finally landed in the promised land.

Furthermore, once the precedent was set that granted leave to any state wanting to secede from the Union, that pattern would have continued. Soon, America would have broken into many countries, like Central America. The united power for good that the United States eventually became would never have materialized. In the years to come, millions would have then suffered under tyranny throughout the world because that powerhouse for good, the United States of America, would not have been there for them.

The Confederate flag.

Also, if Lincoln had failed to maintain the Union, the nations of the world might well have lost hope in democracy. They might have thrown up their hands and realized the aristocracy was right—people can't self-govern without breaking apart and destroying the government. America was the first to try a republic on a large scale. If it succeeded, others would follow. If it failed, freedom would have failed everywhere. How could the Restoration grow throughout the world then? It becomes clear why Satan wanted Lincoln and the North to lose.

Finally, and perhaps most importantly, had the South gained independence, or had there not been a war, the prophecies would not have been fulfilled. America would have remained unchanged and unpurged (the North included), and God's Church and kingdom would have remained obstructed and exiled by wicked politics.

Is it not confusing that many of the same LDS students of the Constitution who declare the South was right and should have been allowed to leave the Union are the ones who love to quote

D&C 101, which teaches that God created the Constitution (verses 77–80)? What do they think the Constitution was? The whole point of it was to create *a more perfect Union*—to bring these independent states together in order to produce the freest and most powerful country in the history of the world. Are we to suppose that God, who brought the states together under scriptural approbation, approved of their separation by the very next American generation? Did God just want that union to last a few years and be done? Did He think it a righteous move for the South to pull away so that it might continue to codify sin in His land? Does that make any sense at all?

But D&C 101 becomes an even greater stumbling block for the critics. For it also declares the obvious point that men should be free from "bondage one to another" (verse 79). I have been absolutely astonished at the lengths to which the critics are willing to go in order to blame their woes on Lincoln and his war. You see, they want to make their argument about federal growth and states' rights, but they don't know what to do about that slavery thing. Indeed, it gets in their way, since it was federal growth and an attack on states' rights that ultimately destroyed slavery. They must get around this somehow, so they deny that slavery was the cause of Southern secession; they claim that slavery would have died on its own, without the war.

These matters—of slavery and liberty—have always been at the core of God's plan and at the core of His fight against the adversary. That said, we cannot afford to make light of them when reading American history. The truth about American slavery could not be clearer. Due to the growing antislavery movement, and in the wake of the antislave Republican Party's rise to power, the South seceded because of their desire to maintain the ability to enslave human beings. They seceded once Lincoln was elected.

That is the reason. End of story. They wrote it in black and white for all to see in their secession documents—in their declarations of independence.[7] I can't say it better than Professor Chandra Manning: "[It is] patronizing and insulting to Confederate soldiers to pretend they did not understand the war as a battle for slavery when they so plainly described it as exactly that."[8] The Prophet Joseph saw this in revelation. Indeed, when God told Joseph of the coming civil war to begin in South Carolina, He stated clearly that the war would arise over and "through the slave question" (see D&C 87:1–4; 130:12–13). If the war was not over slavery, as many critics proclaim, then the Lord certainly has a strange scriptural explanation for it.

The vast majority of trained American historians agree that "it is not an exaggeration to say that the Civil War was about slavery and, in the long run, *only* about slavery."[9] Fine, respond the critics, but Lincoln only freed the slaves as a political move, not as a moral or spiritual one. The Emancipation Proclamation, they claim, did not free a single slave. They say this because the Proclamation only freed slaves in Southern territory, leaving in chains the slaves in the states loyal to the Union. Therefore, they claim, Lincoln freed only the slaves he had no access to and did nothing for those within his reach. So, no slave was actually freed. I enjoy this argument because it reveals how shortsighted the critics are and to what great lengths they are willing to go in order to justify their anti-Lincoln sentiments. Based on the evidence I provided in earlier chapters, to deny Lincoln's spiritual experience and heaven's clear hand in the decision to issue the Proclamation is quite bold. To say it did not free slaves completely defies all logic.

Lincoln had to couch the Proclamation in a political principle that would allow it to remain untouched by the very racist

Supreme Court (which had not long before issued the despicable and racist *Dred Scott* decision. Indeed, much of the Court was pro-South and proslavery). And so, as slaves were viewed as property by the South, even property that was forced to labor in the war effort, Lincoln could constitutionally "confiscate them" (really, free them) as a military necessity granted to the president by the Constitution. In order to use this constitutional justification for the Proclamation, however, he could only target the slaves in enemy territory. He could only "confiscate" or free the slaves being used to fight the North. This kept his power to emancipate safe until he could get the Thirteenth Amendment passed, which he knew would then liberate the rest of the slaves in the country and which he knew—being that it was a constitutional amendment as opposed to a mere executive order—was something even the racist Court could not abolish.

At one point toward the end of the war, the South wanted to finally discuss Lincoln's early proposal to allow the South to keep their precious slavery in exchange for reunification. But by then, Lincoln had taken that option off the table. After his great conversion, he knew definitively that he was under orders from God to destroy the demon slavery, no matter the consequence. In fact, he refused to even discuss a peace treaty with the South unless they would agree beforehand to a strict principle that was, as written in a memo by his own hand, "the abandonment of slavery."[10] As Lincoln biographer Doris Goodwin pointed out, "Nothing on the home front . . . engaged Lincoln with greater urgency than the passage of the Thirteenth Amendment."[11] And so you see, it would be a mistake to suggest Lincoln fought only to restore the Union or that slavery meant little more to him than a means to gaining that Union.

Notwithstanding the need for the Thirteenth Amendment,

it is still equally incorrect to suggest, as some critics do, that the Emancipation Proclamation itself freed no slaves. "The old cliché," wrote Civil War expert James McPherson, "that the proclamation did not free a single slave because it applied only to the Confederate states where Lincoln had no power, completely misses the point. The proclamation announced a revolutionary new war aim—the overthrow of slavery by force of arms if and when Union armies conquered the South."[12] Without the Proclamation, Union soldiers might have continued occupying Southern states, but they would have left slavery alone in those states. For example, early in the conflict, local emancipation orders by Union Generals Fremont and Hunter were rescinded.[13] They had been commanded to continue to retake the South, but to free no slaves. And so, yes, the Proclamation was necessary. Slavery was going nowhere without it.

With the Proclamation, however, once the South was conquered, the slaves *were* freed; and thus, the Proclamation did accomplish much. For critics to say (as they do) that the Proclamation did nothing is like saying the U.S. declarations of war against Imperial Japan and Nazi Germany during World War II did nothing because initially they were just declarations. Upon their issuance, Imperial Japan and Nazi Germany remained a force largely undeterred and untouched by America. If we had to add the obvious fact that these declarations eventually led the U.S. to defeat these foreign enemies, it would be embarrassing. So it is with the Proclamation.

An added point of frustration to those critics who call the Proclamation useless is the fact that the Proclamation grew into the Thirteenth and Fourteenth Amendments (even those acts that reflected Joseph Smith's *provision*). Freedom for *all* the oppressed (Mormons included) began to ring loud and clear for the first time in our history. Indeed, history has proven that the Proclamation was a clarion call that led to the greatest of freedoms for the oppressed.

Fine, the critics respond, *but slavery would have died soon enough without this needless war and this needless federal growth.* I recently found myself in the audience of an LDS lecturer promoting this idea to an LDS audience. As I was attempting to ask him what he thought of my premise about the Civil War and its gospel implications, he stated what he clearly felt was ironclad evidence of his position on slavery (a position I had heard other critics regularly parrot). *No other country in the world,* he explained, *ever required a civil war to eradicate slavery.* The implication was clear: The Civil War should not have been slavery's remedy.

The problem is that this popular argument is based on the faulty premise that slavery has been eradicated throughout the world. It has not! There are more slaves today—human beings forced to labor for the master—than ever existed during the nineteenth century. Indeed, there are an estimated twenty-seven million slaves suffering in the world today.[14] Perhaps a portion of those slaves would still be toiling in America had there not been a Civil War. How can the critic prove otherwise? Perhaps there should by now have been other demonstrations of the righteous use of force, such as Lincoln used, to free these other millions of slaves still suffering. That is what they need today. It is what American slaves in the nineteenth century needed. Nobody, on the other hand, is helped by arguments with a faulty premise.

That said, I will concede that other nations have been able to eradicate slavery without a war. But I would ask the critic the following questions about those other nations: Were they large agricultural nations whose slave populations were growing rapidly, jumping from 800,000 to 4,000,000 in just two generations?[15]

Did those other nations have a rebel/separatist government recently created whose purpose was to preserve slavery at almost any cost? Did they have temples of God in their lands that were being destroyed, confiscated, and burned? Did they have prophets of God in their lands who were being shot and killed? Did they have prophets who, through the priesthood of God, declared in scripture that a vexatious war would come to them as a result of this sin, even calling out specific states or regions in the land that were to be targeted most severely? Were those prophecies then fulfilled to the letter? Did they have presidents who, through miracles and revelations, learned things about slavery in their lands that were completely consistent with these scriptural prophecies? Were they covenant lands, as defined by scripture? The answers to these questions are too obvious for discussion. There is a different story and a different set of rules in a covenant land, which makes it impossible to compare it to other lands. Not knowing or applying this principle leads to mistaken interpretations.

But let's give the critics the benefit of the doubt. Let's say that, notwithstanding the many unsuccessful efforts made to end American slavery over hundreds of years, and notwithstanding slavery's rapid growth in the country, let's just suppose it *would* have ended on its own, without a war. When? How long would the critic be willing to wait for the suffering to end? One decade? Two decades? How long must the promised land endure this? And how does one sit back and patiently predict the death of something that is only growing and thriving? Not only had more than four million slaves been added to the forced-labor rolls in just two generations, but a mere four years before Lincoln took office, slavery had received further bolstering from the Supreme Court decision in *Dred Scott* (1857). Black Americans, declared the Court, even free ones, "are not included, and were not intended to be included, under the word 'citizen' in the Constitution."[16] If that were not enough, an entire government (the Confederate States of America) had just been created with the express purpose of ensuring slavery's existence and growth.

What if one of the critics' own children were a slave child like young Harriett Jacobs, the object of the master's lust I wrote about in an earlier chapter, even that child who represents millions of others forced to confront the demon? Would the critic say, *Don't worry, my child. It will all end soon. Though all indications are that it will continue to grow, it has ended in other countries in years past. Just hang in there. We are not going to do anything drastic here, my dear. We certainly won't pick up our firearms and cause the abuser any harm. Perhaps if we're lucky, though, your grandchildren won't have to deal with this beast.* You know the answer to that absurdity.

The modern-day critics do not have to deal with the ugly fact that one-third of slave marriages ended in a greedy business decision by the master, and over one-half of all slave children lost at least one of their parents (and many times both of their parents) for the same reason.[17] They don't have to deal with the fact that the Southern system had legally institutionalized the destruction of the most important unit in God's plan—the family. They don't have to deal with witnessing the extreme physical and sexual abuse hurled upon the slaves throughout the land. They don't have to deal with seeing advertisements lining the streets on their way to the grocery store, such as the following (which actually existed): "I will at all times pay the highest cash price for Negroes of every description, will also attend to the sale of Negroes on commission, having a jail and yard fitted up expressly for boarding them." Another read, "For sale—several likely girls from 10 to 18 years old, a woman 24, a very valuable woman 25, with three very likely children."[18] And they certainly don't have to see these poor humans being lined up in shackles, ready to be sold like cattle. Lincoln had to see this when, as a young man, he did business in the South. Shocked, he immediately turned to his companion and stated, "Boy, let's get away from this. If ever I get a chance to hit that thing, I'll hit it hard."[19]

Again I ask, if the critics' children or spouses were thrust into this captivity, would they say what they say today about American slavery? Would they say, *Just hang in there, it will all work itself out someday?* Of course not. And they would not let some vague interpretation of the Constitution get in the way of their doing all they could to end their children's suffering now, no matter the consequence to the brutal offenders. They would have applied the solution that the former slave Frederick Douglass proposed for slavery: "It is not light that is needed, but fire; it is not the gentle shower, but thunder. We need the storm, the whirlwind, and the earthquake."[20] They would have, like Harriet Beecher Stowe, invoked "the wrath of Almighty God!" in order to save their children.[21]

Frederick Douglass.

I recognize that my own experience in fighting up close and personal against the evil that enslaves children today gives me clarity. I wish I could take the critics to work with me and let them look into the eyes of a slave child. I wish they could hold a slave child in their arms like I have had to do. I wonder if this would bring them clarity on the issue of the Civil War and of the responsibility a free and covenant people have under God Almighty.

In irony so thick I can scarcely understand it, these critics who claim to come closer to understanding liberty than any other group sit back and side with the team that fought to preserve the most hideous, perverse, oppressive, tyrannical, and evil system ever to lurk in America.

Why do I care about this even now? Because if "liberty lovers" like these critics can justify away tyranny and blind themselves to the truth behind the most oppressive evil ever to hit the land, then what hope do we have today? We have evil today all around us seeking to destroy liberty. If those who claim themselves to be the pillars of liberty in our modern society can't see this nineteenth-century struggle for what it so obviously was— the powers of darkness pitted against the powers of God and light—then I fear for us.

And then that D&C 101 prophecy goes from being a stumbling block for the critics (particularly for the LDS critics) to being a downright embarrassment for them. Why? Because, as I explained earlier, God *told* Joseph and the Saints to seek federal intervention—He told them to do that which the anti-Lincoln critics claim was at the core of the war's mistake. Joseph reacted by passionately condemning "the states' rights doctrine," then promoting an increase in federal authority to restore liberty (what would become the Thirteenth and Fourteenth Amendments). He specifically stated that "the Constitution is . . . not broad enough to cover the whole ground." He then identified the missing piece as the authority for federal intervention to "punish those . . . states, or communities who interfere with the rights of the people." He unapologetically declared that the federal government should have "full power to send an army to suppress mobs" without the invitation of the states.[22]

I have heard some LDS critics say, *Yes, but that was just Joseph the man reacting. That was just his opinion.* Though it is tempting to give them the benefit of the doubt on that one, I realize I can't give it to them when reminded that Joseph's "opinion" was eternally tethered to numerous prophecies about a war in the land to induce repentance and restore the covenant. No, I won't give them the benefit of the doubt when reminded that it was *God* who specifically told Joseph to seek federal intervention (D&C 101:88) and then sustained Joseph's politics by activating the prophecies after the prophet-candidate, while at the height of espousing these ideas to the nation, was killed.

What would those critics say if Joseph had been elected and actually legislated his proposed policies? This would cause quite a predicament for them. Joseph had clearly identified the wicked system of government produced by the politics the critics seem to applaud—a system that disallows federal intervention and thus permits states to do what they want to the suffering minority. What the critics portray as a wonderful, liberty-bearing concept (the doctrine of "states' rights")—even that great thing they claim "the people lost" during the "Great War of Coercion"—was *not* wonderful to the Prophet. Again, Joseph declared, "The states' rights doctrine . . . are a dead carcass, a stink and they ascend up as a stink offering in the nose of the Almighty." Was Joseph wrong? Do the critics understand the Constitution, particularly in a nineteenth-century context, better than Joseph did?

Please do not get me wrong. I do understand the critics' argument. But notwithstanding the inevitable negative externalities (for example, the eventual abuse of power by the federal government that *would* come and against which we *do* need to fight today), the bottom line is this: Lincoln had to do what he did. He had to grow the federal government, notwithstanding some people's modern-day objections. The states could have chosen righteousness on their own; they had their chance. They refused, and as a result people were enslaved. Temples and convents were burning. Children were suffering and dying. Apostles were being murdered. God's Church had been exiled. God's prophet on the earth had called for the same solution Lincoln brought. And then that prophet had died for it!

He was not the only one. Another died a violent death for the cause: Abraham Lincoln. He suffered like no human should have to in order to bring a new birth of freedom under God. Where temples once burned under the states' rights doctrine, now they thrive. Notwithstanding all he gave, even for the critics who now bask in the freedom he brought, they desecrate him and spit upon his name just to justify a myopic political claim. He has become the focal point upon which they place the blame for the federal growth that haunts them today. Yet, all he did was bring about the change called for by James Madison and pled for by Joseph Smith. That others came along later and used Lincoln's inspired acts to justify unconstitutional growth is no fault of Lincoln. To say otherwise is akin to saying that because God gave us the Internet to conduct family history research, He is also responsible for the pornography that came with it. Furthermore, whatever increases in federal abuses of power have come about since the Civil War (and, admittedly, we must push back against those abuses today), they do not even approximate the sins derived of "states' rights'" that prevailed before the war. They do not even hint at enslaving races, exiling and murdering the Saints and their prophets, or burning down God's temple. Is it too much to ask for a reasonable amount of common-sense perspective?

And yet the critics despise Lincoln for what he did. But thus it has always been. The servants of God will always be attacked by those who do not understand. Notwithstanding those attacks, the testators, like Joseph Smith and Abraham Lincoln, are always willing to give the ultimate sacrifice because of the covenant.

Late one night, as I was writing this chapter, I found myself ranting and raving to my wife about these modern-day critics, many of whom were friends and scholars of liberty that I wanted to respect. My wife listened, then told me that she had just read that day about such critics in the classic book by Victor Hugo, *Les Misérables*. (I do not think her timing was a coincidence.) She said Hugo too was disturbed by those who refused to see plain truth simply because they had drawn up a nice little box and filled it with notions of how things were always meant to be. In the case of the anti-Lincoln critics, these notions include that states have the right to secede from the Union, and the federal government cannot grow. When the critics identify violations of their notions, they refuse to see anything outside their little box, so in desperation they scream foul. Unable to see anything outside—unable to see that God is working a great work before them—they simply become trapped inside their box. This trap can easily lead them to call good evil and evil good. Confused, they begin to yelp for

> "It is distressing to see the condition our nation is in, but I cannot help it. Who can? The people *en masse*, by turning to God, and ceasing to . . . persecute the honest and the truth-lover. If they had done that thirty years ago, it would have been better for them today. . . . Did not Joseph Smith tell them in Washington and Philadelphia, that the time would come when their State rights would be trampled upon?"
>
> —*Brigham Young, 1864*[23]

liberty with so much fire that the very thing that brings their liberty ends up burnt. Hugo calls it being "ultra."

> To be ultra is to go beyond. It is to attack the scepter in the name of the throne, and the miter in the name of the altar; it is to mistreat the thing you support . . . it is to insult through an excess of respect; it is to find too little papistry in the pope, in the king too little royalty, and too much light in the night; it is to be dissatisfied with the albatross, with snow, with the swan, and the lily for not being white enough; it is to champion things to the point of becoming their enemy; it is to be so pro you become con.[24]

Intrigued by Hugo's words, from a novel I have always loved, I decided to look further into the French philosopher, as I knew he was a contemporary of Lincoln. I found some fascinating facts. First, Hugo's words here were published in the spring of 1862, even as the Civil War raged. More specifically, they were published during the exact months Lincoln was passing through his deep conversion to the covenant. Second, a few short years after the Civil War and Union victory, the inspired Hugo stood in Paris, rallying a massive group of freedom lovers to stand on true principles related to God and country. Hugo noticed that the U.S. embassy was in view of the crowd. He pointed to the U.S. flag flying high and noble. He then declared the following: "That banner of stars speaks today to Paris and France proclaiming miracles of power which are easy to a great people, contending for great principle, the liberty of every race and the fraternity of all."[25] And third, I was pleased to note that on the same ledger Lincoln used to check out the Book of Mormon, he had also checked out a book by Victor Hugo.

Victor Hugo.

If we would all just view the Civil War (and everything else past, present, and future in America) as a product of the covenant on our land, then we would not fall into the trap Hugo warned us of. Consider the enormity of what the critics miss concerning Lincoln and the war because they blind themselves to the covenant at play, because they do not read American history with the scriptures of the Restoration in their hands. What else might they, or any of us, be missing in our vision and responsibility as citizens of this land because we do not see the covenant? If we blind ourselves to this covenant, which is deeply connected to all important American events, then we will, as the scriptures warn, be "tossed to and fro, and carried about with every wind of doctrine" (Ephesians 4:14). As Americans living in these crucial times, we can't afford to do this.

William Seward had his moment of clarity, and he manifested it in a speech he gave (which really ruffled feathers in the

South). Amidst Southerners' interpretation of the Constitution, even their efforts to justify the legality of human bondage, he stood before the nation and declared: "There is a higher law than the Constitution, which regulates our authority over this domain, and devotes it to the same noble purposes. . . . Does it therefore follow that Congress may amend the ten commandments, or reverse the principles of Christ's Sermon on the Mount . . . ? Man could not, by any law, make right what God and his own conscience declared wrong."[26]

The people of Lincoln's day learned the hard way what we Americans need to learn immediately, particularly as we continue to legislate and codify immorality in the land. They learned that things will turn out very badly if man attempts to amend or reinterpret the American covenant. One cannot employ darkness under the banner of God's promised land. The covenant rules won't permit it.

The Lincoln critics make the fatal mistake of not seeing the national covenant in the Civil War and instead get stuck in their myopic interpretation of the "states' rights doctrine." Ironically, that doctrine becomes more important to them (albeit unintentionally) than their ultimate goal—liberty in the land! What they need to understand is that the "states' rights doctrine" of today (something that actually needs to be strengthened in the land) is not the same as it was in Joseph Smith's or Abraham Lincoln's America. Please understand this: The "states' rights doctrine" of their day was destroying the Church and the purposes of America. The "states' rights doctrine" served to protect an evil social order. God had placed Lincoln under orders to destroy that evil. So he did it. He did it by employing Joseph's *provision,* or, in other words, the Civil War amendments. These amendments would be, as Lincoln declared, "a King's cure for all the evils."[27]

Yes, even the evils of slavery and beyond. "In *giving* freedom to the *slave*," pronounced Lincoln, "we *assure* freedom to the *free*."[28]

One of our most important Founding Fathers seemed to understand some of these concepts in a way that is almost too astonishing to believe. In 1820, just months after Joseph's First Vision, the elderly Thomas Jefferson declared that "if the freedom of religion, guaranteed to us by law *in theory*, can ever rise in *practice* . . . truth will prevail . . . and the genuine doctrines of Jesus, so long perverted by his pseudo-priests, will again be restored to their original purity."[29] Jefferson knew what Joseph was about to learn. Jefferson knew that, even in his twilight years, at the very end of the revolutionary generation, the glorious Constitution was yet but a *theory*.

The anti-Lincoln critics call the Revolution "The First Founding"—splendid and wonderful. They call Lincoln's actions "The Second Founding"—destructive and tragic. Jefferson could have told them that the First Founding was indeed glorious, but sadly it had not, as of yet, risen from *theory* to *practice* (something black Americans, Mormon Americans, and other nineteenth-century minority Americans could attest to). Wicked men had hijacked its original intent, thus requiring God's intervention. His intervention is clearly reflected in history and scripture. Indeed, history and scripture fulfilled Jefferson's prophecy. For Lincoln did take this *theory* and, at the direction of God Almighty, seized upon Joseph's vision, grabbed his "provision," and brought that *theory* into *practice*. What the critics lament so much, what they call "The Second Founding," was simply the Prophet's solution, which had at last come to America and brought the Constitution—for the first time—into *practice*. As a result, and as Jefferson predicted, *the genuine doctrines of Jesus . . . have again been restored to their original purity*. And they have taken root in the land, and gone forth more boldly than ever, because of that liberty won by Lincoln and the Civil War.

The conclusion is as clear as it is sad. Blinded by their preconceived political agendas, and ignoring both scriptural and historical evidence, critics continue to frame the war as North: oppressors of states' rights, versus South: noble freedom fighters. All evidence points in the opposite direction. It was, in actuality, North: bearers of the covenant blessings of liberty, versus South: preservers of a state's right to rule with blood and horror over the innocent—to legally enslave a race and to legally issue an extermination order against the Saints of God. The Civil War was clearly a battle of oppression versus freedom, as prophesied by scripture and as understood by the Prophet of the Restoration.

After Thomas Jefferson declared that the Constitution would usher in a restoration of the doctrines of Jesus in their original purity, he concluded: "This reformation will advance with the other improvements of the human mind, but *too late for me to witness*."[30] Six years after making this prediction, Jefferson died on July 4, 1826—the fiftieth anniversary of the Declaration of Independence. Four years after his death, The Church of Jesus Christ of Latter-day Saints was established in the America he had been so instrumental in building.

CHAPTER 13

Brigham, Lincoln, and the Dispatch

As Brigham Young led the exodus out of America and into the western frontier, he knew what was going to happen to his dear land. He had walked with Joseph and knew the prophecies. He even issued some of his own:

> Thy brethren have rejected you and your testimony, even *the nation* that has driven you out; and now cometh the day of their calamity, even the days of sorrow, like a woman that is taken in travail; and their sorrow shall be great unless they speedily repent, yea, very speedily. For they killed the prophets, and them that were sent unto them; and they have shed innocent blood, which crieth from the ground against them. (D&C 136:34–36, emphasis added)

It certainly is not the fault of God's prophets that the nation refused to listen. They did all in their power to warn their countrymen. The people of the nation simply closed their eyes, ears, and hearts. The day of their calamity and sorrow then followed. It *had* to.

Brigham Young was no fan of Abraham Lincoln in the beginning. Why should he be? Though as an Illinois legislator Lincoln did assist the Saints in getting their city charter for Nauvoo, and though he was kinder to the Saints than most politicians in the state were, and though he did admit once that "Joseph Smith is an admirer of mine,"[1] in the end, Lincoln failed the Saints like everyone else did. He did not stand up for them in their darkest hours.

As a result, when Lincoln took his presidential post in early 1861, Brigham made a few stinging comments about him, fully expecting that he would, like his predecessors, persecute the Latter-day Saints. And why would he not? Lincoln's Republican Party, after all, was almost as antipolygamy as it was antislavery. Indeed, before Lincoln became converted to God's purposes, there was little reason to believe he would be any different from the other political leaders the Saints had dealt with.

Looking back, Brigham Young and the Saints saw the whole picture. As the war crashed down upon America, the Saints were mostly neutral at first. Of course they were! For they knew the secret the rest of America did not know—that this war was a punishment upon North and South. How many prophecies about the bloody national scene did those early Mormons possess? I've documented many of them throughout this book, and there are still more I have not included. When news of the war hit Salt Lake, it was reported that Brigham "seem[ed] pleased." Speaking about the Civil War, he declared that God's purpose in "vex[ing] the nations" was to "break down the barriers that have prevented His Elders from searching out the honest among all peoples."[2] As we have seen, that *is* what happened.

With the war raging in the East, Brigham simply declared, "Joseph's prediction is being fulfilled, and we cannot help it."[3] Yes, the Saints were neutral; Brigham said in early 1861: "The Curse of God will be upon the Nation. . . . They have persecuted the Saints of God and the Rulers would do nothing for us but

all they Could against us and they will now get their pay for it."[4]
Therefore, Brigham admitted during the first year of war that he
"earnestly prayed for the success of both North & South," desiring that "both parties might be used up" unto the purging of sin.[5]
He understood it all immediately!

But as the nation changed (and
this is the important part!), so did the
Saints. Within weeks of Abraham's
entering his "process of crystallization," indeed, within weeks of his
ordering up a copy of the Book of
Mormon, we see the Saints break
from their neutrality. On October
18, 1861, Brigham Young sent a tele-
gram to the eastern states drawing a
line in the sand and choosing sides once and for all: "Utah has not
seceded," he proudly declared, "but is firm for the Constitution
and laws of our once happy country."[7]

> "Never be anxious for the Lord
> to pour out his judgments
> upon the nation; many of you
> will see the distress and evils
> poured out upon this nation
> till you will weep like children."
> —Joseph Smith[6]

Once the North began to climb on board the train of righteousness, Brigham saluted them and supported them. For, just
as he knew the war would purge the entire nation, he also knew
that it would eventually redeem it. And he knew it fell upon the
newly converted North to lead that charge. By 1862, nobody
could claim the Saints were neutral. During Independence Day
of that year, the Salt Lake mayor, Abraham O. Smoot, proposed
toasts to Lincoln's health and to the Union's success. In 1863, the
Saints celebrated the Emancipation Proclamation and the Union
battlefield victories, while Brigham Young stated that such Union
victories would ultimately "give freedom to millions that are
bound."[8] After Lincoln's reelection in 1864, the citizens of Salt
Lake celebrated with a mile-long parade and many toasts to and

FLEEING TO THE MOUNTAINS

As the Saints were commencing their exodus out of main America in 1847, Brigham Young revealed his knowledge about what would happen next: "The whisperings of the Spirit to us have invariably been of the same import, to depart, to go hence, to flee into the mountains, to retire to our strongholds that we may be secure in the visitation of the judgments that must pass upon this land, that is crimsoned with the blood of Martyrs; and that we may be hid, as it were, in the clefts of the rocks, and in the hollows of the land of the Great Jehova[h], while the guilty land of our fathers is purifying by the overwhelming scourge."[9]

The Saints found safety in the refuge
of the mountain wilderness.

prayers for the president's health. When Lincoln was killed a year later, something happened in Zion that had perhaps never happened before in the history of latter-day Israel: the Saints mourned their national leader. Upon hearing the news of their president's death, Brigham Young declared a day of mourning. Businesses closed, the city was draped in crepe, and the Church held a memorial service for Lincoln in the old Tabernacle. Wilford Woodruff and other Apostles eulogized the fallen president.[10]

But of all the Mormon manifestations of support and love for Lincoln, I am most touched by the willingness of the Latter-day Saints to put their own skin in the game. The Mormons responded quickly to a request from Lincoln to guard, in the name of the Union, the western transcontinental telegraph and western transportation routes. The Saints also responded immediately to a request from Congress that the Utah Territory supply $26,982 annually toward the war effort— no small sacrifice for the struggling Saints. And finally, in the only direct military effort rendered by the Saints, President Young responded to Lincoln's request in the spring of 1862 for a cavalry unit to be organized and dispatched to secure western routes. (Interestingly, at the time he received this request, President Young

Since his death, Lincoln has been quoted in general conference more than two hundred times. Elder Hyrum M. Smith declared, "I believe Abraham Lincoln was raised up to do God's will." President Heber J. Grant declared: "Perhaps no other people in all the world look upon Abraham Lincoln as an inspired servant of God, a man raised up by God to occupy the presidential chair, as much as do the Latter-day Saints." And during the nation's bicentennial year, the First Presidency went so far as to ask members of the Church to read and ponder Lincoln's words regarding God's hand in the affairs of men.[11]

Brigham Young became a supporter of the Union's cause.

was no longer governor of the territory, and was acting only in his higher calling as a prophet of God. Perhaps it is telling that Lincoln skipped the territorial governor and instead directed his request to the prophet.) Immediately, President Young organized a 120-man unit and sent them off to war. Brigham said he sent the Mormon soldiers "to prove our loyalty to the Constitution and not to their infernal meanness . . . to fight the battles of a free country to give it power and influence, and to extend our happy institutions in other parts of this widely extended republic."[12]

The turning point of the Lincoln-Mormon relationship truly did revolve around Lincoln's conversion to the truth of what this war was really all about. And no event manifested the improved relationship more than the dispatch Lincoln sent to Brigham Young. I recently came across a *New York Times* piece that was written a few years ago by Ted Widmer, an author and speechwriter for Bill Clinton. I thought his perspective on this event as a non-Mormon American historian made it quite valuable. I want to share with you an excerpt from his article, which he titled, "Lincoln and the Mormons." He was discussing how Lincoln's Republican Party was hammering on the Mormons because of polygamy. (And they were!) They even got a bill passed (the Morrill Anti-Bigamy Act) that made polygamy illegal. They were targeting the Mormons, and it was Lincoln's job, as chief executive, to fire away at them. What would he do?

According to that *New York Times* article, "Instead of ordering an invasion, Lincoln ordered information. Specifically, he asked the Library of Congress to send him . . . 'The Book of Mormon' in its original 1831 edition. . . . Fortified by his reading, Lincoln came to a great decision. And that decision was to *do nothing*."[13]

Lincoln wanted Brigham to know. So he sent a message to the Mormon prophet through an emissary, T. B. H. Stenhouse of the *Deseret News*. "Stenhouse," Lincoln began, "when I was a boy on the farm in Illinois there was a great deal of timber on the farms which we had to clear away. Occasionally we would come to a log which had fallen down. It was too hard to split, too wet to burn and too heavy to move, so we plowed around it. That's what I intend to do with the Mormons. You go back and tell Brigham Young that . . . I will let him alone."[15]

> "I always had a liking for Abe Lincoln, and if he had come out here and known us, he would have understood us and liked us."
> —*Brigham Young*[14]

And Lincoln backed this promise with action. In June 1863, Lincoln fired the territorial governor of Utah, Stephen Harding, after learning that he was hard on the Church and had participated in persecuting Joseph Smith, even during Joseph's early days as a very young prophet in Palmyra. Lincoln promptly replaced

Harding with James Doty, someone Lincoln knew to be a "very discreet gentleman" who would support Lincoln's policy of leaving the Saints alone.[16]

President Lincoln's tolerance toward the Mormon people (something they had rarely enjoyed from their government) allowed them to divert attention from politics, diplomacy, and conflict, and to finally redouble their missionary efforts. Not insignificantly, one of the great missionary surges in Church history occurred during the tenure of President Lincoln. Between 1861 and 1868, more than 16,000 souls joined the Saints in Utah and assisted greatly in the building of the kingdom.[17]

This was one happy chapter in an otherwise sad story of war.

CHAPTER 14

The Gettysburg Prayer

At noon on October 18, 1863, Lincoln and Seward boarded the four-car train with its adornments of red, white, and blue bunting. They were off to visit Gettysburg, Pennsylvania, to help dedicate the new national cemetery, which had been created to receive the thousands of dead of that great battle. Lincoln had been asked to give an address. At least one reporter caught a glimpse of the duo boarding the train at Washington and felt inclined to report that, once again, Seward had chosen to go out in public wearing "an essentially bad hat."[1]

It was a strange train ride. Lincoln was so pensive, it was as if he had entered some other realm. Some spiritual realm, perhaps. The feeling emanating from Lincoln and the North during this time was silent and somber, but somehow bright. Paradoxically, the light was connected to and couched in events surrounding the Battle of Gettysburg, which had shaken the land with immense death and destruction a little more than two months earlier. Notwithstanding the horror of it all, the battle had also proved to be a glorious Union victory and a sign that the American covenant had been activated—that God was on the side of the Union. All this was reflected in Lincoln as he sat quietly on the train. It was a somber brilliance, a sad triumph, a heavy victory. Indeed, it was a strange train ride.

As was the custom, the train made several stops for

well-wishers along the route who were hoping to get a glimpse of the president, hoping to hear him expound upon the war, the country, anything. He would poke his head out and wave, but he did not have it in him to say anything. Ducking back into the train car, he turned to Seward and said, "Seward, you go out and repeat some of your 'poetry' to the people."[2]

The same thing happened when they arrived at Gettysburg. Lincoln resided in the Wills residence while Seward stayed in a private home next door to him. Once word arrived that the president was in town, crowds flocked to the residence. Lincoln stepped out briefly, then dismissed the crowd using the classic Lincolnian technique—humor. He said he had to be careful not to say anything foolish and that the best way to do that was to say nothing at all. As the crowd laughed, he waved and ducked back into the house.

The unsatisfied crowd sought a consolation prize. They went next door and called out Seward's name.[3]

Happy to help his best friend, Seward stood and spoke from his heart. He started with a joke: "I am now sixty years old," he said. "I have been in public life, practically, forty years of that time, and yet this is the first time that any community so near the border of Maryland was found willing to listen to my voice." They liked it. Then, trying to capture the truth of the moment, the truth that was congealing in Lincoln's mind, Seward said: "I thank my God that this strife is going to end in the removal of [slavery]. . . . I thank my God for the hope that this is the last fratricidal war which will fall upon the country which is vouchsafed to us by Heaven."[4]

After the crowd dispersed, Lincoln snuck over to Seward's residence with his draft documents for the address he was to give the following day. They spent an hour discussing. Seward later

The battlefield at Gettysburg.

admitted that he could do very little to improve the address. Looking back, perhaps the most important thing that came out of their little discussion was the formalization of a new policy that affects all Americans even today. Lincoln granted Seward permission to institutionalize the celebration of Thanksgiving—that's Thanksgiving *to God,* for those of us (too many of us) who have forgotten the meaning of that holiday. Fittingly, in Gettysburg they made it the national holiday it is today.[5]

Early the next morning, Lincoln and Seward got up and toured the battlefield in a carriage. They could not believe their eyes. The terrifying evidence of bloody war lay all about them. Decaying horse corpses were strung about the landscape. Knapsacks, canteens, soldiers' coats, and shoes were scattered all over the rolling hills—their owners gone forever, unable to reclaim their once precious items.[6] Near the cemetery they viewed seemingly innumerable coffins stacked upon each other waiting for interment. Lincoln was overcome as he walked through these death fields. One witness heard him whisper, "I gave myself to God, and now I can say that I do love Jesus."[7]

Jesus. According to our scripture, America is a "choice land" to be "free from bondage" as long as the people adhere to the "God of the land, who is Jesus Christ" (Ether 2:12). He is the God of this land and the God of the covenant. Perhaps this was why Lincoln had shown such deep emotion since boarding the train for Gettysburg. The nation was in the moment of change, the moment of conversion to that covenant. This battle had led them there. Gettysburg was *the* pivotal point. As Edward Everett would say later that day during his keynote address at the Gettysburg ceremony, this battle was going to determine whether America "should live, a glory and a light to all coming time, or should expire like the meteor of a moment."[8] You see, Confederate General Robert E. Lee had come to Gettysburg to score a Southern victory in Northern territory—something he had not yet been able to do. If he had been successful, nothing would have stopped his march into the U.S. capital. The war would have been over. The only thing standing in Lee's way at that moment was the covenant on this land—the God of this land.

But had America done enough at that point to reactivate the covenant in order to utilize its power at this do-or-die battle? Had the humbling effects of war brought enough of its people to their knees? Had they felt the mighty change of heart experienced by their president? Would God intervene on the battlefield in favor of the Northern cause? These were the important questions during those days and hours leading up to the battle at Gettysburg. And the world was about to discover the answers. But Lincoln was prepared to find out first.

As the battle began to rage in Gettysburg, Lincoln dropped

to his knees. He had come to believe in the covenant, for he had seen its effects. On behalf of the nation, he would invoke it once again. He would "pray in" the victory. And he did! The North won. After the battle ended, and Lee was running back to the South, Lincoln visited Union General Dan Sickles in a military hospital. The general had been severely wounded at the battle and was fighting for his life. Lincoln felt impressed to share his prayer experience with the bedridden general. According to Sickles and General James Rusling, who was also present, Lincoln recounted the following:

> In the pinch of the campaign up there [at Gettysburg] when everybody seemed panic stricken and nobody could tell what was going to happen, oppressed by the gravity of our affairs, I went to my room one day and locked the door and got down on my knees before Almighty God and prayed to Him mightily for victory at Gettysburg. I told Him that this war was His war, and our cause His cause. . . . And I then and there made a solemn vow to Almighty God, that if He would stand by our boys at Gettysburg, I would stand by Him. And He did stand by your boys, and I will stand by Him. . . . Never before had I prayed with so much earnestness. I wish I could repeat my prayer. I felt I must put all my trust in Almighty God. He gave our people the best country ever given to man. He alone could save it from destruction. I had tried my best to do my duty and found myself unequal to the task. The burden was more than I could bear. I asked Him to help us and give us victory now. . . . And after that, I don't know how it was, and I cannot explain it, but soon a sweet comfort crept into my soul. The feeling came that God had taken the whole business into His own hands

and that things would go all right at Gettysburg. And that is why I had no fears about you.[9]

As Lincoln stood to leave General Sickles's bedside, the general related that "Mr. Lincoln took my hand in his and said with tenderness, 'Sickles, I have been told, as you have been told perhaps, that your condition is serious. I am in a prophetic mood today. You will get well.'" And he most certainly did.[10]

I can't help but share one more tidbit, one that connects this prayer experience to the Book of Mormon. Perhaps it means nothing, but I must share it with you in case it does. As I ponder Lincoln's prayer, I can't help but see that wonderful military character in the Book of Mormon named Helaman. There is something about Helaman that reminds me of Lincoln and his Gettysburg experience. Perhaps it was Lincoln's continued reference to the Gettysburg soldiers as "your boys." Helaman, you will recall, repeatedly called his young stripling warriors "my two thousand sons," "those sons of mine," "my little sons" (Alma 56:10, 17, 30). The same tenderness was there. Or perhaps it was the heavenly assurance Lincoln received prior to the Gettysburg victory—God told him the North would win. Similarly, God told Helaman that his sons would see victory in their battle: "Yea, and it came to pass that the Lord our God did visit us with assurances that he would deliver us; yea, insomuch that he did speak peace to our souls . . . that we should hope for our deliverance in him" (Alma 58:11). Lincoln's cause and covenant and American land were, of course, Helaman's *same* cause, *same* covenant, and *same* American land. "[We] were fixed with a determination to conquer our enemies, and to maintain our lands . . . and the cause of our liberty" (Alma 58:12).

But the connections continue—and this part stunned me. Interestingly, it was my eleven-year-old son, Jimmy, who pointed this startling fact out to me during a family reading session of the fifty-sixth chapter of Alma.

Of all my children, Jimmy reminds me of how I imagine young Willie Lincoln to have been—thoughtful, analytic, sometimes too smart for his age, and always ready to deliver a good prank. Willie was Jimmy's age when he died, which somehow helps me to imagine some of the pain Lincoln felt. Months before this insight from my Jimmy, I had taken him by himself on a special trip to Gettysburg. As we walked the battlefield together, I told him what had happened there and what Lincoln had been doing back at home to usher in the victory. It was one of the most memorable experiences of my life.

Anyway, the point I want to make—the insight Jimmy gave me—was the fact that Helaman provided the exact day of the first battle his sons were engaged in: "the third day of the seventh month" (Alma 56:42). Now, I do not know how the Nephite calendar worked, but I do know the book was written for us. And I do know that the third day of the seventh month *to us* is, as Jimmy pointed out, July 3. "Dad," Jimmy interrupted our reading session excitedly, "July 3 is the very day the Battle of Gettysburg raged!"

As you might imagine, when I visited the Library of Congress to review the Lincoln Book of Mormon, I made sure not to skip the part where Helaman tells this story. In that first edition copy, the entire Helaman epistle, in which he writes about his sons and their battles (everything I just quoted), is contained in *one single* chapter. (In later editions, the Church divided the book into additional, smaller chapters.) But to Lincoln, the whole Helaman army experience—the covenant, the spiritual assurances, the battles, and everything—was all contained in one single chapter. I kid you not when I tell you this: of the relatively few dog-eared

pages in that Lincoln Book of Mormon, this Helaman chapter—
the very first page of it!—was one of them. Somebody reading
this copy many years ago felt inclined to mark it well.[11]

But I digress. Let's go back to Lincoln on the battlefield. . . .

As I think about that scene of Lincoln touring the battlefield,
these are the thoughts that fill my mind—covenant, repentance,
choice land, the Christ. I wonder if these things were brimming
in Lincoln's soul as he walked over that sacred ground where so
many had made the ultimate sacrifice for this righteous cause. At
last, with this victory, Lincoln could see the silver lining amidst
the dark clouds of war. As I mentioned earlier, the news of Union
victory at Gettysburg was accompanied by news of another
Union victory in the western theater—the battle at Vicksburg.
Both victories culminated on July 4, which the nation took as a
sign that God had blessed their arms and that He was on their
side. In hindsight, we can see through the many Northern writings and publications leading up to the battle (which writings and
publications I discussed in an earlier chapter) that the North had
become sufficiently repentant. This is what activated the covenant
blessings. The victories confirmed the truth of it. One Union officer spoke for the rest after the Gettysburg-Vicksburg victories
when he said that now the "nation will be purified" and "God
will accomplish his vast designs."[12]

This was the message Lincoln was about to give that very day
in his Gettysburg Address.

Lincoln and Seward left the battlefield together, returned to
their houses to change their clothes, then joined the procession
to the cemetery. The president and Seward were ushered to the
raised platform and took their seats right next to each other. They
looked upon the crowd—about 25,000 people had gathered.[13]
Perhaps, as they looked out among the thousands of faces, they

pondered the sickening fact that this enormous crowd was equal to only *half* of the number of the Gettysburg dead.

The chaplain stood to open the ceremony. He prayed, "Oh God, our Father, for the sake of Thy Son, our Saviour, inspire us with Thy Spirit." His prayer continued on and recognized the war as a fight about "Liberty, Religion, and God." Perhaps Seward and the others on the stand noticed that many in the crowd were looking at Lincoln during the prayer, for Lincoln had, once again, become flooded with emotion, wiping tears from his face.[14]

At last it was his turn to speak. And when he did, he kept the Spirit alive in Gettysburg.

> Fourscore and seven years ago, our fathers brought forth upon this continent a new nation, conceived in liberty and dedicated to the proposition that all men are created equal. Now we are engaged in a great civil war, testing whether that nation, or any nation so conceived and so dedicated, can long endure.

We should not take for granted these familiar lines. Listen to

Lincoln delivers his Gettysburg Address.

what Lincoln is saying. Consider the gospel implications of his message. *God gave us this covenant land*—the only land of liberty on the face of the planet at that time, the only land capable of supporting something like the Restoration. If the North failed now, the rest of the world would be able to maintain their long-held belief that self-government and the pure liberty it provides is not possible. Indeed, it was a *test* to see if our nation *or any nation so conceived . . . can long endure.* If it could, democracy would be emulated and would grow, and the gospel would find safe haven throughout the world. If not, Satan would chalk up a victory against righteousness.

As was said by scholar Gabor Boritt (one of the world's foremost experts on Gettysburg), the Gettysburg Address "reached beyond the American problem of slavery to the global problem of liberal democracy."[15] Indeed, Lincoln often said the same thing— that this civil war is "an important crisis which involves, in my judgment, not only the civil and religious liberties of our own dear land, but in a large degree the civil and *religious liberties of mankind in many countries and through many ages.*"[16] On another occasion, he declared that in this war "constitutional government is at stake. This is a fundamental idea, going down about as deep as any thing."[17]

No wonder Lincoln in general, and the Gettysburg Address in particular, have been quoted by freedom fighters the world over—from Gandhi in India, to revolutionaries for democracy in Latin America, to Mandela in South Africa, and to independence-loving student movements in Hungary (1956), Iran (1979), and China (1989).[18] No wonder Lincoln called America "the last best hope of earth."[19]

Make no mistake, the future cause of the restored gospel hung in the balance of the Civil War.

Handwritten draft of the Gettysburg Address.

Which makes the concluding words of Lincoln's address all the more potent:

> It is rather for us to be here dedicated to the great task remaining before us—that from these honored dead we take increased devotion to that cause for which they gave the last full measure of devotion—that we here highly resolve that these dead shall not have died in vain, that this nation, under God, shall have a new birth of freedom, and that government of the people, by the people, for the people, shall not perish from the earth.[20]

This was the call to the covenant! We must now *take increased devotion to that cause!* We must continue forward! We must not give up on that God-given liberty that leads to the salvation of mankind!

Almost in the instant it was given, reporters telegraphed the words of the Gettysburg Address throughout the North. Those millions of now-converted American souls read and understood.

They committed to rally around Lincoln and accept his call. As Boritt wrote, the nation devoured Lincoln's words, thus "immersing [themselves] in one fastening ritual, creating community."[21] It was a *covenant community.*

One minister from Gettysburg confirmed the national sentiment: "The deadly war that is now waging, is, on the one hand, the price we are paying for past and present complicity with iniquity; on the other, it is the cost of . . . the realization of the grand idea enunciated in the Declaration of Independence." The North must accept Lincoln's call to fight and destroy that "mortal antagonist of Democratic Institutions," and usher in "a higher, purer, nobler national life and character." And so, concluded the Gettysburg minister, echoing Lincoln's call to endure this awful crisis: "God forbid" the war should stop "short of this glorious end."[22]

In the moment Lincoln finished his short and powerful address, he stood silently on the stage, likely wondering what response he would receive from the crowd. Seward, sitting behind him and also looking out over the people, must have wondered the same thing. The people also stood or sat there silently for a moment, their eyes fixed on their president, their minds and hearts still absorbing the powerful message. Then something happened that many would never forget. Eyes began to focus in on a young army captain in the crowd. In many ways, he represented all of America—the whole nation. For, though he was wounded (he was missing an arm), just as the whole nation was wounded, he stood tall and determined and full of God's light. Overcome with emotion like the rest, the soldier buried his weeping and shaking face into his good arm and cried aloud, "God Almighty bless Abraham Lincoln," to which it seemed the crowd responded solemnly, "Amen."[23]

CHAPTER 15

The Hymn

It's like an onion. That's what many of my friends say when I share this research with them. I am familiar enough with the Civil War basics, they say, but this takes it to a whole new level. It's like layers and layers of an onion being peeled back. Allow me now to peel back yet another layer.

Her name was Julia Ward Howe—a spiritual giant in and of the North. I'll let her explain what happened to her one night in the middle of the war.

> I awoke in the grey of the morning, and as I lay waiting for dawn, the long lines of the desired poem began to entwine themselves in my mind, and I said to myself, "I must get up and write these verses, lest I fall asleep and forget them!" So I sprang out of bed and in the dimness found an old stump of a pen, which I remembered using the day before. I scrawled the verses almost without looking at the paper.[1]

I don't know what you think, but to me that sounds an awfully lot like she was receiving personal revelation. And the inspired words she wrote concerned all we have discussed about the true meaning of this war. You know these words already, for you have heard them countless times. They are the words that became the lyrics to the famous "Battle Hymn of the Republic." But after truly understanding what God revealed through her, you will never be able to sing that hymn the same way again. You will not be able to sing it without the Spirit testifying to you about the truth behind Lincoln, Joseph Smith, the war, and the covenant on this land.

Julia Ward Howe.

Howe nailed it from the beginning. She revealed what the war was about in one line—one line that most people sing without a clue as to what they are singing about: "He is trampling out the vintage [the yield of wine during one season] where the grapes of wrath [the wicked] are stored." In this line she sums up what Joseph was trying to tell the nation. *The judgment of God is coming to America,* he said. *He will compel our humility unto repentance for national sin,* he said. Howe repeated the prophetic warning. Joseph declared that God would come out of hiding and vex the nation with a furious vexation. Howe agreed, and saw fulfillment in the Civil War: "He hath loosed the fateful lightning of His terrible swift sword."

Like Joseph, Howe identified the solution to the crisis, and she saw that solution formulating in the Northern cause. "I have seen Him in the watch-fires of a hundred circling camps; they have builded him an altar in the evening dews and damps." Yes, the conversion would happen among the armies of God—the armies of latter-day Israel. History proves that this happened. Once the national heart began to change and turn toward God, the Northern people saw themselves as the *circling camps* of Israel, *building altars* and praising God. They began to see themselves as the "New Israel," just as George Washington and his revolutionaries did in their day.

One day, just outside Lincoln's White House, witnesses remember seeing a congregation worshipping. The pastor, praising God, pled aloud, "O Lord command the sun & moon to stand still while your Joshua Abraham Lincoln fights the battle of freedom."[5] Was that not a sign of the national change of heart? A similar sign rippled through the rank and file of Northern troops: "Failure now is failure forever," they said. They recognized that "the day of national judgment" was upon the land, and if Lincoln did not prevail, then "we may write 'Ichabod' on the wall of its Temple of Liberty."[6] This particular warning, published in a Union paper, was especially poignant. For the Hebrew word *Ichabod* translates into the phrase: "The glory is departed from Israel."[7] Yes, Howe's

Lincoln explained that the war had brought him to a place and time "when I felt that slavery must die that the nation might live," to which, with the help of a scriptural allusion, he added that he had at last hearkened to "the groaning of the children of Israel whom the Egyptians kept in bondage."[2] His secretary of war, Edwin Stanton, echoed the allusion: "Our national destiny is as immediately in the hands of the Most High as ever was that of the Children of Israel."[3] And clergyman and reformer Henry Ward Beecher continued the metaphor: "Right before us lies the Red Sea of war. It is red indeed. There is blood in it. We have come to the very edge of it, and the word of God to us today is, 'Speak unto this people that they go forward.'"[4]

hymn reflected exactly how the North was discovering the roots of the covenant.

But of all the signs, the one I find most tender was the scriptural allusion repeated through the streets and over the hills of the battlefield. It was the sign that brought tears to many eyes. It was the title the converted soldiers began to place upon their leader: "Father Abraham."[8] By invoking this title, they knew what they were doing. They knew that the great patriarch of the Old Testament was the father of the covenant and that *their* Abraham represented an extension of that covenant. The people entered this covenant, and the soldiers renewed it by singing that old improvised song that brought joy and courage:

> *We are coming, Father Abraham, 300,000 more,*
> *From Mississippi's winding stream and from New England's*
>   *shore.*
> *We leave our plows and workshops, our wives and children*
>   *dear,*
> *With hearts too full for utterance, with but a silent tear.*
> *We dare not look behind us but steadfastly before.*
> *We are coming, Father Abraham, 300,000 more!*[9]

And what were they coming to do? I turn your attention back to Mrs. Howe: "Let the Hero, born of woman, crush the serpent with his heel." They had to win. They had to purge sin by destroying the system that perpetuated it. It was indeed a war between heaven and hell.

But Julia Ward Howe knew that only through answering Lincoln's call to the covenant would the nation be victorious. And so she wrote: "He is sifting out the hearts of men before His judgment-seat; Oh, be swift, my soul, to answer him! be jubilant, my feet! Our God is marching on!"

But the single most important line—the one whose full meaning is all but lost today—is my favorite (and probably yours as well). Howe gets right to the heart of the matter: Jesus Christ and His Atonement. She knew the Atonement was everything—and she knew the Atonement was at the center of this war. After we sing about Christ being "born across the sea" and how we access His atoning sacrifice that "transfigures you and me," we sing: "As he died to make men holy, let us live to make men free." Think on this doctrine! Unless people are free, there is no way for them to fully access the gospel and the Atonement. There was not enough freedom in the land before the war to allow for a temple to be built in the main body of the country, and temple worship is paramount for the fulness of the Atonement to be applied. And so, freedom had to be brought! Lincoln and his boys were trying to bring it!

Which brings me to a particularly tender part of the story. You see, somewhere along the way, we changed the original lyrics. Mrs. Howe wrote, "As he died to make men holy, let us *die* to make men free."[10] That is what she understood. Those are the words the soldiers sang as they marched to battle. Yes, that song became very popular to that modern army of Israel, even to those boys in blue. They were willing to *die* for that freedom that would ultimately bring in the gospel, the temple, and the fulness of Christ's Atonement. And that, my friends, sums up the Civil War. That is what we should think about as we sing that repeated refrain: "His *truth* is marching on!"

This hymn was being published for the first time during those same weeks and months in 1862 that Abraham Lincoln was passing through his worst trials and growing in faith like never before. It was published just when Willie was dying, when Lincoln had his Book of Mormon, when he was studying the gospel with Nurse Pomroy, and when he was praying for help and receiving answers. Fittingly, the hymn landed just as Lincoln was coming to learn, through God and personal revelation, the very principles taught in the hymn. It was published under the name: "Battle Hymn for the Northern Republic During the Civil War."

One of the first people to perform the hymn in public was Army Chaplain Charles Caldwell McCabe. The response to his performance was described as "magical, people shouted, wept, and sang together." And this part is key: Abraham Lincoln was present. Perhaps he was thinking, *Thank the Lord someone else gets it too! I'm not alone! The nation needs to learn this message—it's the one I have been trying to teach them!* As the chaplain finished, and notwithstanding the cheers of the people, one familiar voice was heard above the rest. The people followed the sound of the voice and knew it was coming from their president. There they saw him, "the tears roll[ing] down his cheeks." In that famous high-pitched voice—though this time it crackled with emotion—Father Abraham sweetly demanded, "Sing it again!"[11]

Like I said, you will never hear or sing that hymn the same way again.

CHAPTER 16

The Fall and Rise of Richmond

William Seward got hurt—really badly hurt. It was the strangest thing. The team of horses pulling his carriage got spooked and ran like lightning, and the next thing he knew, he was thrown to the hard ground. And I mean *hard* ground. With broken limb and jaw, he found himself fully bedridden.[1] The timing could not have been worse; it all happened just as the war was winding down. He would miss the victorious conclusion. Perhaps the hardest thing to miss in those final days was Lincoln's experience at Richmond, Virginia.

How far Richmond had fallen from grace! Richmond was, at one time, the hub of American patriotism. It was Richmond where, in 1775, George Washington and Thomas Jefferson and many other patriots had witnessed Patrick Henry's spiritually gripping "Give me liberty or give me death" speech. It was Richmond where Jefferson had served as Virginia's governor and where he and Madison had crafted the inspired legislation that would block government from meddling in the church, which would one day help bring forth the First Amendment.[2] It was a city of the covenant. But during the war, it was anything but. It was the capital city of that system that sought to preserve the national sin and to destroy Lincoln, his boys, and (most important) their shared vision under God. For this reason, Lincoln had tried tirelessly, year after year, to enter that city, to take it back and redeem it. Hundreds of thousands of lives were lost in that effort.

On April 2, 1865, Richmond fell at last to Union forces. A few days later, Seward fell from his carriage. He would not get to be with Lincoln as he fulfilled his dream of entering that city and watching the stars and stripes fly over it once again. Against the request of his military advisers, who told him it would not be safe for him to enter Richmond, Lincoln had packed his bags and was on his way. Nothing could stop him. Days later he returned to Washington. His first stop upon his return was to Seward's room. Seward would remember the happy anxiousness in his eyes and the wide smile on his face. He had a story to tell his best friend.

This is what happened. As Lincoln reached the landing at Richmond, the unexpected occurred. Almost immediately, he found himself surrounded by a growing group of now freed black men, women, and children who shouted, "Bress de Lord! . . . Dere is de great Messiah! . . . Glory Hallelujah!" The former slaves then, one by one, began falling on their knees before Lincoln in deep respect and emotion. Lincoln, himself now becoming shocked and emotional, pleaded with the group, saying, "Don't kneel to me, that is not right. You must kneel to God only, and thank him for the liberty you will hereafter enjoy." The newly freed then stood, joined hands, and began to sing a hymn of praise to God. The streets, which up until that point had been "entirely deserted," became alive with happiness and jubilee as black people all around began "tumbling and shouting, from over the hills and from the water-side."[3] One witness reported to Lincoln that he had seen an elderly, white-haired former slave exclaim, "Massah Linkum, he eberywhar. He know eberyting. He walk de earf like de Lord!"[4] Upon hearing this, Lincoln became silent for several moments, then solemnly stated, "It is a

Lincoln on the streets of Richmond.

momentous thing to be the instrument, under Providence, of the liberation of a race."[5]

With the liberated slaves all about him in the streets of Richmond, Lincoln spontaneously decided to do something extraordinary. He had become fully convinced of the reality of the American covenant. In fact, it was this covenant that had allowed him to be where he was in that very moment. Fittingly, he wasted no time in calling the now-liberated black Americans to the same covenant. For freedom comes at a cost. As the hero Martin Luther King Jr. would say decades later: "We usually think of freedom *from* something, but freedom is also *to* something. It is not only breaking loose from some evil force, but it is reaching up for a higher force. Freedom from evil is slavery to goodness."[6]

Declared Lincoln in Richmond:

> I am but God's humble instrument, but you may rest
> assured that as long as I live no one shall put a shackle on
> your limbs, and you shall have all the rights which God
> has given to every other free citizen of this Republic. . . .
>
> My poor friends, you are free—free as air. You can
> cast off the name of slave and trample upon it. . . .
> Liberty is your birthright. . . . But you must try to deserve
> this priceless boon. Let the world see that you merit it,
> and are able to maintain it by your good works. Don't let
> your joy carry you into excesses. Learn the laws and obey
> them.[7]

Though Richmond had fallen, it was now on the rise. The
beginnings of its redemption began with these words spoken by
God's humble servant as he stood in the streets of that old city.

Now, I do not want to break the spirit of this narrative, but I
must digress for a moment. You see, when I first read these words
Lincoln recited at Richmond, they resonated deep down inside.
"I am but God's humble instrument," were the words I could not
shake. It seemed from all my reading that he had said these same
words before, perhaps many times before.

I began poring over documents and books. I thought I should
perhaps start rereading material from Lincoln's magical year of
conversion—1862. It was, after all, during those spiritual months,
when he had his Book of Mormon, that things began to be clear.
Sure enough, I found the same phrase there! He was in his office
meeting with a group of Quakers. Lincoln's secretary was surprised when he poked his head in and found the president par-
ticipating in a "prayer meeting," kneeling with his visitors in the
office. After the prayer, Lincoln said those words, calling himself

"a humble instrument in the hands of our Heavenly Father. . . . I have sought his aid." Lincoln then added that God "permits [this war] for some wise purpose of His own."[8]

As I have read and reread Lincoln's writings, I have confirmed my initial intuition again and again. He seemed to love that phrase, "instrument in the hands of God," and used it on a number of occasions. My curiosity compelled me to do a word search. Perhaps that glorious phrase was in the Bible. But it was not—not one reference there. You know where I went next . . . I ran the same check against the Book of Mormon. Stunning. No fewer than a dozen times did that phrase appear.[9] I suppose it makes sense that Lincoln, in his quest to make and keep the American covenant, would use words from the book that does more than any other to testify of that covenant.

After leaving Seward's bedside, Lincoln knew he had to go to the people now and issue the message of God's intervention once again. He returned home and watched from his window as the once sad, dark town of Washington, D.C., transformed into a place of light and celebration. The war was over! The capital instantly became a city of gratitude to the God who had blessed the nation with Union victory. During those nights right after the war ended, the Capitol Building was lit, as were the homes of the citizenry. People took to the streets in celebration. An enormous, gaslit transparency printed with oversized letters was stretched across the entire length of the Capitol's western portico for all to see. Borrowing words from the Bible, it read, "This is the Lord's doing; it is marvelous in our eyes."[10]

It was only a matter of time before the jubilant citizens would make their way to Lincoln's home to celebrate with him. He knew he would have his chance to address them there. Indeed, the joyous crowd eventually gathered at the foot of his residence.

As Lincoln entered the north portico of the Executive Mansion, his face lit by a lantern held by his son Tad, he declared to the elated crowd, "We meet this evening . . . in gladness of heart. . . . In the midst of this, however, He from Whom all blessings flow, must not be forgotten . . . no part of the honor . . . is mine." Then, in a forward-looking effort to begin the reconstruction of the nation, Lincoln proposed, albeit informally, the induction of blacks not only as citizens but as voting citizens.[11] He had shone a light on the path that would soon lead to not only the Thirteenth Amendment but the Fourteenth as well. It was revolutionary. It was the last speech Lincoln gave in mortality.

An astonishing thing then happened in Richmond, Virginia. Remember, I mentioned earlier that, though Richmond had fallen, it was now being redeemed. Even though what I am about to reveal to you seems too amazing to be true—too "scripture-like" (for some) to be true—it is true. It actually happened. If there is one thing you should now understand about a covenant land, it is this: its story is always scriptural. Indeed, you will see strange things happen in a covenant land, things that may seem rare in "real life" although we read about them frequently in the Bible and in the Book of Mormon. But if you are paying attention, you will also see them happening all the time in the history of the United States of America, for it is also a covenant land. And so, without further ado, I take you back to Richmond in the days immediately following the end of the war.

The mostly evacuated former Southern capital had recently been all but burned to the ground by Confederates not wanting to leave anything for the Union. Then, just weeks after the Union had occupied the city, as reported by the *Richmond Times,* "the very floodgates of heaven seemed to open." The rains poured down violently. According to the *Times,* "Never within

Richmond in ruins.

'the recollection of the oldest inhabitant' has such a destructive rainstorm occurred in this city. . . . And so great was its effect that the whole city was soon submerged in water, overflowing all the streams and washing from their banks a number of small houses, trees, [etc.]." Some believed all this (the combination of the fires, the occupation, and the storms) was "a plague of almost biblical proportions," while others knew it to be a baptism of sorts, a renewal, a cleansing, and the dawning of a new era for America.[12]

CHAPTER 17

Upon the Altar

The war was over. Yet there is so much more I want to tell you about it. The things I want to share next represent at once the saddest and the happiest moments of this narrative. But is it not a scriptural pattern that some of the happiest moments in many stories are preceded by the saddest? Think on the Savior's final days. Well, this was no exception. As a true gospel story, the Civil War was no exception.

To set the stage for what I am about to share with you, I quote historian William J. Wolf, who wrote:

> Lincoln is one of the greatest theologians of America—not in the technical meaning of producing a system of doctrine, certainly not as the defender of some one denomination, but in the sense of seeing the hand of God intimately in the affairs of nations. Just so the prophets of Israel criticized the events of their day from the perspective of the God who is concerned for history and Who reveals His will within it. Lincoln stands among God's greatest latter-day prophets.[1]

A latter-day prophet indeed. That is why we should not be surprised by the final outcome of his story. So often the Lord's anointed—especially those who had to go to hell and back to redeem a people or a nation—have been required to make the ultimate sacrifice. So often they have sealed their testimonies with their own blood. The Prophet Joseph Smith had to do this. And so did Abraham Lincoln. In fact, the circumstances surrounding those martyrdoms were quite similar.

Like Joseph, Abraham saw it coming. Both men knew they had fulfilled their missions. Weeks before his death, Joseph knew he had by then delivered the final revelations, authorities, and ordinances to the Twelve—his part in the building of the kingdom on earth had been completed. He knew it was over. It was time to go home. While on his way to Carthage and an imminent martyrdom, Joseph declared, "I am going like a lamb to the slaughter." He turned to his close friends who were accompanying him and said somberly, "I am willing to die." He knew, and thus told them, "My work is finished."[2]

Similarly, just days before his own death, Abraham had brought the nation to victory over sin. The war was over; he had redeemed the national covenant. Having completed his unbearable task, he too knew the end of his life was coming soon. His friends should not have taken for granted the prophecy he once uttered: "Whichever way [the war] ends," he said, "I have the impression I shan't last long after it's over."[3] Days before he died, he had a dream that he shared with his wife and inner circle. He saw his own body laid to rest—a victim of an assassin's bullet.[4]

Then, on Good Friday, April 14, 1865, Lincoln sat hand in hand with his wife enjoying a play at Ford's Theatre. According to Mary, at one point during the play Lincoln leaned over and, as a reflection of the spiritual high he was experiencing, told her that he wanted to "visit the Holy Land and see those places hallowed by the foot-steps of the Savior."[5] Mary later said, "There is no city on earth he so much desired to see as Jerusalem."[6] Within moments of these whisperings to his dear wife, a shot rang out through the walls of the theater. The demon had shot the president in the back of the head.

A few days earlier, the assassin, John Wilkes Booth, had been standing with the elated crowd at the foot of Lincoln's residence listening to him praise God and then propose what would eventually become the Fourteenth Amendment. After the speech, Booth turned to his accomplice and said, "That means nigger citizenship. Now, by God, I'll put him through." As he walked from the event in demonic hatred, he squealed to another accomplice, "That is the last speech he will ever give."[7]

After Booth pulled the trigger that night, Lincoln never regained consciousness. He died early the next morning.

Compare these circumstances to the death of Joseph Smith. Two men of the same generation (born just a few years apart), both came to earth in extremely humble circumstances, both became unlikely national figures, both were sustained by God, both saw the national sin and called the people to repentance, both foresaw their imminent murders, both were cut down in their prime by assassins' bullets, and both were buried in Illinois. Upon Joseph's death, one of his brethren declared: "He lived great, and he died great in the eyes of God and his people; and like most of the Lord's anointed in ancient times, has sealed his mission and his works with his own blood" (D&C 135:3). Similarly, upon Lincoln's death, one of his brethren declared: "A martyr's blood has sealed the covenant we are making with posterity," forever securing "the rights of men, the truth of the Gospel, the principles of humanity, the integrity of the Union, the power of Christian people to govern themselves, the indefeasible equality of all creatures of God."[8]

But these were the least of Joseph's and Abraham's similarities.

THE DEATH OF THE PRESIDENT

News of the murderous act spread immediately and rapidly through the city that night. Lincoln's young son Tad was sitting with his caretaker in a nearby theatre. A messenger took to the stage and emotionally revealed the tragic news (perhaps not knowing or remembering that young Tad was in attendance). Tad was immediately ushered back to the Executive Mansion, where he collapsed into the arms of a staffer. "They've killed Papa dead!" he cried out. "They've killed Papa dead!"[9]

Lincoln's deathbed.

THE NATION GRIEVES

Acclaimed Lincoln biographer Richard Carwardine studied the hundreds of Lincoln eulogies offered by the grieving nation. Quoting directly from these eulogies, he offered his own summary of the national sentiment.

"Lincoln's religious credentials and role as liberator of an enslaved people cast him as a latter-day Moses (though one who had freed even more slaves than the Old Testament leader, 'and those not of his kindred or his race'); he had taken 'this Israel of ours' over 'the blood-red sea of rebellion' and, like Moses, had been allowed to see, but not to enter, the Promised Land. More compelling still were the Christ-like characteristics of the murdered president. Vicarious sacrifice for his people on Good Friday succeeded a Palm Sunday on which Lincoln had in humble triumph entered the Confederate capital of Richmond: 'As Christ entered Jerusalem, the city that above all others hated, rejected, and would soon slay Him . . . so did this, His servant, enter the city that above all others hated and rejected him, and would soon be the real if not the intentional cause of his death.' . . . God had taken Lincoln, 'the Saviour of his country,' from the American people, just as he had taken Moses and Jesus when their tasks were done. In the future, urged Gilbert Haven [a religious historian and Lincoln peer], his death should be commemorated not on the calendar date, but on every Good Friday, as 'a movable fast' to be kept 'beside the cross and the grave of our blessed Lord, in whose service and for whose gospel he became a victim and a martyr.'"[10]

Something much deeper connected them. And it begins with a dream Lincoln often had and often spoke of. "[I] seemed to be in some singular, indescribable vessel," he would say, " . . . moving with great rapidity towards an indefinite shore." Lincoln claimed that he had had this same dream before "every great and important event of the war."[11] He reported to the cabinet on the very morning of the day he would be killed that he had received that dream the night before. The final "great event" was upon him that day. Lincoln would at last enter that "indefinite shore" and land in the bosom of his God. But there is more. That shore and that God would offer him the reward for his sacrifice.

Knowledge of Lincoln's eternal reward comes from the testimony of one of Joseph Smith's dear friends, Wilford Woodruff. This testimony provides proof that something greater than us all bound Joseph Smith and Abraham Lincoln together forever. It begins with Wilford Woodruff's report of a visitation he received in August 1877 while in the St. George Temple.

> Two weeks before I left St. George, the spirits of the dead gathered around me, wanting to know why we did not redeem them. Said they, "You have had the use of the Endowment House for a number of years, and yet nothing has ever been done for us. We laid the foundation of the government you now enjoy, and we never apostatized from it, but we remained true to it and were faithful to God." . . . I straightway went into the baptismal font and called upon brother McAllister to baptize me for the signers of the Declaration of Independence, and fifty other eminent men.[12]

On the same day these ordinances were performed . . . Sister Lucy Bigelow Young went forth into the font and was Baptized for . . . seventy (70) of the Eminent women of the world.[13]

One of the temple clerks, James G. Bleak, added the following report:

I was also present in the St. George Temple and witnessed the appearance of the Spirits of the Signers . . . the spirits of the Presidents . . . And also others . . . Who came to Wilford Woodruff and demanded that their baptism and endowments be done. Wilford Woodruff was baptized for all of them. While I and Brothers J.D.T. McAllister and David H. Cannon (who were witnesses to the request) were endowed for them.[14]

Elder Woodruff recorded that he spoke with these individuals (he uses the word "argued"), and that they "pled" with him that their ordinances be done "as a man pleading for his life." Later, upon performing the baptisms, Elder Woodruff noted that it seemed as if "the room was filled as with flaming fire."[15]

So, who exactly was on that temple list? Who were the people of the visitation? Whose work was performed pursuant to that miracle? I have seen and studied the list. Not *all* the Founding Fathers were there. Not *all* the presidents who had died up until that point were there. It was a unique privilege, not some formalistic ritual.

Abraham Lincoln was there!

This event represented the climax of the Civil War story. Like Washington and his revolutionaries, Lincoln had lived and died to make men free. Those free men used that freedom to build the

Copy of the St. George Temple records showing Abraham Lincoln's name.

kingdom of God—to build the temples that now dot the globe. And it all came full circle in August 1877. Those who had made the temple possible at last enjoyed the ultimate fruit of their earthly labors—eternity and salvation.

This all makes me ponder a single event in my life that changed me forever. It was *the* event that served as the catalyst that began my entire investigation into Lincoln well over a decade ago. It happened on the night of my very first visit to Washington, D.C. I had arrived earlier that day, along with my wife, our firstborn, and what few possessions we owned at the time. We had come to fulfill a full-time assignment with the Central Intelligence Agency. Though it was very late when we finally unpacked and got settled into our little apartment, I insisted that we go downtown and visit the Lincoln Memorial immediately. I had never been there before, and I could not wait any longer.

It was so late when we arrived that we were pretty much the only visitors there. As I approached the memorial with my baby son in my arms, I was immediately impressed by the overwhelming spirit surrounding the ninety-nine foot marble edifice that houses the grand sculpture of Lincoln. I walked up the majestic stairway leading to the entrance hall and was overcome by the building's radiant glow against the backdrop of night. I found myself mesmerized as I gazed at the sculpture representing this great man and pondered his profound words as they appeared memorialized within the walls of the structure.

Yet it wasn't the words on the walls—the Gettysburg Address and Lincoln's Second Inaugural Address—that struck me the deepest; nor was it the edifice or sculpture alone that created the lasting effect. As meaningful as these were, it was the profound spiritual manifestation I received that night, testifying to me that the United States of America is truly one nation under God, set apart as a choice land and commissioned with a divine purpose.

But there was something else I felt—something that deeply (and quite curiously) connected Abraham Lincoln to the Restoration of the gospel. At that time, I certainly knew nothing of the facts and ideas I would later learn. I was surprised to have received such an unexpected impression. I had no idea why I felt

IN THIS TEMPLE
AS IN THE HEARTS OF THE PEOPLE
FOR WHOM HE SAVED THE UNION
THE MEMORY OF ABRAHAM LINCOLN
IS ENSHRINED FOREVER

The Lincoln Memorial in Washington, D.C.

it or what it meant. But the impression had in fact come, and I could not shake it. It was actually this impression that sent me on my decade-long investigation into Lincoln. In that moment, as I stood in the memorial, I knew I had to learn what this feeling was all about, and I was determined to stop at nothing to find out.

In the midst of these spiritual promptings, I raised my eyes above the sculpture of Lincoln, which sits majestically in the center of the grand structure. The words engraved on the wall above and behind his head are words I would never forget, and they played profoundly into the whole experience I was having. But as important as these words became to me at that moment, they would eventually become infinitely more meaningful toward the end of my investigation, especially as I learned of Lincoln's death and his subsequent connection to Wilford Woodruff and the events at St. George. The words read: "*In this temple,* as in the hearts of the people for whom he saved the Union, the memory of Abraham Lincoln is enshrined forever" (emphasis added).

I would later learn something else about how important the temple and its sealing power might have been for Lincoln. Before Lincoln's funeral train left the D.C. station, a hearse had arrived from Oak Hill Cemetery in Georgetown. It carried the body of little Willie Lincoln. He was to travel with his father to Springfield, where they would be buried together.[16] You will recall that some three years earlier, upon Willie's death, Lincoln mourned deeply; but he mourned with hope. He often recited to himself: "I shall see my boy again."[17] I believe he did! I believe he does! On February 12, 1909, on Lincoln's one-hundredth birthday, Elder Matthias F. Cowley entered the temple and helped perform the sealing ordinance for Abraham Lincoln and Mary Todd. Willie was then vicariously baptized, confirmed, and sealed to his parents; Abraham was sealed to his son—his best friend, whom he had missed so dearly during mortality.[18]

Abraham and many who loved him had suffered like no mortal should. They did so for freedom. But God remembers all who labor and sacrifice in His vineyard. The freedom they bought with their blood, sweat, and tears came back to bless them forever— worlds without end. I can't emphasize enough how fitting this all is. Remember, before Lincoln and the war, temples were confiscated, burned, or not permitted to be built. With the power of God manifested through Lincoln and his people, all that changed forever. Temples were at last protected by the Constitution. And the Lincoln family was sealed in one of them.

But let us not forget the others who also shed blood, sweat, and tears for this liberty unto salvation. Let us not forget the soldiers and their families. We can scarcely comprehend their suffering. The war caused more American deaths (more than 600,000) than were suffered in every war from the Revolutionary War through World War II combined.[19] To help you better understand this tragic number, I will give it to you in terms of our own current population. As a percentage of total population, it would be like losing more than five million Americans today. Not one home went unaffected.

Should we not expect a glorious reward for those who died or suffered for righteousness—a sacrifice for God, country, and human liberty? Lincoln seemed to hope so. Upon receiving a report in 1864 that a Mrs. Lydia Bixby had recently lost five sons in the war, Lincoln wrote her the following: "I pray that our Heavenly Father may assuage the anguish of your bereavement, and leave you only the cherished memory of the loved and lost, and the solemn pride that must be yours, to have laid so costly a sacrifice upon the altar of Freedom."[20] *A sacrifice upon the altar!* That is what they did—the soldiers, Lincoln, the nation. That is what they did for *us!*

In 1864, Lincoln was up for reelection. He did not believe he would win, nor did his advisers believe it. Earlier, we discussed George McClellan, the Union commander who treated Lincoln and his team so horribly. Lincoln had learned that McClellan did not want to fight for the purpose of human freedom. He wanted slavery left alone. Once Lincoln learned God's true intent for the war, he wondered how he could keep McClellan as the commanding officer of his army. Lincoln became concerned that McClellan's prejudice was the motive for his slow advances against the Confederates.[21] Right after the battle at Antietam,

McClellan's presidential campaign poster made his intentions clear.

even that spiritual event that became Lincoln's sign to emancipate the slaves, and even though McClellan was hailed as the hero of the battle, Lincoln fired him. He had to. In return, McClellan ran against Lincoln on the 1864 Democratic ticket. His platform was to end the war immediately, preserve slavery, and allow the continuation of the wicked political system that had crushed blacks, Mormons, and other minorities. The Democrats, under McClellan, were pushing for peace and reunification with the South at the sacrifice of emancipation, promising that, if McClellan were elected, America would happily have "the Constitution as it is, and the nigger where he was."[22]

Poor Lincoln had a tough go at that election. Lincoln had promised God that he would not end the war before he could eradicate the evil. This placed McClellan in a fortuitous position. While he could promise that if he were elected, the soldiers would go home to their families, Lincoln had to admit that if he were elected, the soldiers would likely have to die—for he would not give up the ship.

How do you win that election? You pray!

During the campaign, instead of stumping around the country for votes, Lincoln took a different approach. He very naturally and calmly turned the nation once again to God, knowing that only the Almighty could convince the people, voter by voter, to hang on and let His work and glory prevail in the matter. First on September 10, 1864, then again on October 20, 1864, Lincoln called for days of national fasting, prayer, and thanksgiving. Lincoln dedicated these sacred days in a public proclamation to "our Heavenly Father" in the hopes for "an ultimate and happy deliverance" and the triumph of "the cause of freedom and humanity."[23]

Then the miracle followed. Lincoln got the soldier vote. Eighty percent of those who suffered the most voted to keep their commander-in-chief, knowing that such a vote would keep them on the bloody battlefield until victory was achieved, which would mean they were quite possibly voting in their own death warrants.[24] It was an amazing testament to the converted state of the North. Lincoln had become the first president reelected to a second term since 1836.[25] God could easily bless such a nation.

Yes, they would die to make men free. They would give the last full measure of devotion. They prayed for Lincoln even as Lincoln prayed for them. No person who was not a part of this can understand this bond. And have you seen the photos of Lincoln? See what he looked like in 1860 upon his first election; then review the photos taken just a few years later, right before his death. The man aged twenty years, it seems. A friend of Lincoln attested to the fact that the "happy-faced lawyer" from 1861 had evolved into a lowly, sad and stooped man, with a "sunken deathly look about the large, cavernous eyes."[26] May we see his soldiers' faces in that sunken, deathly look. For they all suffered together *upon the altar.* Father Abraham and so many of his soldiers even shared a similarly violent death. Perhaps that is how it was meant to be.

I keep coming back to Lincoln's chosen words for Mrs. Bixby—three words that ultimately applied to himself and all his people; three words that describe how we sacrifice for God and country; three words that define our willingness to obey. In light of the fact that the Civil War experience culminated in the temple (whether we are talking about the St. George Temple experience or about the temple experience of any other soul, living or dead, at last free to worship therein), Lincoln's words are indeed fitting: "Upon the altar"!

> With the war over and Lincoln recently buried, the hero of Gettysburg, General Joshua Chamberlain, reflected: "We miss the deep, sad eyes of Lincoln coming to review us after each sore trial. Something is lacking in our hearts now—even in this supreme hour."[27]

◆　◆　◆

We have finally reached the point in our narrative where I need to share perhaps the most important fact about the primary witness in this Lincoln investigation. I need to tell you about how it all ended with William H. Seward.

The night Lincoln was shot, something else happened that terrorized Seward's soul for the rest of his mortal life. The assassin's plot had been a conspiracy to kill him as well. While Booth was shooting Lincoln, his accomplice Lewis Powell was entering Seward's home and attacking him and his family. Seward barely survived the bowie knife strikes to his face. In the monster's wake, bodies lay everywhere in his home. Seward's son almost

Lincoln in 1860 (left) and in 1865.

succumbed to his injuries, and his wife eventually died as a result of the attack. In the end, Seward also learned the deepest meaning of sacrifice.

In retrospect, I think I understand why Seward had to share with Lincoln, to at least some degree, in this violent experience. It has to do with the God-ordained role that was always Seward's to play. If Abraham was a type or shadow of Joseph, then Seward was his Hyrum. The elder brother sent to comfort, aid, and be there when nobody else would or could. The unheralded who did not want to be heralded. The unsung hero, who did not believe he was a hero but only wanted to serve God's burdened servant.

The Lord does create types and shadows, and the Hyrum-Seward parallel reflects this principle in other powerful ways. You may recall that at the onset of the Restoration, Hyrum sought to be one of the first missionaries called to serve. To Hyrum's disappointment, the Lord did not immediately call him, but instead called others (see D&C 11:21). Some of those others ultimately betrayed Joseph and left the Church. Yet Hyrum stayed true and fiercely loyal to Joseph, and in the end he received the corresponding blessings reserved for the faithful.[28] One of those blessings was, strangely, the privilege to fall along with Joseph at Carthage.

And so it was for Seward. He too was initially disappointed at not having received the honor to do that which was reserved for Abraham. Remember, Seward was the senior statesman of the two and the leading presidential candidate in 1860. But in the end, while almost every member of the cabinet betrayed the president at one time or another, Seward stayed humble and loyal. As with Hyrum, it was Seward's blessing and burden to be one of the precious few who stood completely unwavering. And as with Hyrum, it was Seward's blessing and burden to fall along with his "brother" on that fateful and murderous night.

At one point during the war, radical Republicans in the Senate were led to believe horrible and false rumors about Seward, which caused them to call for his resignation as secretary of state. Instead of adding yet another burden on Lincoln, Seward decided to send him his resignation.

When Lincoln realized that he might lose Seward, he fumed—the accusations are "a lie," he insisted, "an absurd lie!" Notwithstanding the political consequences to himself personally, he would refuse the resignation at all costs. He then told a friend, "I have been more distressed [by this] than by any event of my life."[29] *Any event?* This was a man of deep sorrows, who had recently lost a child and was being crushed on so many other levels. Seward meant that much to Lincoln.

Almost immediately after Seward knew Lincoln had received his resignation, there was a knock on the door of the Seward residence. Seward lived near the Executive Mansion and likely knew

LINCOLN'S EULOGY BY HIS SECRETARY, JOHN HAY

"The history of governments affords few instances of an official connection hallowed by a friendship so absolute and sincere as that which existed between these two magnanimous spirits. Lincoln had snatched away from Seward at Chicago [at the Republican National Convention] the prize of a laborious life-time, when it seemed within his grasp. Yet Seward was the first man named in his Cabinet and the first who acknowledged his personal preeminence. . . . From the beginning of the Administration to that dark and terrible hour when they were both struck down by the hand of murderous treason, there was no shadow of jealousy or doubt [that] ever disturbed their mutual confidence and regard."[30]

Fittingly, John Hay had also written the account of Joseph and Hyrum Smith's martyrdom for the *Atlantic Monthly*.[31]

Lincoln with John Hay.

who had come knocking. When the president entered Seward's room, Seward was calm about the situation. He expressed his relief at getting out of the political scene. Seward's comments were met by the president's kind but stern glare: "Ah yes, Governor," Lincoln replied, "that will do very well for you, but I am like [the caged bird]: I can't get out!"[32] Seward was taken aback. How could he leave the president now? He had become the Hyrum Smith. He realized he would be with Lincoln until the end . . . even until his Carthage.

Perhaps all this sheds light on Seward's reaction to Lincoln's death, as recorded in the first chapter of this book. When Seward awoke that Easter morning of 1865, filled with pain and with death and terror lingering all about his home, one thing overshadowed even that misery. It was his realization that morning that Lincoln was dead.

Perhaps Seward was remembering in that moment how he had just seen his best friend in that very room a few days earlier—*how could he now be gone?* As you recall, when the demon had attacked, Seward was already convalescing after that horrible carriage accident. As you also recall, Lincoln had returned from Richmond just days before the attack, and the first place he visited upon his return was Seward's bedside. After seeing how his friend was recovering from the carriage accident, Lincoln spoke to him about Richmond. Seward just lay there in bed absorbing the wonders of what Lincoln was recounting. Seward's son, also in the room, recorded that Lincoln spoke gently to his father, casually stretching his elongated body out on the bed with his hand supporting his tilted head. He stayed, according to Seward's son, conversing and encouraging, until his loyal friend and secretary of state had drifted off to sleep.[33]

On that Easter morning, as he pondered over Lincoln's death,

I imagine Seward thought about that last moment they had shared in mortality. I imagine he thought of all the other moments they had shared. He clearly missed his friend immediately. Perhaps, as he was pondering his own situation, even as his own death still appeared imminent, Seward wondered if he would be going to where Lincoln was.

As it turned out, Seward would not get an immediate answer to such an eternal question. Instead, he survived the attack. With the war at last behind him, with slavery at last eradicated, and with the Union at last secured, what would Seward do next? He was left a widower in a crippled body to await the answer to that eternal question.

With little else to do, he decided to travel the world. He justified his travels by saying, "At my age, and in my condition of health, 'rest was rust,' and nothing remained, to prevent rust, but to keep in motion."[34] He even made a stop in Salt Lake City. It happened to be a Sunday, and Brigham Young invited him to worship with the Saints in the Tabernacle. Upon meeting, Seward and President Young may have reminisced over the fact that, as a young carpenter, Brigham had built the fireplace in Seward's New York home.[35] When they passed the bread and water, Seward decided to partake. Later, he wrote home explaining that he did it "regardless of the religious and political differences."[36] That decision, while carrying little meaning at the time, would perhaps mean much more to Seward at a later date. You see, something was about to happen to Seward that might possibly make his sacrament meeting experience with the Mormons much more memorable and might shed light on how powerful and everlasting his "Hyrum role" really was in the end. But I'm getting ahead of myself.

As he continued his travels week after week and month after

month, it eventually became apparent to Seward that his days were coming to an end. His failing health forced him to return home. The answer to his eternal question was soon to be delivered. It all culminated on October 10, 1872. The end was upon him. He wanted to leave some parting words to his family, who lovingly surrounded his deathbed. After all he had been through, those last words came easily, simply. "Love one another," he pled with them. Then it was over. He was buried four days later. His tombstone simply read: "He was faithful."[37] And he was.

So, what of the eternal question? Would he follow Abraham? Could he go where Lincoln went? As I stated before, I have pored over the St. George Temple records. It was a select group of people who ended up on the list for vicarious ordinances to be performed for them. Again, not all the deceased Founding Fathers or the deceased presidents ended up on that miraculous temple list derived of the visitation. And few, if any, presidential advisers were there. Seward died in 1872, some five years before Wilford Woodruff saw what he saw and recorded what he recorded.

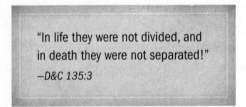

"In life they were not divided, and in death they were not separated!"
—D&C 135:3

We might imagine William Seward standing shoulder to shoulder with his best friend Abraham in the St. George Temple—for William Seward was also on the list.[38]

As we ponder that scene, we would all do well to consider the grand purposes of America—from the Revolution to the Civil War and into the present day—and to consider our own responsibilities in this grand American saga, which God has rolled out as a fundamental element in His plan of happiness.

CHAPTER 18

For We Shall Meet Again

I almost ended this book with that wonderful mental picture of Lincoln and Seward in the temple. But then I realized that the message of this book is really not about Lincoln or Seward. The take-home message is about *you!* It's about *us!* It's about our application today of the lessons Lincoln and the war have left for us. It's about the breach of the American covenant I fear we are witnessing at present. I fear that consequences like those detailed in the history we have just explored may befall us if we continue down the path we are on.

Years ago, I came across a letter written by a Union soldier who understood God, country, and covenant. He was one of us—an ordinary American living out his ordinary life, just like anyone else. It seems to me that if he figured out his responsibility toward the American covenant and gave his last full measure of devotion for it, then so can any one of us. Yes, there is hope. Notwithstanding our severe problems, I believe so many Americans are, deep down inside, like this young man. His name was Sullivan Ballou.

I want to share his letter with you, for it sums up all that I believe Lincoln would have you know. But in order to do so properly, I need to exercise a little literary license to put the letter into the context in which Sullivan wrote it.

A MODERN PROPHET SPEAKS OUT

"For a good while, there has been going on in this nation a process that I have termed the secularization of America. . . . We as a nation are forsaking the Almighty, and I fear that He will begin to forsake us. We are shutting the door against the God whose sons and daughters we are. . . .

"Future blessings will come only as we deserve them. Can we expect peace and prosperity, harmony and goodwill, when we turn our backs on the Source of our strength? If we are to continue to have the freedoms that evolved within the structure that was the inspiration of the Almighty to our Founding Fathers, we must return to the God who is their true Author. . . .

"God bless America, for it is His creation."

—*President Gordon B. Hinckley*[1]

I ask you to remember: though I am telling it to you in an imagined form, this is a true story.

Major Sullivan Ballou mounted his horse. Things were getting bad. Though the Union soldiers had begun the battle with vigor and success, the rebels were gaining on them. With men confused and dropping all around him (he lost ninety-three of his men that day), he knew he had to lead from a mounted position. He also knew this would make him a target and likely lead to his death. At that moment, the words from his letter, written days earlier to his wife, flashed through his mind:

My very dear Sarah:

The indications are very strong that we shall move in a few days—perhaps tomorrow. Lest I should not be able to write again, I feel impelled to write a few lines that may fall under your eye when I shall be no more. . . . "Not my will, but thine, O God be done." If it is necessary that I should fall on the battlefield for my Country, I am ready.

I have no misgivings about, or lack of confidence in, the cause in which I am engaged, and my courage does not halt or falter. I know how strongly American Civilization now leans on the triumph of the Government, and how great a debt we owe to those who went before us through the blood and sufferings of the Revolution. And I am willing—perfectly willing—to lay down all my joys in this life, to help maintain this Government, and to pay the debt. . . .

Rebel guns jolted his mind back to the scene of war. He resolved to have the courage he knew was in him. "Forward, men!" was his cry. He knew what was at stake in this war: it was God's gift to America. As an orphan child living in Rhode Island, Sullivan had never imagined his future would be so bright. But he was, nonetheless, an American living in God's land! Overcoming all odds, young Sullivan had grown into a successful man. He was a sought-after lawyer, the Speaker of the Rhode Island House of Representatives, and now the judge advocate for the Rhode Island militia and a major in the Union army—and all this by the age of thirty-two. But his greatest success and happiness was his family. He had been blessed with a wonderful wife, his dear Sarah, and two young sons, Edgar and Willie. He had lived the American dream. With this dream now in decline for millions, he would march forward and, as he had promised to do, "pay the debt."

Sullivan peered up on the ridge before him and caught a glimpse of the revered Confederate General Thomas Jackson, who defiantly sat upright on his undaunted horse, rallying his men to sure victory. "Look at Jackson standing there like a stone wall," he thought he heard someone yell.

He then heard something else above all the noise of the battlefield—the loudest, most earth-shattering noise he had ever heard. Somehow he knew that cannon blast was intended for him. The six-pound ball was too much for his mount to handle; the horse dropped with a squeal and a thud. Sullivan was in such shock that he did not even notice at first that his right leg had been completely torn off by the ball. As he lay on his back, his head propped up by the corpse of his horse, the blue sky above him looked so peaceful. The battlefield din began to vanish as the sound of what appeared to be a heavenly choir slowly filled his soul. He closed his eyes and saw his letter to his Sarah—it was seared into his memory. He continued to review it in his mind's eye:

I cannot describe to you my feelings on this calm Summer Sabbath night, when two-thousand men are sleeping around me, many of them enjoying perhaps the last sleep before that of death, while I am suspicious that death is creeping around me with his fatal dart, as I sit communing with God, my Country and thee. I have sought most closely and diligently and often in my heart for a wrong motive in thus hazarding the happiness of those I love, and I could find none. A pure love of my Country and of the principles I had so often advocated before the people—another name of Honor that I love more than I fear death, has called upon me and I have obeyed.

Sarah my love for you is deathless, it seems to bind me with mighty cables that nothing but Omnipotence could break; and yet my love of Country comes over me like a strong wind and burns me unresistably on with all these chains to the battle field. . . . I have, I know, but few and small claims upon Divine Providence, but something whispers to me—perhaps it is the wafted prayer of my little Edgar, that I shall return to my loved ones unharmed. If I do not my dear Sarah, never forget how much I love you, and when my last breath escapes me on the battle field, it will whisper your name. . . .

Images of his dear Sarah filled his head as warm feelings filled his heart. He loved her so much. As he lay on the soft grass, hardly able to breathe, he did whisper her name . . . then drifted off to sleep.

What seemed like moments later, Sullivan slowly, barely, awoke from his unconscious state. The battle had ended—was it hours ago? Days ago? He did not know. He was very weak,

Sullivan Ballou.

but he was aware that whatever had been left of his destroyed leg had been amputated. Would the painful emergency surgery save his life? Fearful that he would slip back into unconsciousness, he wanted to use whatever lucid moments he had left to think upon his family.

> But, O Sarah! if the dead can come back to this earth and flit unseen around those they loved, I shall always be near you; in the gladest days and in the darkest nights, advised to your happiest scenes and gloomiest hours, always, always, and if there be a soft breeze upon your cheek, it shall be my breath, as the cool air fans your throbbing temple, it shall be my spirit passing by. Sarah do not mourn me dead; think I am gone and wait for thee, for we shall meet again. . . .

The pain was gone. The heavenly choir he had heard on the battlefield was in full swing. It was the most beautiful thing he had ever heard. He knew he was being carried to the bosom of his God.

> I must watch you from the Spirit-land and hover near you, while you buffit the storm, with your precious little freight, and wait with sad patience, till we meet to part no more. . . .
>
> As for my little boys—they will grow up . . . and never know a father's love and care. Little Willie is too young to remember me long—and my blue eyed Edgar will keep my frolicks with him among the dim memories of childhood. Sarah I have unlimited confidence in your maternal care and your development of their characters, and feel that God will bless you in your holy work.
>
> . . . O! Sarah I wait for you there; come to me and lead thither my children.

Sullivan Ballou died a hero just days after penning his letter. Sarah never remarried. She lived with her son Willie, who took care of her until she passed away at age eighty-two in 1917. Sullivan and Sarah are now buried next to each other at Swan Point Cemetery in Providence, Rhode Island.[2]

Sullivan Ballou had a vision. He understood why he was placed on this earth, and he fulfilled his duty. The liberty he died for is that most precious gift of God. It is a gift given to America and destined to fill the whole earth. It is a gift that allows mankind to seek, find, and live the religion of true salvation. For Sullivan, that religion would offer an eternal world in which he and his family might live "and part no more." He had faith that Sarah would join him: "Come to me and lead thither my

Gravestones of Sullivan and Sarah Ballou.

children," was his final plea and hope. "Think I am gone and wait for thee, *for we shall meet again.*"

And this leads us to the point of it all (which I shall repeat yet one more time): *God's temples.* Those sacred edifices, which offer that eternal hope and promise Sullivan sought for his family, indeed represent the point of all we have been discussing in this book. Before Sullivan and Sarah made the ultimate sacrifice, temples of God were scarcely permitted to survive in the promised land. After the war—or, better said, *because* of the war—all that changed forever. Because of the liberty purchased by the sacrifices of Americans like Sullivan and Sarah, temples returned to stay. One of those temples is found in Mesa, Arizona. And according to Church records, it was in that temple that Sullivan, Sarah, young Edgar, and little Willie were sealed vicariously for time and all eternity.[3] Their husband and father gave them up in mortality so that he could have them in eternity. And that sums up this book.

Such salvation with and under God Almighty is something all can attain. And America is part of the plan—a base of operations from which God carries out His work to save all those who will come unto Him. He has blessed America with the gifts of liberty, protection, and prosperity to facilitate this eternal prospect.

But these gifts are not free. Freedom is not free! The Almighty offers these gifts contingent upon our willingness to turn to Him as a nation. It is a covenant relationship. That covenant is in force today, and the rules still apply.

As I pointed out earlier, George Washington understood these rules—what he called "the eternal rules of order and right, which Heaven itself has ordained." And he knew that breaking these rules would lose us the blessings—or, as he stated, it would lose us "the smiles of Heaven." He also knew what sins would lead to our national destruction. Washington identified the twin evils as "the sweeping torrent of boundless ambition on the one side, aided by the sapping current of corrupted morals on the other." Such evil would prevail, stated Washington, so long as there exists in the land a "Supineness or venality of [the] Constituents." In other words, so long as we the people remain lethargic, apathetic, and uncaring about our responsibilities, we will lose the covenant blessings. All the while, according to Washington, "those who are entrusted with the management of this government . . . [will] overleap the known barriers of the Constitution and violate the unalienable rights of humanity."[4]

Does this sound like America today? Boundless governmental ambition? Corrupted morals? Apathetic citizens? An ignored Constitution? The loss of unalienable rights? How long will we let America continue to sink? Will we learn the lessons God left for us in the history of the Civil War?

As President Gordon B. Hinckley stated, the "blessings will come only as we deserve them. . . . If we are to continue to have the freedoms that evolved within the structure that was the inspiration of the Almighty to our Founding Fathers, we must return to the God who is their true Author."[5]

We must stand and fight like Washington and Lincoln and

all those who followed them to hell and back. We must move forward with the faith and courage of Sullivan Ballou, with a willingness to put it all on the line. If we don't, consider what we risk. Ask Joseph what we risk! He lived through the consequences of an apathetic and sinful populace. Ask the Nephites, especially those at the end of the Book of Mormon story, what we risk! They too saw the devastations of a people unwilling to stand and fight with and for the God of the land. When the covenant blessings of liberty are lost, temples begin falling with them; the gospel begins to come under fire. This is why Satan has hated liberty from the beginning and has sought to thwart it wherever he can on earth. It is why we need to take a stand against evil and fight now for liberty!

It's not enough to do our home and visiting teaching and go to the temple and fulfill our priesthood covenants (though these temple covenants *are* the most important promises to fulfill). We must also remember the *national* covenant so long as we live in the promised land. Are we willing to receive and carry forward the torch of the American covenant that the likes of Washington, Lincoln, and Sullivan have passed on to us? Is salvation worth it?

I pray we will take our cues from Washington and Lincoln, who learned the secret and masterfully employed it. I pray we will turn America back to its God! Turn America back to its covenant!

If we don't do it, who will?

A Final Note from the Author

We have sifted through a lot of information—facts, theories, hopes, projections. Much of this information has been substantiated and corroborated, while some is simply speculation based on indirect evidence. And other ideas in this book fall somewhere in between these two spectrums. For example, if I were a court witness on the stand, and I were asked, "Mr. Ballard, did Abraham Lincoln read and/or utilize the Book of Mormon in any significant way?" I would have to answer, "I don't know for certain, but the investigation into that question tells an amazing story and leaves us with important truths to ponder regarding America and our responsibility to God and country."

For all that I don't know, there is so much that I do. And I would be remiss not to share my final witness with you as we close out this study.

I know that Joseph Smith Jr. was a prophet of God. I know that as a seer and revelator he revealed many great, important, and true prophecies pertaining to the promised land of America, including prophecies regarding the American Civil War (see D&C 87, for example). I know that Abraham Lincoln was a man inspired by God to bring the nation closer to heaven and to healing. I know he invoked a covenant relationship between America and its Maker not unlike the national covenants invoked by righteous leaders in the Book of Mormon. And I know he was ultimately successful in his endeavor for America. I also know that Joseph Smith and Abraham Lincoln had very similar ideas about how the nation might be healed under the God of this land. I know that their shared solutions, particularly their well-documented and joint belief that national repentance would heal the land, are the same solutions we the people of America desperately need to apply today.

Finally, though Joseph and Abraham might have a fascinating connection through the Book of Mormon, perhaps the only real connection is that both men were being guided by the same Heavenly Father and were being given the same heavenly solutions to America's challenges.

And if that were the *only* real connection here, then it was still a book worth writing and hopefully a book worth reading.

Notes

Introduction

1. See UNICEF, "The State of the World's Children 2005: Childhood under Threat," 26. Accessed online at http://www.unicef.org/publications/files/SOWC_2005_(English).pdf.

Chapter 1: Easter Sunday, 1865

1. See Doris Kearns Goodwin, *Team of Rivals: The Political Genius of Abraham Lincoln* (New York: Simon & Schuster, 2005), 735–37.
2. Noah Brooks, in Goodwin, *Team of Rivals,* 744–45.
3. Letter from Seward to Frances Seward, March 26, 1837, in Frederick Seward, *William H. Seward,* 3 vols. (New York: Derby and Miller, 1891), 1:325, 329; Letter from Seward to T. Weed, January 16 and March 26, 1837, in Walter Stahr, *Seward: Lincoln's Indispensable Man* (New York: Simon & Schuster, 2012), 49–50.

Chapter 2: The Witness

1. See John M. Taylor, *William Henry Seward: Lincoln's Right Hand* (New York: HarperCollins, 1991), 127.
2. Frederick Seward, *William H. Seward,* 3 vols. (New York: Derby and Miller, 1891), 1:162; see also Taylor, *William Henry Seward,* 28.
3. Charles Frances Adams, *Charles Frances Adams, 1835–1915: An Autobiography* (New York: Houghton Mifflin, 1916), 59–61.

4. In Walter Stahr, *Seward: Lincoln's Indispensable Man* (New York: Simon & Schuster, 2012), 213.
5. Fanny Seward Diary, September 1, 1860, in Stahr, *Seward,* 174, 201.
6. Doris Kearns Goodwin, *Team of Rivals: The Political Genius of Abraham Lincoln* (New York: Simon & Schuster, 2005), 488.
7. See ibid., 387–88.
8. In Richard Carwardine, *Lincoln: A Life of Purpose and Power* (New York: Alfred A. Knopf, 2006), 197.
9. In Goodwin, *Team of Rivals,* 534.
10. In Carwardine, *Lincoln,* 97.
11. William Lee Miller, *President Lincoln: The Duty of a Statesman* (New York: Alfred A. Knopf, 2008), 171–73; Goodwin, *Team of Rivals,* 383; History Channel, "General McClellan Snubs President Lincoln," available at http://www.history.com/this-day-in-history/mcclellan-snubs-lincoln.
12. See Miller, *Duty of a Statesman,* 171–173; Goodwin, *Team of Rivals,* 380; History Channel, "General McClellan Snubs President Lincoln."
13. In Gordon Leidner, *Lincoln on God and Country* (Shippensburg, PA: White Mane Books, 2000), 18.

Chapter 3: The Covenant Day

1. George Washington's First Inaugural Address, April 30, 1789, in William J.

Bennett, *The Spirit of America* (New York: Touchstone, 1997), 382.

2. See "Inaugural History," *PBS NewsHour,* accessed online at www.pbs.org /newshour/updates/white_house-jan -june01-inauguration_01-20/; see also Bruce Feiler, *America's Prophet* (New York: HarperCollins, 2009), 28, 78.

3. George Washington, January 22, 1777, in Steven Waldman, *Founding Faith: Providence, Politics, and the Birth of Religious Freedom in America* (New York: Random House, 2008), 70. The full story of the fog, along with detailed source citations, is documented in Timothy Ballard, *The American Covenant: One Nation under God,* 2 vols. (New York: Digital Legend Press, 2011), 1:249–56.

4. Thomas Fleming, "Unlikely Victory," in *What If? The World's Foremost Military Historians Imagine What Might Have Been,* Robert Cowley, ed. (New York: G. P. Putnam's Sons, 1999), 179.

5. William J. Bennett, *America: The Last Best Hope* (Nashville, TN: Nelson Current, 2006), 29.

6. See Joseph J. Ellis, *Patriots: Brotherhood of the American Revolution* (audiobook), lecture 7, track 6, minute 2:15; see also Fleming, "Unlikely Victory," 180–81.

7. Fleming, "Unlikely Victory," 180.

8. Ibid., 181.

9. Ibid., 182.

10. George Washington, in Marshall Foster and Mary Elaine Swanson, *The American Covenant: The Untold Story* (Thousand Oaks, CA: Mayflower Inst., 1982), 163.

11. In Michael Novak and Jana Novak, *Washington's God* (New York: Basic Books, 2006), 66.

12. Walter Stahr, *Seward: Lincoln's Indispensable Man* (New York: Simon & Schuster, 2012), 519.

13. See Walter Nugent, *Habits of Empire: A History of American Expansion* (New York: Alfred A. Knopf, 2008), 251–54; Stahr, *Seward,* 159.

14. Stahr, *Seward,* 413, 429.

15. In Michael Parker, *John Winthrop: Founding the City upon a Hill* (New York: Routledge, 2014), 191–92.

16. For more information on how this prophecy connects to the New World, see *Old Testament Student Manual,* 2nd ed. rev. (Salt Lake City: The Church of Jesus Christ of Latter-day Saints, 1981), 98–99; *Old Testament Seminary Student Study Guide* (Salt Lake City: The Church of Jesus Christ of Latter-day Saints, 2002), 40–41.

17. The Lord refers to these blessings and obligations throughout the Book Mormon. Examples of such include 1 Nephi 13:15, 16, 19; 22:7; 2 Nephi 10:10–12; and many others.

18. That Washington had his Bible opened to Genesis 49 during his swearing-in ceremony is documented in H. Paul Jeffers, *The Freemasons in America* (New York: Kensington Publishing Corp., 2006), 28.

Chapter 4: Joseph, Abraham, and the Breach

1. In Roy P. Basler et al., eds., *The Collected Works of Abraham Lincoln,* 9 vols. (New Brunswick, NJ: Rutgers University Press, 1953), 1:111; emphasis added. For Lincoln's full address, known as the Lyceum Address, see pp. 108–15.

2. Joseph Smith Jr., *History of the Church of Jesus Christ of Latter-day Saints,* 7 vols. (Salt Lake City: Deseret Book, 1973), 5:394.

3. Joseph Smith, Letter to the Elders of the Church, November 1835, in Richard Vetterli, *Mormonism, Americanism and Politics* (Salt Lake City: Ensign Publishing, 1961), 172–73.

4. Basler et al., *Collected Works,* 1:112.

5. Basler et al., *Collected Works,* 1:108–15.

6. Smith, *History of the Church,* 5:394.

7. In Vetterli, *Mormonism, Americanism and Politics,* 202.

8. Peter A. Lillback, *George Washington and Israel* (King of Prussia, PA: Providence Forum Press, 2012), 40–41.

9. William J. Bennett, *The Spirit of America* (New York: Touchstone, 1997), 366.

10. See Bruce Feiler, *America's Prophet: Moses and the American Story* (New York: HarperCollins, 2009), 92–93.

11. In Lillback, *George Washington and Israel,* 34–35.

12. Ibid.

13. Harriet Jacobs, *Incidents in the Life of a Slave Girl* (New York: Dover Publications, 2001), 26. Originally published in 1861.

14. Ibid., 59–60, 64.

15. Ibid., 48.

16. Ibid., 65.

17. Leland H. Gentry and Todd M. Compton, *Fire and Sword: A History of the Latter-day Saints in Northern Missouri, 1836–39* (Salt Lake City: Greg Kofford Books, 2010), 325.

18. Ibid., 329. The author has taken slight literary license to place the account in the context of a story.

19. Ibid., 334–37.

20. Ibid., 335–37.

21. Ibid., 319.

22. Ibid., 329.

23. Ibid., 327–28.

24. As described by Civil War journalist Noah Brooks, in Michael Burlingame, ed., *Lincoln Observed: Civil War Dispatches of Noah Brooks* (Baltimore, MD: Johns Hopkins University Press, 1998), 41–42.

25. From Henry McHenry, *Abraham Lincoln Papers at the Library of Congress.* Transcribed by the Lincoln Studies Center, Knox College, Galesburg, Illinois. Notes from May 1860. Accessed online at http://memory.loc.gov/ammem/alhtml/malhome.html.

26. Letter from Mary Vineyard to William Herndon, in Douglas L. Wilson and Rodney O. Davis, eds., *Herndon's Informants: Letters, Interviews, and Statements about Abraham Lincoln* (University of Illinois Press, 1998), 262.

27. William Lee Miller, *Lincoln's Virtues* (New York: Alfred A. Knopf, 2002), 364.

28. Linda King Newell and Valeen Tippetts Avery, "Jane Manning James: Black Saint, 1847 Pioneer," *Ensign,* August 1979, 26–29. Read the full story at www.lds.org/ensign/1979/08/jane-manning-james-black-saint-1847-pioneer?lang=eng.

29. In Richard Carwardine, *Lincoln: A Life of Purpose and Power* (New York: Alfred A. Knopf, 2006), 146.

30. Smith, *History of the Church,* 5:498.

Chapter 5: The Prophet for President

1. See John M. Taylor, *William Henry Seward: Lincoln's Right Hand* (New York: HarperCollins, 1991), 17, 24.

2. See Richard Lyman Bushman, *Joseph Smith: Rough Stone Rolling* (New York: Alfred A. Knopf, 2005), 236.

3. See ibid., 393, 396.

4. See ibid., 397, 512.

5. See Steven Waldman, *Founding Faith: Providence, Politics, and the Birth of Religious Freedom in America* (New York: Random House, 2008), 52–53, 136, 173–74.

6. In Bushman, *Rough Stone Rolling,* 514.

7. In Richard Vetterli, *Mormonism, Americanism and Politics* (Salt Lake City: Ensign Publishing Company, 1961), 107.

8. Joseph Smith Jr., *History of the Church of Jesus Christ of Latter-day Saints,* 7 vols. (Salt Lake City: Deseret Book, 1973), 5:384.

9. Joseph Smith Jr., *Teachings of the Prophet Joseph Smith,* selected and arranged by Joseph Fielding Smith (Salt Lake City: Deseret Book, 1976), 326–27.

10. Ibid.
11. In Michael I. Meyerson, *Endowed By Our Creator: The Birth of Religious Freedom in America* (New Haven, CT: Yale University Press, 2012), 165; emphasis added.
12. Ibid.
13. Ibid.
14. Ibid., 164–65.
15. In Bushman, *Rough Stone Rolling,* 514.
16. In Toby Mac and Michael Tait, *Under God* (Minneapolis: Bethany House, 2004), 287.
17. In Arnold K. Garr, "Joseph Smith: Campaign for President of the United States," *Ensign,* February 2009, 50.
18. In Bushman, *Rough Stone Rolling,* 516.
19. See Garr, "Joseph Smith: Campaign," 50.
20. Ezra Taft Benson, "Beware of Pride," *Ensign,* May 1989, 4.
21. In Vetterli, *Mormonism, Americanism and Politics,* 173.
22. In Richard Bushman, "Mormonism and Politics: Are They Compatible?," speech given at the Pew Forum's biannual Faith Angle Conference on Religion and Public Life, May 14, 2007, accessed online at www.pewforum.org/2007/05/14/mormonism-and-politics-are-they-compatible/.
23. In Vetterli, *Mormonism, Americanism and Politics,* 197.

Chapter 6: The Civil War Prophecies

1. In Richard Vetterli, *Mormonism, Americanism and Politics* (Salt Lake City: Ensign Publishing Company, 1961), 173.
2. In Gerald N. Lund, *The Coming of the Lord* (Salt Lake City: Deseret Book, 2005), 54.
3. Vetterli, *Mormonism, Americanism and Politics,* 230.
4. In ibid., 172–73.
5. *Merriam-Webster's Collegiate Dictionary,* 11th ed. (Springfield, MA; Merriam-Webster, Inc., 2005), s.v. "vex."
6. Dallin H. Oaks, "Love and Law," *Ensign,* November 2009, 27.
7. In Vetterli, *Mormonism, Americanism and Politics,* 173.
8. In Kenneth L. Alford, ed., *Civil War Saints* (Provo, UT: Religious Studies Center, Brigham Young University, 2012), 96, 116.
9. See William J. Bennett, *America: The Last Best Hope* (Nashville, TN: Nelson Current, 2006), 323, 330–32, 350.
10. "Madison Debates, Tuesday, August 22, 1787," in *The Avalon Project: Documents in Law, History and Diplomacy.* Accessed online at http://avalon.law.yale.edu/18th_century/debates_822.asp.
11. Thomas Jefferson, *Notes on the State of Virginia,* 289–90. Accessed online at http://web.archive.org/web/20110221131430/http://etext.lib.virginia.edu/etcbin/toccer-new2?id=JefVirg.sgm&images=images/modeng&data=/texts/english/modeng/parsed&tag=public&part=18&division=div1.
12. Joseph Smith Jr., *History of the Church of Jesus Christ of Latter-day Saints,* 7 vols. (Salt Lake City: Deseret Book, 1973), 5:394.
13. In Richard Bushman, "Mormonism and Politics: Are They Compatible?," speech given at the Pew Forum's biannual Faith Angle Conference on Religion and Public Life, May 14, 2007, accessed online at www.pewforum.org/2007/05/14/mormonism-and-politics-are-they-compatible/.
14. *Discourses of Brigham Young,* John A. Widtsoe, ed. (Salt Lake City: Deseret Book, 1954), 365.
15. In Tad R. Callister, *The Inevitable Apostasy and the Promised Restoration* (Salt Lake City: Deseret Book, 2006), 361.
16. Ibid.
17. Vetterli, *Mormonism, Americanism and Politics,* 149.

Chapter 7: Lincoln's First Holy Field: Willie and the Divine

1. Memory from Horatio Taft, in David Von Drehle, *Rise to Greatness: Abraham Lincoln and America's Most Perilous Year* (New York: Henry Holt and Company, 2012), 76.
2. In Von Drehle, *Rise to Greatness*, 77.
3. Ibid.
4. Ibid., 196.
5. Ibid.
6. In Doris Kearns Goodwin, *Team of Rivals: The Political Genius of Abraham Lincoln* (New York: Simon & Schuster, 2005), 328.
7. Larry Schweikart and Michael Allen, *A Patriot's History of the United States* (New York: Sentinel/Penguin Books, 2004), 313.
8. See Harold Holzer, *Father Abraham: Lincoln and His Sons* (Honesdale, PA: Calkins Creek, 2011), 129.
9. In Von Drehle, *Rise to Greatness*, 76–78.
10. Goodwin, *Team of Rivals*, 419.
11. Ibid., 419–20.
12. In Holzer, *Father Abraham*, 130.
13. See Ron L. Andersen, *Abraham Lincoln: God's Humble Instrument* (Salt Lake City: Millennial Mind Publishing, 2010), 196.
14. In Holzer, *Father Abraham*, 131.
15. In Andersen, *Lincoln: God's Humble Instrument*, 197.
16. Francis Carpenter, in Richard Carwardine, *Lincoln: A Life of Purpose and Power* (New York: Alfred A. Knopf, 2006), 314.
17. In Carwardine, *Lincoln*, 223.
18. Ibid.
19. Ibid., 314.
20. In Toby Mac and Michael Tait, *Under God* (Minneapolis: Bethany House, 2004), 165.
21. In Carwardine, *Lincoln*, 223.
22. Ibid.
23. In Von Drehle, *Rise to Greatness*, 79–80.
24. Ibid., 111–12.
25. In Carwardine, *Lincoln*, 227.
26. Ibid., 210.

Chapter 8: Lincoln's Second Holy Field: The Grassy Meadow of Frederick

1. In Richard Carwardine, *Lincoln: A Life of Purpose and Power* (New York: Alfred A. Knopf, 2006), 217.
2. In Doris Kearns Goodwin, *Team of Rivals: The Political Genius of Abraham Lincoln* (New York: Simon & Schuster, 2005), 364.
3. In Ron L. Andersen, *Abraham Lincoln: God's Humble Instrument* (Salt Lake City: Millennial Mind Publishing, 2010), 132–33.
4. See Carwardine, *Lincoln*, 7, 311–12.
5. In Andersen, *Lincoln: God's Humble Instrument*, 127.
6. In Newt Gingrich, *Rediscovering God in America* (Nashville, TN: Integrity Publishers, 2006), 55.
7. Ibid.
8. In Andersen, *Lincoln: God's Humble Instrument*, 6.
9. Carwardine, *Lincoln*, 227–28.
10. Ibid., 210.
11. Ibid., 235.
12. Ibid., 223.
13. Walter Stahr, *Seward: Lincoln's Indispensable Man* (New York: Simon & Schuster, 2012), 339–40.
14. In Goodwin, *Team of Rivals*, 468.
15. In Matthew S. Holland, *Bonds of Affection: Civic Charity and the Making of America—Winthrop, Jefferson, and Lincoln* (Washington, D.C.: Georgetown University Press, 2007), 209.
16. Ibid.
17. In Carwardine, *Lincoln*, 210.
18. James M. McPherson, "If The Lost Order Hadn't Been Lost," in *What If? The World's Foremost Military Historians Imagine What Might Have Been*, Robert Cowley, ed. (New York: G. P. Putnam's Sons, 1999), 231–32.
19. See ibid.
20. Ibid., 232.
21. In Carwardine, *Lincoln*, 210.
22. In Geoffrey Perret, *Lincoln's War: The*

Untold Story of America's Greatest President as Commander in Chief (New York: Random House, 2004), 294.

23. In Carwardine, *Lincoln,* 228, 210.

24. In Bruce Feiler, *America's Prophet: Moses and the American Story* (New York: HarperCollins, 2009), 162.

25. Larry Schweikart and Michael Allen, *A Patriot's History of the United States* (New York: Sentinel/Penguin Books, 2004), 328.

Chapter 9: Lincoln's Third Holy Field: The Book of Mormon

1. See Michael K. Winder, *Presidents and Prophets* (American Fork, UT: Covenant Communications, 2007), 107. Lincoln presented his first draft of the Proclamation to his cabinet on July 22. On September 22, after the Battle of Antietam, he issued the preliminary document—the Emancipation Proclamation—that would go into effect on January 1, 1863.

2. In Gordon Leidner, *Lincoln on God and Country* (Shippensburg, PA: White Mane Books, 2000), 113–14.

3. See Ron L. Andersen, *Abraham Lincoln: God's Humble Instrument* (Salt Lake City: Millennial Mind Publishing, 2010), 300.

4. In *Old Testament: 1 Kings–Malachi, Student Manual,* 2nd ed. rev. (Salt Lake City: The Church of Jesus Christ of Latter-day Saints, 1982), 142.

5. Ibid., 141.

6. In Kenneth Alford, ed., *Civil War Saints* (Salt Lake City: Deseret Book, 2012), 50.

7. *Old Testament: 1 Kings–Malachi,* 142.

8. See Donald W. Parry, Jay A. Parry, and Tina M. Peterson, *Understanding Isaiah* (Salt Lake City: Deseret Book, 2009), 57.

9. See Andersen, *Lincoln: God's Humble Instrument,* 300.

10. *Old Testament: 1 Kings–Malachi,* 140.

11. In Richard Carwardine, *Lincoln: A Life of Purpose and Power* (New York: Alfred A. Knopf, 2006), 227, emphasis added.

12. In Leidner, *Lincoln on God and Country,* 107.

13. Ibid., 110.

14. Ibid., 107–8.

15. See Carwardine, *Lincoln,* 223.

16. David Von Drehle, *Rise to Greatness: Abraham Lincoln and America's Most Perilous Year* (New York: Henry Holt and Company, 2012), 219.

17. In Roy P. Basler et al., eds., *The Collected Works of Abraham Lincoln,* 9 vols. (New Brunswick, NJ: Rutgers University Press, 1953–55), 7:535–36; emphasis added.

18. Ibid., 536.

19. Von Drehle, *Rise to Greatness,* 369.

20. In Carwardine, *Lincoln,* 279.

21. In James L. Swanson, *Manhunt: The Twelve-Day Chase for Lincoln's Killer* (New York: HarperCollins, 2006), 2.

22. In Andersen, *Lincoln: God's Humble Instrument,* 291.

23. In Matthew S. Holland, *Bonds of Affection: Civic Charity and the Making of America—Winthrop, Jefferson, and Lincoln* (Washington, D.C.: Georgetown University Press, 2007), 4.

24. In Jon Meacham, *American Gospel: God, the Founding Fathers, and the Making of a Nation* (New York: Random House, 2006), 121.

Chapter 10: National Repentance

1. In Ron L. Andersen, *Abraham Lincoln: God's Humble Instrument* (Salt Lake City: Millennial Mind Publishing, 2010), 277.

2. Ibid.

3. See David Von Drehle, *Rise to Greatness: Abraham Lincoln and America's Most Perilous Year* (New York: Henry Holt and Company, 2012), 217.

4. In Richard Carwardine, *Lincoln: A Life of Purpose and Power* (New York: Alfred A. Knopf, 2006), 227.

5. Ibid., 234.

6. In Newt Gingrich, *Rediscovering God in America* (Nashville, TN: Integrity Publishers, 2006), 52.

7. In Gordon Leidner, *Lincoln on God and Country* (Shippensburg, PA: White Mane Books, 2000), 107.

8. In Don E. Fehrenbacher and Virginia Fehrenbacher, eds., *Recollected Words of Abraham Lincoln* (Stanford, CA: Stanford University Press, 1996), 500.

9. Ibid; emphasis added.

10. See Larry Schweikart and Michael Allen, *A Patriot's History of the United States* (New York: Sentinel/Penguin Books, 2004), 307–8.

11. In Carwardine, *Lincoln,* 234.

12. Letter from Private Levi Hines, in Chandra Manning, *What This Cruel War Was Over: Soldiers, Slavery, and the Civil War* (New York: Alfred A. Knopf, 2007), 119.

13. In Manning, *What This Cruel War Was Over,* 188–89.

14. Ibid., 85.

15. Ibid.

16. Ibid., 113.

17. Ibid., 165.

18. Ibid., 26.

19. In Kenneth Alford, ed., *Civil War Saints* (Provo, UT: Religious Studies Center, Brigham Young University, 2012), 49–50.

20. In Roy P. Basler et al., eds., *The Collected Works of Abraham Lincoln,* 9 vols. (New Brunswick, NJ: Rutgers University Press, 1953), 5:212–13.

21. Manning, *What This Cruel War Was Over,* 118–19.

22. Ibid., 6.

23. Ibid., 211.

24. From the official website of the United States Treasury, available at http://www.treasury.gov/about/education/Pages/in-god-we-trust.aspx.

25. Von Drehle, *Rise to Greatness,* 379.

Chapter 11: A Fight between Heaven and Hell

1. See Melissa Sanford, "Illinois Tells Mormons It Regrets Expulsion," *New York Times,* April 8, 2004. President George W. Bush honored President Gordon B. Hinckley with the United States Medal of Freedom (see Michael K. Winder, *Presidents and Prophets* (American Fork, UT: Covenant Communications, 2007), 394.

2. See Jessica Garrison and Joanna Lin, "Prop. 8 protesters target Mormon temple in Westwood," *Los Angeles Times,* November 7, 2008, available at www.latimes.com/news/local/la-me-protest7–2008nov07,0,3827549.story. For images of police in riot gear protecting the temple, see www.youtube.com, video number 0EtD0Bu9Bie.

3. See "The Mormons," produced and directed by Helen Whitney, *PBS Special: American Experience, Frontline;* airdate: April 30, 2007, program available at http://www.pbs.org/mormons/.

4. In Richard Carwardine, *Lincoln: A Life of Purpose and Power* (New York: Alfred A. Knopf, 2006), 122.

5. Ibid., 143.

6. In an 1862 speech to the Emancipation League in Boston, accessed online at http://en.wikiquote.org/wiki/Frederick_Douglass.

7. In Neil Kagan and Stephen G. Hyslop, *Eyewitness to the Civil War* (Washington, D.C.: National Geographic Society, 2006), 23.

8. I am aware of the Libertarian-based arguments on this point that the South was not really fighting for slavery, that slavery was going to die out on its own, that Lincoln's reaction to Southern slavery actually destroyed freedom in the end, and so forth. These arguments discount the many evidences that tie the war and Lincoln to the Restoration.

9. In Gordon Leidner, *Lincoln on God*

and Country (Shippensburg, PA: White Mane Books, 2000), 75.

10. In Larry Schweikart and Michael Allen, *A Patriot's History of the United States* (New York: Sentinel/Penguin Books, 2004), 350.

11. Ibid.

12. In Scott Berg, *Thirty-Eight Nooses* (New York: Pantheon Books, 2012), 63.

13. In Schweikart and Allen, *A Patriot's History,* 298.

14. "Declaration of the Immediate Causes Which Induce and Justify the Secession of South Carolina from the Federal Union and the Ordinance of Secession" (Charleston, SC: Evans and Cogswell, Printers to the Convention, 1860), 7–10.

15. In Schweikart and Allen, *A Patriot's History,* 302.

16. Ibid.

17. Chandra Manning, *What This Cruel War Was Over: Soldiers, Slavery, and the Civil War* (New York: Alfred A. Knopf, 2007), 64.

18. Ibid., 36–37.

19. Schweikart and Allen, *A Patriot's History,* 325–26; see also 301, 307.

20. Chris Stewart and Ted Stewart, *Seven Miracles That Saved America* (Salt Lake City: Shadow Mountain, 2009), 163.

21. In William Lee Miller, *President Lincoln: The Duty of a Statesman* (New York: Alfred A. Knopf, 2008), 150.

22. In Richard Lyman Bushman, *Joseph Smith: Rough Stone Rolling* (New York: Alfred A. Knopf, 2005), 514.

23. In Toby Mac and Michael Tait, *Under God* (Minneapolis: Bethany House, 2004), 287.

24. See *Autobiography of Parley P. Pratt,* revised and enhanced edition, edited by Scot Facer Proctor and Maurine Jensen Proctor (Salt Lake City: Deseret Book, 2007), 570–72.

25. See B. H. Roberts, *New Witnesses for God* (U.S.A: Published by Lynn Pulsipher, 1986), 88–90; as originally published in *Millennial Star,* 50:44–47.

26. Richard Vetterli, *Mormonism, Americanism and Politics* (Salt Lake City: Ensign Publishing Company, 1961), 81.

27. In Bushman, *Rough Stone Rolling,* 357.

28. In Vetterli, *Mormonism, Americanism and Politics,* 218.

29. See Roberts, *New Witnesses for God,* 88–90; as originally published in *Millennial Star,* 50:44–47.

30. Manning, *What This Cruel War Was Over,* 115.

31. Ibid., 157.

32. In Leidner, *Lincoln on God and Country,* 108.

33. David McCullough, *Truman* (New York: Simon & Schuster, 1992), 26–28.

34. Ibid.

35. In Vetterli, *Mormonism, Americanism and Politics,* 297.

36. From *St. Joseph Herald,* as reprinted in *Deseret News,* October 18, 1863; Kenneth Alford, ed., *Civil War Saints* (Provo, UT: Religious Studies Center, Brigham Young University, 2012), 102.

37. General Order No. 11 (1863), available at http://en.wikipedia.org/wiki/General_Order_No._11_(1863).

38. Ibid.

39. In Richard J. Ellis, *To the Flag: The Unlikely History of the Pledge of Allegiance* (Lawrence, KS: University Press of Kansas, 2005), 210–11.

40. In *Church History in the Fulness of Times,* 2nd ed. (Salt Lake City: The Church of Jesus Christ of Latter-day Saints, 2000), 382.

41. In Carwardine, *Lincoln,* 122.

Chapter 12: Answering the Critics

1. See the research of Stephen Pratt at http://www.libertyandlearning.com/downloads/an-heuristic-exploration-of-the-union. See also Stephen Pratt, "The Three Foundings" (video presentation), available at www.libertyandlearning.com/videos; and Stephen Pratt,

"The Second Founding," video available at www.libertyandlearning.com. I encourage all to read Pratt's conclusions on Lincoln and compare them with the research in this book. Other prominent sources that use similar allegations to paint Lincoln in a very negative light include Thomas J. DiLorenzo, *Lincoln Unmasked: What You're Not Supposed to Know About Dishonest Abe* (New York: Three Rivers Press, 2006); Jeffrey Rogers Hummel, *Emancipating Slaves, Enslaving Free Men: A History of the American Civil War* (Chicago: Open Court, 1996); Allen Buchanan, *Secession: The Morality of Political Divorce from Fort Sumter to Lithuania and Quebec* (Boulder, CO: West View Press, 1991); Robert Higgs, *Crises and Leviathan: Critical Episodes in the Growth of American Government* (New York: Oxford University Press, 1987). These authors and presenters represent some of the sources I refer to as "the critics."

2. John V. Denson, *A Century of War: Lincoln, Wilson and Roosevelt* (Auburn, AL: Ludwig von Mises Institute, 2006), 22, as quoted and supported by Stephen Pratt, "Empire of Debt," DVD available at www.libertyand learning.com; see Pratt's research on the subject, also available at http://libertyandlearning.com/downloads/that-troublesome-word-sovereignty.

3. In Richard Carwardine, *Lincoln: A Life of Purpose and Power* (New York: Alfred A. Knopf, 2006), 227.

4. See Timothy Ballard, *The American Covenant: One Nation Under God,* 2 vols. (New York: Digital Legend Press, 2011), 2:210–27. See also Timothy Ballard, *Lincoln, the Covenant, and the War* (El Centro, CA: Title of Liberty Press, 2012), chapter titled "The Anti-Lincolnites."

5. In Kenneth Alford, ed., *Civil War Saints* (Provo, UT: Religious Studies Center, Brigham Young University, 2012), 113.

6. *The Writings of James Madison, comprising his Public Papers and his Private Correspondence, including his numerous letters and documents now for the first time printed,* ed. Gaillard Hunt (New York: G. P. Putnam's Sons, 1900), vol. 9, chapter *TO N. P. TRIST. mad. mss.* Accessed at http://oll.libertyfund.org/title/1940/119377.

7. See the insert in chapter 11 titled "Southern Intent" (pages 144–45).

8. Chandra Manning, *What This Cruel War Was Over: Soldiers, Slavery, and the Civil War* (New York: Alfred A. Knopf, 2007), 32. The scope of this study does not permit an exhaustive list of the many publications, sermons, and other communications in the South that clearly show that the Southern war cause was sustained by a passion to preserve the practice of slavery. For more on this, see David Goldfield, *America Aflame: How the Civil War Created a Nation* (New York: Bloomsbury Press, 2011), 183–96.

9. Larry Schweikart and Michael Allen, *A Patriot's History of the United States* (New York: Sentinel/Penguin Books, 2004), 302.

10. Doris Kearns Goodwin, *Team of Rivals: The Political Genius of Abraham Lincoln* (New York: Simon & Schuster, 2005), 647.

11. Ibid., 686.

12. In Linda R. Monk, *The Words We Live By: Your Annotated Guide to the Constitution* (New York: Hyperion, 2003), 208.

13. See Carwardine, *Lincoln,* 180, 203.

14. These millions of slaves—no more free than American slaves were—find themselves captive in many regions of the world, including the Middle East, South Asia, Africa, and Eastern Europe. For more details, see Schweikart and Allen, *A Patriot's History,* 351; Kevin Bales, *Disposable People: New Slavery in the Global Economy* (California: University

of California Press, 1999); U.S. State Department, "Trafficking in Persons Report" (2013), as reported in "27 Million People Said to Live in 'Modern Slavery,'" *New York Times,* June 20, 2013; "Millions Forced into Slavery," *BBC News,* May 27, 2002; www.free theslaves.net.

15. See Manning, *What This Cruel War Was Over,* 14.

16. Dred Scott v. Sandford, 19 Howard 393 (1856). Accessed online at supreme .justia.com/cases/federal/us/60/393 /case.html.

17. See Manning, *What This Cruel War Was Over,* 49.

18. Ron L. Andersen, *Abraham Lincoln: God's Humble Instrument* (Salt Lake City: Millennial Mind Publishing, 2010), 22.

19. Ibid.

20. In Toby Mac and Michael Tait, *Under God* (Minneapolis: Bethany House, 2004), 266–67.

21. In Matthew S. Holland, *Bonds of Affection: Civic Charity and the Making of America—Winthrop, Jefferson, and Lincoln* (Washington, D.C.: Georgetown University Press, 2007), 166.

22. Joseph Smith Jr., *Teachings of the Prophet Joseph Smith,* selected and arranged by Joseph Fielding Smith (Salt Lake City: Deseret Book, 1976), 326–27; Joseph Smith Jr., *History of the Church of Jesus Christ of Latter-day Saints,* 7 vols. (Salt Lake City: Deseret Book, 1973), 6:206.

23. In Alford, ed., *Civil War Saints,* 50–51.

24. Victor Hugo, *Les Misérables* (New York: Penguin Books, 1987), 621–22 (originally published in 1862).

25. In Chris Stewart and Ted Stewart, *Seven Miracles That Saved America* (Salt Lake City: Shadow Mountain, 2009), 195.

26. In Goldfield, *America Aflame,* 67.

27. In Goodwin, *Team of Rivals,* 686.

28. In Carwardine, *Lincoln,* 217.

29. In Tad R. Callister, *The Inevitable Apostasy and the Promised Restoration* (Salt Lake City: Deseret Book, 2006), 106.

30. Ibid; emphasis added.

Chapter 13: Brigham, Lincoln, and the Dispatch

1. In Michael K. Winder, *Presidents and Prophets* (American Fork, UT: Covenant Communications, 2007), 106.

2. In Kenneth Alford, ed., *Civil War Saints* (Provo, UT: Religious Studies Center, Brigham Young University, 2012), 118.

3. Ibid., 116.

4. Ibid., 109.

5. Ibid., 118.

6. Ibid., 51.

7. Ibid., 72.

8. Ibid., 74, 113.

9. Ibid., 95.

10. Ibid., 76.

11. Winder, *Presidents and Prophets,* 111–12.

12. In Alford, ed., *Civil War Saints,* 138.

13. Ted Widmer, "Lincoln and the Mormons," *New York Times,* November 17, 2011, accessed online at http:// opinionator.blogs.nytimes.com/2011 /11/17/lincoln-and-the-mormons/?_r =0; emphasis added.

14. In "Lincoln frequently worked with LDS faithful," *Deseret News,* September 19, 2008.

15. In *Church History in the Fulness of Times,* 2nd ed. (Salt Lake City: The Church of Jesus Christ of Latter-day Saints, 2000), 383.

16. Winder, *Presidents and Prophets,* 109.

17. See *Church History in the Fulness of Times,* 388–89.

Chapter 14: The Gettysburg Prayer

1. Walter Stahr, *Seward: Lincoln's Indispensable Man* (New York: Simon & Schuster, 2012), 384.

2. John M. Taylor, *William Henry Seward: Lincoln's Right Hand* (New York: HarperCollins, 1991), 223.

3. See Stahr, *Seward*, 384–85.
4. Taylor, *William Henry Seward*, 223–24.
5. See ibid., 224.
6. See Stahr, *Seward*, 386.
7. In Richard Carwardine, *Lincoln: A Life of Purpose and Power* (New York: Alfred A. Knopf, 2006), 320. Lincoln's quotation here, though quoted by many, has never been fully substantiated.
8. Gabor Boritt, *The Gettysburg Gospel: The Lincoln Speech That Nobody Knows* (New York: Simon & Schuster, 2006), 129.
9. In Newt Gingrich, *Rediscovering God in America* (Nashville, TN: Integrity Publishers, 2006), 54; see also Chris Stewart and Ted Stewart, *Seven Miracles That Saved America* (Salt Lake City: Shadow Mountain, 2009), 190–91.
10. In Don E. Fehrenbacher and Virginia Fehrenbacher, *Recollected Words of Abraham Lincoln* (Stanford, CA: Stanford University Press, 1996), 406.
11. These observations were made by the author as he studied that first edition copy of the Book of Mormon in the Library of Congress.
12. In Chandra Manning, *What This Cruel War Was Over: Soldiers, Slavery, and the Civil War* (New York: Alfred A. Knopf, 2007), 157.
13. See Stahr, *Seward*, 386.
14. In Boritt, *Gettysburg Gospel*, 97.
15. Ibid., 117.
16. In Roy P. Basler et al., eds., *The Collected Works of Abraham Lincoln*, 9 vols. (New Brunswick, NJ: Rutgers University Press, 1953), 5:212; emphasis added.
17. In William Lee Miller, *President Lincoln: The Duty of a Statesman* (New York: Alfred A. Knopf, 2008), 151.
18. See Boritt, *Gettysburg Gospel*, 202.
19. In Carwardine, *Lincoln*, 217.
20. In William J. Bennett, *The Spirit of America* (New York: Touchstone, 1997), 368.
21. Boritt, *Gettysburg Gospel*, 122.
22. Ibid., 17.
23. Ibid., 118.

Chapter 15: The Hymn

1. In Thomas R. Valletta, gen. ed., *Great American Documents for Latter-day Saint Families* (Salt Lake City: Deseret Book, 2011), 135.
2. In William J. Bennett, *America: The Last Best Hope* (Nashville, TN: Nelson Current, 2006), 348.
3. In Richard Carwardine, *Lincoln: A Life of Purpose and Power* (New York: Alfred A. Knopf, 2006), 225.
4. In Bruce Feiler, *America's Prophet: Moses and the American Story* (New York: HarperCollins, 2009), 159.
5. In Carwardine, *Lincoln*, 279.
6. Ibid., 305.
7. From *Easton's 1897 Bible Dictionary*, retrieved by http://dictionary.reference.com/browse/ichabod.
8. Bennett, *America: The Last Best Hope*, 348.
9. In David Von Drehle, *Rise to Greatness: Abraham Lincoln and America's Most Perilous Year* (New York: Henry Holt and Company, 2012), 241.
10. In Valletta, ed., *Great American Documents*, 139; emphasis added.
11. Ibid., 137.

Chapter 16: The Fall and Rise of Richmond

1. See Walter Stahr, *Seward: Lincoln's Indispensable Man* (New York: Simon & Schuster, 2012), 431.
2. See Bill O'Reilly and Martin Dugard, *Killing Lincoln: The Shocking Assassination That Changed America Forever* (New York: Henry Holt and Company, 2011), 38.
3. In Doris Kearns Goodwin, *Team of Rivals: The Political Genius of Abraham Lincoln* (New York: Simon & Schuster, 2005), 719.
4. In Gordon Leidner, *Lincoln on God and Country* (Shippensburg, PA: White Mane Books, 2000), 33–34.
5. Ibid.
6. In Bruce Feiler, *America's Prophet: Moses*

and the American Story (New York: HarperCollins, 2009), 248; emphasis added.

7. James L. Swanson, *Bloody Crimes: The Chase for Jefferson Davis and the Death Pageant for Lincoln's Corpse* (New York: HarperCollins, 2010), 45–46.

8. David Von Drehle, *Rise to Greatness: Abraham Lincoln and America's Most Perilous Year* (New York: Henry Holt and Company, 2012), 317.

9. See 2 Nephi 1:24; 3:24; Mosiah 23:10; 27:36; Alma 1:8; 2:30; 17:9, 11; 26:3, 15; 29:9; 35:14.

10. Swanson, *Bloody Crimes,* 93.

11. In James L. Swanson, *Manhunt: The 12-Day Chase for Lincoln's Killer* (New York: HarperCollins, 2006), 4–6.

12. Swanson, *Bloody Crimes,* 331–32.

Chapter 17: Upon the Altar

1. In Ron L. Andersen, *Abraham Lincoln: God's Humble Instrument* (Salt Lake City: Millennial Mind Publishing, 2010), 235.

2. In *Church History in the Fulness of Times,* 2nd ed. (Salt Lake City: The Church of Jesus Christ of Latter-day Saints, 2000), 277.

3. In Neil Kagan and Stephen Hyslop, *Eyewitness to the Civil War* (Washington, D.C.: National Geographic, 2006), 376.

4. See Ward Hill Lamon, *Recollections of Abraham Lincoln: 1847–1865* (Lincoln, NE: University of Nebraska Press, 1994), 116–17.

5. In Matthew S. Holland, *Bonds of Affection: Civic Charity and the Making of America—Winthrop, Jefferson, and Lincoln* (Washington, D.C.: Georgetown University Press, 2007), 252.

6. In Bruce Feiler, *America's Prophet* (New York: HarperCollins, 2009), 170.

7. In James L. Swanson, *Manhunt: The 12-Day Chase for Lincoln's Killer* (New York: HarperCollins, 2006), 6.

8. In Richard Carwardine, *Lincoln: A Life of Purpose and Power* (New York: Alfred A. Knopf, 2006), 320–21.

9. In Bill O'Reilly and Martin Dugard, *Killing Lincoln: The Shocking Assassination That Changed America Forever* (New York: Henry Holt and Company, 2011), 214.

10. Carwardine, *Lincoln: A Life of Purpose and Power,* 320.

11. In James L. Swanson, *Bloody Crimes: The Chase for Jefferson Davis and the Death Pageant for Lincoln's Corpse* (New York: HarperCollins, 2010), 112.

12. In *Journal of Discourses,* 26 vols. (London: Latter-day Saints' Book Depot, 1854–86), 19:229.

13. In Vicki Jo Anderson, *The Other Eminent Men of Wilford Woodruff* (Malta, ID: Nelson Book, 1994), 419–20.

14. Ibid., 420.

15. Truman G. Madsen, *The Presidents of the Church: Insights into Their Lives and Teachings* (Salt Lake City: Deseret Book, 2004), 105.

16. See Swanson, *Bloody Crimes,* 208–9.

17. In Andersen, *Lincoln: God's Humble Instrument,* 197.

18. See Michael K. Winder, *Presidents and Prophets* (American Fork, UT: Covenant Communications, 2007), 112; see also http://new.familysearch.org. Search Abraham, Mary Todd, and William Wallace Lincoln (1850–1862).

19. See Larry Schweikart and Michael Allen, *A Patriot's History of the United States* (New York: Sentinel/Penguin Books, 2004), 306.

20. In Gordon Leidner, *Lincoln on God and Country* (Shippensburg, PA: White Mane Books, 2000), 112.

21. See Doris Kearns Goodwin, *Team of Rivals: The Political Genius of Abraham Lincoln* (New York: Simon & Schuster, 2005), 451–52, 484–86.

22. Carwardine, *Lincoln: A Life of Purpose and Power,* 305.

23. Ibid., 298.

24. See Chandra Manning, *What This Cruel*

War Was Over: Soldiers, Slavery, and the Civil War (New York: Alfred A. Knopf, 2007), 185.

25. See William Lee Miller, *President Lincoln: The Duty of a Statesman* (New York: Alfred A. Knopf, 2008), 377.

26. In Carwardine, *Lincoln*, 222–23.

27. In Swanson, *Bloody Crimes*, 336–37.

28. See Cecil O. Samuelson Jr., "Stand by My Servant Joseph," *Ensign*, February 2013, 34–39.

30. In Goodwin, *Team of Rivals*, 744–45.

31. See Winder, *Presidents and Prophets*, 106.

29. David Von Drehle, *Rise to Greatness: Abraham Lincoln and America's Most Perilous Year* (New York: Henry Holt and Company, 2012), 353.

32. Ibid., 351.

33. See Goodwin, *Team of Rivals*, 724–25.

34. In Walter Stahr, *Seward: Lincoln's Indispensable Man* (New York: Simon & Schuster, 2012), 541.

35. See Goodwin, *Team of Rivals*, 13.

36. Stahr, *Seward*, 538.

37. Anderson, *Other Eminent Men*, 347.

38. Another seemingly surprising name on the temple list was Thomas "Stonewall" Jackson, Confederate commander who died in battle (see Anderson, *Other Eminent Men*, Preface). As I stated earlier, many Southern soldiers fighting in the war had their own purposes, notwithstanding the obvious fact that the Southern leadership was fighting to preserve slavery. Jackson, for example, did not join the cause in deference to any race, but for what he interpreted to be loyalty to his country. In fact, before the war, he had set up a Sunday school (at his own expense and at the risk of breaking certain laws and customs) for the religious instruction of black persons within his community (see Anderson, *Other Eminent Men*, 226). All this brings up another fascinating thought. If God needed the purging effect of the Civil War to induce real national repentance, the war had to last long enough to create that effect. In other words, a quick Northern victory would have halted God's goal here. So, might He have influenced some of the Southern victories to keep the refiner's fire burning bright? Now, we are getting into deep waters here, and I do not pretend to know the inner workings of God in this matter. But I am at least willing to entertain the notion that perhaps He placed inspired leaders on both sides of the war in order to work through both sides and keep the vexation alive. Jackson might have been one who fit this bill. The Book of Mormon teaches us that enemies of God's people may be utilized to "stir [God's people] up in the ways of remembrance" when God's people have fallen into sin (1 Nephi 2:24). Enemies of the Nephites were clearly given the green light from God "to stir [the Nephites] up in remembrance of me; and . . . they shall scourge [the Nephites] even unto destruction" (2 Nephi 5:25). "And thus we see that except the Lord doth chasten his people with many afflictions, yea, except he doth visit them with death and with terror, . . . they will not remember him" (Helaman 12:3). "Therefore, thus saith the Lord: Because of the hardness of the hearts of the people of the Nephites, except they repent . . . I will turn the hearts of their brethren against them" (Helaman 13:8). "But, behold, the judgments of God will overtake the wicked; and it is by the wicked that the wicked are punished" (Mormon 4:5).

Chapter 18: For We Shall Meet Again

1. Gordon B Hinckley, *Standing for Something* (New York: Times Books, 2000), xviii, xxiii, xxv.

2. Letter to Sarah Ballou from Sullivan Ballou, July 14, 1861, from Camp Clark, Washington; in Neil Kagan and

Stephen Hyslop, *Eyewitness to the Civil War* (Washington, D.C.: National Geographic, 2006), 72; see also Evan Jones, "Sullivan Ballou: The Macabre Fate of an American Civil War Major," accessed online at www.historynet .com/magazines/american_civil_war /3033061.html. Liberties were taken in the way Ballou's letter was presented. The facts surrounding his death and the writing of the letter are accurate.

However, there is no way to know exactly what was going through his mind, including his proposed reflection upon the letter, while in the process of dying.

3. See https://new.familysearch.org. Search for Sullivan, Sarah, Edgar, and William Ballou.

4. In Peter A. Lillback, *George Washington and Israel* (King of Prussia, PA: Providence Forum Press, 2012), 34–35.

5. Hinckley, *Standing for Something,* xxiii.

Index

of, 172–73, 225–26; Brigham Young on, 179–80; relationship of, with Mormons, 179–80, 184–86; Mormon support for, 181–83; travels to Gettysburg, 187–88; addresses crowd in Gettysburg, 188; tours battlefield at Gettysburg, 189–90, 194; gives Gettysburg Address, 195–98; as Joshua, 201; as father of covenant, 202; and "Battle Hymn of the Republic," 204; and fall of Richmond, 205–8; and end of Civil War, 209–10; assassination of, 212–17; bound to Joseph Smith, 214–17; temple work for, 217–19, 222; reelection of, 223–25; and resignation of William H. Seward, 228–30; eulogy of, 229; author's testimony of Joseph Smith and, 243–44

Lincoln, Mary Todd, 81, 83–84, 122, 213, 222

Lincoln, Tad, 80, 84, 215

Lincoln, Willie, 77–83, 222

Lincoln Memorial, 220–22

Long Island, Battle of (1776), 20

Los Angeles Temple, protection of, 139–40

Love: of Abraham Lincoln and Joseph Smith, 45–48; of Abraham Lincoln, 80

Lutz, Donald, 37

Madison, James, 58–60, 148, 159

Manning, Chandra, 135–36, 143–46, 163

Manning, Jane, 46–48

Mason, George, 71

McAllister, J.D.T., 218

McCabe, Charles Caldwell, 204

McClellan, George B.: Lincoln's humble dealings with, 15–17; obtains Special Order #191, 93; presidential campaign of, 223–25

McCullough, David, 153

McPherson, James, 93–94, 165

"Meditation on the Divine Will," 90–91

Merrick, Charley, 44–45

Miller, William Lee, 47

Miner, Noyes, 89

Miracles: during Revolutionary War, 20–23; and oath of George Washington, 31; surrounding Special Order #191, 93–98; and rescue of child slave, 99–105

Missionary work, 110–11, 186

Missouri, 73, 149–50, 153–55

Mitchell, Barton W., 92–93, 97

Monocacy, Battle of, 96

Moore, John, 132

Morals, corrupted, as breach of national covenant, 37, 241

Mormon, 125

Mormons: Stephen Douglas turns against, 75–76; freedom for, 87; change in attitude toward, 139–41; Lincoln's dealings with, 179–80, 184–86; views of, on Civil War, 180–82; participation of, in Civil War, 183–84. *See also* Persecution of Saints

Moses, Lincoln as latter-day, 216

National covenant: Washington invokes, 18–20, 25–27; America under, 27–28; need for, 28–30; breach of, 34–40, 240–41; Civil War and, 51; in Book of Mormon, 108–10, 114; reactivation of, 150–51, 194; and end of slavery, 167; blindness to, 175–77; Jesus Christ as God of, 190; Lincoln invokes, 191; and Gettysburg Address, 197–98; Lincoln as father of, 202; freed slaves called to, 207–8; in force today, 240–41; remembering, 241–42. *See also* Covenant land; National repentance; National sin

National repentance: Lincoln calls people to, 115; Abraham Lincoln on, 116; need for, 125–26; and prophecies regarding Civil War, 126–28; and purpose of Civil War, 128–31; acceptance of, 131–36; blessings of, 136–38; signs of, 150–51; compelled, 200–201. *See also* National covenant; National sin

National sin: Joseph Smith on, 36; civil rights violations as, 39–40; slavery as, 40–42, 60–61, 71, 109, 132–33; Haun's Mill Massacre as, 42–45; Civil War and, 51, 109; in Isaiah 5, 111–13; Abraham Lincoln on, 116. *See also* National covenant; National repentance

New Israel, 36, 201

Nind, J. G., 151